T0418478

Southern Resistance in Critical Perspective

From the Arab Uprising, to anti-austerity protests in Europe and the US Occupy Movement, to uprisings in Brazil and Turkey, resistance from below is flourishing. Whereas analysts have tended to look North in their analysis of the recent global protest wave, this volume develops a Southern perspective through a deep engagement with the case of South Africa, which has experienced widespread popular resistance for more than a decade. Combining critical theoretical perspectives with extensive qualitative fieldwork and rich case studies, *Southern Resistance in Critical Perspective* situates South Africa's contentious democracy in relation to both the economic insecurity of contemporary global capitalism and the constantly shifting political terrain of post-apartheid nationalism. The analysis integrates worker, community and political party organizing into a broader narrative of resistance, bridging historical divisions among social movement studies, labor studies and political sociology.

Marcel Paret is Assistant Professor in the Department of Sociology at the University of Utah, USA, and Senior Research Associate at the Centre for Social Change at the University of Johannesburg, South Africa.

Carin Runciman is Senior Researcher at the Centre for Social Change at the University of Johannesburg, South Africa.

Luke Sinwell is Senior Researcher at the Centre for Social Change at the University of Johannesburg, South Africa.

The Mobilization Series on Social Movements, Protest, and Culture
Series editor:
Professor Hank Johnston, San Diego State University, United States

For a full list of titles in this series, please visit www.routledge.com

Published in conjunction with *Mobilization: An International Quarterly*, the premier research journal in the field, this series publishes a broad range of research in social movements, protest and contentious politics. This is a growing field of social science research that spans sociology and political science as well as anthropology, geography, communications and social psychology. Enjoying a broad remit, the series welcome works on the following topics: social movement networks; social movements in the global South; social movements, protest and culture; personalist politics, such as living environmentalism, guerrilla gardens, anticonsumerist communities and anarchist-punk collectives; and emergent repertoires of contention.

The Ritual of May Day in Western Europe
Abby Peterson and Herbert Reiter

Economic Crisis and Mass Protest
Jón Gunnar Bernburg
(Routledge, 2016)

Austerity and Protest
Popular contention in times of economic crisis
Edited by Marco Giugni and Maria T. Grasso
(Ashgate, 2015)

Social Movement Dynamics
New perspectives on theory and research from Latin America
Edited by Federico M. Rossi and Marisa von Bülow
(Ashgate, 2015)

Urban Mobilizations and New Media in Contemporary China
Edited by Lisheng Dong, Hanspeter Kriesi and Daniel Kübler
(Ashgate, 2015)

Southern Resistance in Critical Perspective
The Politics of Protest in South Africa's Contentious Democracy

Edited by Marcel Paret, Carin Runciman and Luke Sinwell

LONDON AND NEW YORK

First published 2017
by Routledge
2 Park Square, Milton Park, Abingdon, Oxon OX14 4RN

and by Routledge
711 Third Avenue, New York, NY 10017

Routledge is an imprint of the Taylor & Francis Group, an informa business

© 2017 selection and editorial matter, Marcel Paret, Carin Runciman, Luke Sinwell; individual chapters, the contributors

The right of Marcel Paret, Carin Runciman, and Luke Sinwell to be identified as the authors of the editorial material, and of the authors for their individual chapters, has been asserted in accordance with sections 77 and 78 of the Copyright, Designs and Patents Act 1988.

All rights reserved. No part of this book may be reprinted or reproduced or utilised in any form or by any electronic, mechanical, or other means, now known or hereafter invented, including photocopying and recording, or in any information storage or retrieval system, without permission in writing from the publishers.

Trademark notice: Product or corporate names may be trademarks or registered trademarks, and are used only for identification and explanation without intent to infringe.

British Library Cataloguing-in-Publication Data
A catalogue record for this book is available from the British Library

Library of Congress Cataloging-in-Publication Data
A catalog record for this book is available from the Library of Congress

ISBN: 978-1-4724-7346-2 (hbk)
ISBN: 978-1-315-58501-7 (ebk)

Typeset in Times New Roman
by Apex CoVantage, LLC

Printed and bound by CPI Group (UK) Ltd, Croydon, CR0 4YY

Contents

List of figures and table	vii
Notes on contributors	viii
Preface	xi
List of abbreviations	xiii

1 Southern resistance in critical perspective   1
MARCEL PARET

PART I
Global formations   19

2 Social movements in the neoliberal age   21
MICHAEL BURAWOY

3 South African social movements in the neoliberal age   36
CARIN RUNCIMAN

PART II
Community formations   53

4 Postcolonial politics: theorizing protest from spaces of exclusion   55
MARCEL PARET

5 South Africa 'unrest' or rebellion: a focus on Durban
community protests   72
TOM LODGE AND SHAUNA MOTTIAR

6 Social movements beyond incorporation: the case of the
housing assembly in post-apartheid Cape Town   89
ZACHARY LEVENSON

vi *Contents*

PART III
Local state formations 105

7 **Party politics and community mobilisation in Buffalo City, East London** 107
TATENDA G. MUKWEDEYA AND HLENGIWE NDLOVU

8 **Protests, party politics and patronage: a view from Zandspruit informal settlement, Johannesburg** 118
HANNAH DAWSON

PART IV
Labour formations 135

9 **Changing forms of power and municipal worker resistance in Johannesburg** 137
CARMEN LUDWIG AND EDWARD WEBSTER

10 **Organic intellectuals and leadership in South Africa's contemporary mineworkers' movement** 153
LUKE SINWELL

PART V
Left formations 169

11 **South Africa's new left movements: challenges and hopes** 171
NOOR NIEFTAGODIEN

Index 189

Figures and table

Figures

2.1	Three waves of marketization and their counter-movements	30
3.1	Community protests in South Africa, 2005–2014	41
6.1	Housing assembly districts in relation to the Cape Town city centre	97

Table

4.1	Postcolonial politics: included society vs excluded society	61

Notes on contributors

Michael Burawoy teaches sociology at the University of California, Berkeley and is an Associate of the Society, Work and Development Institute at the University of Witwatersrand, South Africa.

Hannah Dawson is a DPhil candidate in Social and Cultural Anthropology at the University of Oxford and a Research Associate at the South African Chair in Social Change at the University of Johannesburg. She has published in *African Affairs* and the *Journal of Southern African Studies*, amongst others. Her current work explores how young people re-work the meanings of work and it's relationship to personhood, social relationships and the state in a context of mass unemployment and social inequality.

Zachary Levenson is currently completing his PhD in the Department of Sociology at the University of California, Berkeley. His dissertation, *The Post-Apartheid State: The Politics of Housing in South Africa*, is an ethnographic analysis of three mass land occupations in the Cape Flats and proposes a framework for explaining why some occupations are targeted for eviction whereas others are ultimately tolerated. He has published in *International Sociology, Transformation, Contexts*, and elsewhere.

Tom Lodge is Dean of Humanities and teaches peace and development studies at the University of Limerick and is an Honorary Professor at the School of Built Environment and Development Studies at the University of KwaZulu-Natal. He is the author of several books about South African politics, most recently *Sharpeville: An Apartheid Massacre and its Consequences* (Oxford University Press, 2011). At present he is writing a history of the South African Communist Party.

Carmen Ludwig is a postdoctoral researcher at the Institute of Political Science at University of Giessen, Germany. From 2012 to 2014 she joined the 'Decent Work and Development Initiative' cluster at Society, Work and Development Institute (SWOP), University of the Witwatersrand as a visiting scholar. The focus of her dissertation was on trade union strategies in organising solidarity in fragmented workforces in the municipal sector in South Africa. Her current research interest is on organising strategies along global value chains.

Notes on contributors ix

Shauna Mottiar is Senior Lecturer in Development Studies, School of Built Environment and Development Studies at the University of KwaZulu-Natal, South Africa. She obtained a PhD in Political Studies from the University of the Witwatersrand. Her interests include civil society, social movements and social protest in South Africa.

Tatenda G. Mukwedeya is a postdoctoral fellow in Urban Studies and Planning at the University of Sheffield. He is also Visiting Researcher in the school of Architecture and Planning, University of the Witwatersrand. His doctoral thesis focused on the trajectory of factionalism in the African National Congress (ANC), particularly in its local structures post-apartheid. His research interests are in urban governance, everyday politics, development and the state. His work has appeared in *Transformation*, *South African Review of Sociology* and as book chapters. He is currently researching on how transformation in the peripheries of African cities (specifically related to infrastructural investments and economic change), is shaped, governed and experienced.

Hlengiwe Ndlovu is a PhD candidate in Sociology at the University of the Witwatersrand, Johannesburg, South Africa. She is a doctoral fellow at the Public Affairs Research Institute, (PARI) and an associate at the Society Work and Development Institute (SWOP) at the University of the Witwatersrand. Her work engages questions about the state, governance, citizenship, local politics, service delivery and different forms of claim making and resistance.

Noor Nieftagodien is the South African Research Chair in Local Histories, Present Realities, and is the Head of the History Workshop at the University of the Witwatersrand, where he also lectures in the Department of History. He is the co-author, with Phil Bonner, of books on the history of Alexandra, Ekurhuleni and Kathorus, and recently published books on the history of Orlando West and the Soweto uprising; he also co-edited a book on the history of the African National Congress (ANC). In addition, he has published articles and book chapters on aspects of popular insurgent struggles, public history, youth politics and local history. He is currently researching the relationship between local popular movements and the local state in the Vaal.

Marcel Paret is an Assistant Professor in the Department of Sociology at the University of Utah, and Senior Research Associate with the Centre for Social Change at the University of Johannesburg, South Africa. He holds a PhD in Sociology from the University of California, Berkeley. Focusing on the politics of class formation in the United States and South Africa, his work appears in *Review of African Political Economy*, *Critical Sociology*, *Citizenship Studies*, *African Affairs*, *Politikon*, *International Labor and Working Class History*, *International Sociology* and *Latino Studies*, among others.

Carin Runciman is a Senior Researcher at the Centre for Social Change, University of Johannesburg, South Africa. She holds a PhD in Sociology from the University of Glasgow. Her research specializes in the politics of post-apartheid

x *Notes on contributors*

protest and social movements, and has appeared in *Current Sociology* and *Review of African Political Economy*, amongst others. She currently leads the Rebellion of the Poor research team alongside Professor Peter Alexander and Trevor Ngwane, a quantitative and qualitative research project analyzing community protests.

Luke Sinwell is Senior Researcher at the Centre for Social Change at the University of Johannesburg, South Africa. His research interests include the politics and conceptualization of participatory development and governance, social movements and housing struggles, non-violent direct action as a method to transform power relations, ethnographic research methods and action research. He has published widely on contentious politics in South Africa. His most recent book is *The Spirit of Marikana: The Rise of Insurgent Trade Unionism in South Africa* (Pluto Press, 2016).

Edward Webster is Professor Emeritus at the University of the Witwatersrand and the out-going director of the Chris Hani Institute. He was the founder and director of the Society, Work and Development Institute (SWOP) at the University for 25 years. He has written widely on the world of work and his co-authored book, *Grounding Globalisation: Labour in the Age of Insecurity*, was awarded the scholarly monograph prize for the best book on labour by the American Sociological Association. He is currently completing a manuscript on labour after globalisation.

Preface

This project was sparked by the South African Research Chair in Social Change, also known as the Centre for Social Change, which is housed at the University of Johannesburg. Established in 2010 as part of the South African Research Chair Initiative, which is funded by the National Research Foundation and the Department of Science and Technology, the Centre for Social Change has quickly become a leading centre for the study of protest and social movements in South Africa. Deeply committed to social justice, many of the participants in the centre – from senior researchers and postdoctoral fellows to doctoral, master's, and honours students – are activists themselves.

The Centre for Social Change is also committed to critical theoretical perspectives, which are developed and explored through weekly seminars and annual conferences. Given our deep engagement with collective struggles of various kinds, we have often discussed the relevance of the dominant strands of social movement theory – namely the resource mobilization, political process and framing approaches – for making sense of South Africa. While some are sympathetic, wanting to incorporate the best elements of that tradition, others find it wanting, and thus search for alternatives – notably those associated with Marxist traditions. Given the sheer magnitude of resistance, both historically and in the present, there is also a feeling that South Africa is an especially significant site for developing social movement theory.

These inklings were stoked by the massive upsurge of global protest after 2008. Discussions of the 'new global protest' rarely mention South Africa, and this seems both remarkable and disappointing. How could such an important site of resistance not be included in the rapid production of knowledge about current global resistance? For some of us, this overlooking only seems to make the question of South Africa's relationship to social movement studies more relevant and more urgent.

These concerns provided the impetus for a conference, held in May 2014, with the theme of 'Contentious Politics, Capitalism and Social Movement Theory: South Africa in Global Perspective.' All of the chapters that follow were first presented at this conference, which provided space for critical dialogue and feedback. In addition to the authors of this volume, we extend a special thanks to a number of other conference participants: Claire Bénit-Gbaffou, Trevor Ngwane, Prishani xii *Preface*

Naidoo, Elke Zuern, Mosa Phadi, Shannon Walsh, Bridget Kenny and Jacob Mati. Bringing both critical perspectives and substantive contributions, these individuals were absolutely crucial to the success of the conference and thus this volume.

Following the critical dialogue that emerged through the conference, this volume aims to provide a Southern perspective – and in particular a South African perspective – into current global resistance. It is worth mentioning, however, that the producers of this volume symbolize the complicated and power-laden web of global knowledge production. All three of the editors spent their formative years in the North, growing up and earning bachelor's degrees in the United States and the United Kingdom. Two of us completed our PhDs in the North, but spent years in South Africa for dissertation research, and then landed back in the country as postdoctoral fellows with the Social Change research unit. The third completed his PhD in Johannesburg and never left. Of the remaining authors, roughly half are originally from southern Africa, including South Africa and Zimbabwe. The others are older scholars from the North who have either lived in and/or been engaged with South Africa for much of their lifetimes, and younger scholars from the North who are quickly developing close ties with the country.

With all of the cross-pollination it is not surprising that the contributions draw from a mix of theory with roots in both the North and the South. We do not claim to be successful at escaping, or even disrupting, the unequal balance of power between North and South with respect to knowledge production and valuation. What we do provide, instead, is a window into South African struggles that is based on long-term research and lived experience, as well as a deep commitment to the future of the country. For us, this future is crucial to the future of our increasingly interconnected world. We ignore it at our peril.

Marcel Paret, Carin Runciman and Luke Sinwell

Abbreviations

AGM	Anti-Globalisation Movement
AMCU	Association of Mineworkers and Construction Union
ANC	African National Congress
APF	Anti-Privatisation Forum
AZAPO	Azanian People's Organisation
BEE	Black Economic Empowerment
BMWU	Black Municipal Workers' Union
CAHAC	Cape Areas Housing Action Committee
CCMA	Commission for Conciliation, Mediation and Arbitration
CCS	Centre for Civil Society
COPE	Congress of the People
COSATU	Congress of South African Trade Unions
DA	Democratic Alliance
DLF	Democratic Left Front
EFF	Economic Freedom Fighters
GEAR	Growth, Employment and Redistribution
GJM	Global Justice Movement
GJMC	Greater Johannesburg Metropolitan Council
ID	Independent Democrats
IFP	Inkatha Freedom Party
ILRIG	International Labour Research and Information Group
IMF	International Monetary Fund
JCC	Johannesburg City Council
LPM	Landless People's Movement
LRA	Labour Relations Act
NEDLAC	National Economic and Development and Labour Council
NGO	Non-governmental organisation
NUM	National Union of Mineworkers
NUMSA	National Union of Metalworkers South Africa
RDO	Rock Drill Operator
RDP	Reconstruction and Development Programme
SAMWU	South African Municipal Workers Union

xiv *Abbreviations*

SANCO	South African National Civic Organisation
SATAWU	South African Transport and Allied Workers Union
SDCEA	South Durban Community Environmental Alliance
SECC	Soweto Electricity Crisis Committee
TAC	Treatment Action Campaign
TRA	Temporary Relocation Area
UDF	United Democratic Front
UDM	United Democratic Movement
UIF	Unemployment Insurance Fund
UPM	Unemployed Peoples Movement
WDF	Wentworth Development Forum
WSSD	World Summit on Sustainable Development
WTO	World Trade Organisation

1 Southern resistance in critical perspective

Marcel Paret[1]

In August 2012 roughly 28,000 workers at the Lonmin platinum mine, located just outside the small town of Marikana in South Africa's North West province, went on strike for a living wage of R12,500 per month. No union participated in the strike. Instead the workers organised themselves through independent committees, which included members of two rival unions. The strike made international headlines one week after it began, when police gunned down 34 workers and injured many more during a militarised operation. Half of those killed were hit by a flurry of bullets from a police line, as they were leaving the mountain where they had been gathering. Shortly after the initial skirmish, the remaining workers were assassinated by police at close range.[2] Remarkably, and with widespread support from families and the broader community, the workers continued their strike and eventually secured a 22 percent wage increase.

For many observers the Marikana massacre marked an important turning point in South African history. Crucially, it fuelled disaffection with the African National Congress (ANC), the hegemonic leader of the anti-apartheid liberation struggle and the ruling party since 1994. Reminiscent of previous episodes of political repression in Sharpeville (1960) and Soweto (1976), which had been carried out by the apartheid state, the massacre demonstrated an utter lack of respect for the country's poor and working-class black communities. It is thus not surprising that the events at Marikana led to a loss of membership for the National Union of Mineworkers (NUM), which is closely tied to the ANC and understood by many mineworkers to be aligned with mining bosses as well. Likewise, the National Union of Metalworkers South Africa (NUMSA) decided in December 2013 to officially withdraw its support for the ANC, underscoring 'the first post-apartheid massacre' as a key reason: 'As a union we said that after the mowing down of 34 miners in Marikana, it can't be "business as usual" in South Africa.'[3] Finally, Marikana has provided fertile ground for the rise of the Economic Freedom Fighters (EFF), whose firebrand and ex-ANC leader Julius Malema was a key supporter of mineworker struggles both before and after the massacre.[4]

The events at Marikana have also inspired resistance and new forms of solidarity. Following directly on the heels of the massacre, there were wildcat strikes throughout the mining sector and an uprising by farmworkers seeking a living wage in the Western Cape. In a call to action during the strike, a coalition of

2   Marcel Paret

unions, community organisations, non-governmental organisations (NGO)s and farm worker committees exclaimed: 'Marikana has come to the farms!!!'[5] Two years later, in 2014, the demands of the 2012 uprising at Marikana propelled a five-month strike across the platinum belt. Marikana has also inspired resistance within communities. At least four recently created informal settlements have named themselves 'Marikana', and in the protest-affected community of Bekkersdal, the residents refer to the local taxi rank as 'Marikana' because it is where the protests begin, and where residents often face off with police. From workplaces to communities, the threat of 'doing a Marikana' has given renewed confidence to the exploited, poor, and marginalised within South Africa. It is also inspiring a sense of solidarity, with the phrase 'We Are All Marikana' spray-painted on walls across the country.

While Marikana and its immediate aftermath appear to be exceptional, to fully understand the sequence of events we need to take a broader view. To a certain extent, they reflected political dynamics that were already unfolding within South Africa. Rather than an isolated incident, the uprising by Lonmin mineworkers represented a continuation of struggles in workplaces and communities that began to gain prominence in the middle of the 2000s, and accelerated from 2009.[6] For this reason, some have suggested that South Africa is the 'protest capital of the world.'[7] Similar to the mineworker uprising in Marikana, this persistent wave of resistance has highlighted the failure of post-apartheid democracy to reduce inequality and deliver economic security to the black majority.

The recent wave of South African resistance, including the Marikana uprising, must also be situated within the context of increasing resistance internationally. Across the globe, new protest movements erupted in the wake of the 2008 financial crisis. Some have compared the year 2011, in particular, for which *Time* magazine named 'the protester' its Person of the Year, to earlier periods of global resistance in 1848, 1905, 1968, and 1989.[8] Despite the persistently high level of resistance in South Africa, however, it is often overlooked in commentaries that spotlight the recent global protest wave. This absence partially reflects the peculiar features of South African resistance, which are profoundly shaped by the legacy of the post-apartheid transition. Yet there are also important resonances between contemporary protest in South Africa and contemporary protest in the rest of the globe, particularly with respect to their political forms and orientations.

This volume provides a Southern perspective into the current wave of global resistance. We do this by unpacking the politics of protest in contemporary South Africa, but with a consistent eye towards the global context. As the world erupts in collective resistance, it is now important as ever to develop Southern perspectives on protest, social movements, and progressive political formations. The recent global protest wave is pushing scholars of social movements to rebuild, update, and enhance their theoretical tools, and the experiences and insights of the Global South should be incorporated into this process. Not only will it contribute to the democratization of knowledge production, but it will also open additional areas of research and help us to sharpen our theories.

Southern resistance in critical perspective   3

Our analysis is framed by two sets of questions. First, how is the politics of protest in South Africa shaped by the country's position within the global political economy? Here we must attend to the legacy of colonialism/apartheid and liberation, as well as to South Africa's semi-peripheral status within the world economy. Taken together these factors have had a profound impact on both state-society relations and the socio-economic structure, and in turn on contemporary forms of collective resistance. Second, to what extent does collective resistance in contemporary South Africa resonate with episodes of resistance in other parts of the globe? What does the study of protest in South Africa reveal about the dynamics of resistance, including its unevenness, in contemporary global capitalism?

To provide a foundation for the analysis, this Introduction examines the global protest wave and its resonances in South Africa, situates resistance in the post-apartheid period within a historical and global context, interrogates the project of building social theory from the Global South, and highlights the contributions of the chapters that follow.

Global resistance

The current wave of global protest is often traced back to December 17, 2010, when a Tunisian street vendor named Mohamed Bouazizi set himself on fire in a public square after facing consistent harassment by police officials. The following day, protests occurred throughout the country, and within months they had spread to countries throughout North Africa and the Middle East, including the well-known revolution in Egypt. This 'Arab Spring' was followed by uprisings throughout Europe in the middle of 2011, most notably in Portugal, Spain, Italy, and Greece. Later in 2011 the Occupy Movement erupted in the United States and the United Kingdom, and then refracted outwards, with Occupy encampments popping up briefly in cities across the globe. In 2013, major protests spread to Ukraine, Turkey, and Brazil, and since 2011 prominent student protests have also occurred in Mexico, Chile, and Canada.

These uprisings have become iconic examples of the new resistance that is spreading across the globe. They are often lumped together because they are understood as sharing a common politics, including particular motivations, aims, and tactics. Mohammed Bamyeh thus argues that the Tunisian uprising in 2010 gave birth to a 'new global culture of protest' that is defined by six features: opposition to the capture of the 'system' by special interests, and particularly the collusion of financial and political power; frustration that the interests of ordinary people are no longer represented; suspicion of political parties, formal organisations, and leaders, combined with a preference for networks and experimental structures; insistence that alternatives do exist, and that contra the narrative of politicians, genuine opposition to the status quo is possible; an intention to represent 'the people', rather than a specific class or disadvantaged group; and demands that exhibit an 'enticing vagueness', making resistance both less focused but also more accessible to people with a wide range of interests.[9]

4   *Marcel Paret*

The recent proliferation of global protests and their convergence around a common politics is extremely significant. But it is important to note that the most visible examples, noted previously, represent only a portion of recent global resistance. Much of the resistance that is being overlooked is taking place in the Global South. This includes, for example, indigenous struggles against mining companies in Guatemala and Ecuador, ongoing worker protests in China, and anti-corruption struggles in India.[10] With respect to Africa, Clive Gabay suggests that dominant narratives of instability and 'Afro-pessimism' are essentially rendering the continent absent from the new global protest. This is despite the fact, he argues, that 'uprisings, protests, revolts and changes of regime' have recently occurred in many African countries – Cote D'Ivoire, Malawi, Burkina Faso, Gabon, Ethiopia, Swaziland, Uganda, Nigeria, Sudan, and Mozambique – not to mention the fact that the 'Arab Spring' essentially sprung from African soil.[11]

In this respect, it is not unusual that South Africa is rarely included in discussions of the new global protest. It is, rather, one case among many that deserves greater attention from a global audience. This means that making sense of the South African case, as well as its relation to the more visible examples of protest – the Arab Spring, anti-austerity protests in Europe, the Occupy movement – is fruitful in terms of developing a more complete understanding of contemporary global resistance. It is worthwhile to begin such an examination by asking: Why is protest in South Africa not often mentioned with respect to current global protest? Three factors stand out: their class content, their fragmented character, and their repertoires of struggle.

Following Paul Mason's well-known treatise on the recent global protest wave, *Why It's Kicking Off Everywhere*, many commentators discuss the uprisings as a rebellion of 'graduates without a future.' For Mason this is a 'new sociological type' comprising 'educated young people whose life chances and illusions are now being shattered.'[12] Despite their university degrees, they confront a future of precarious work, late retirement, and debt. According to Mason, the graduates without a future are flanked and supported by the urban poor and an increasingly weakened organised working class, but they are the main reason why the protests are 'kicking off' across the globe. This analysis does not fit easily with the South African context, where until very recently university students and graduates played a relatively minor role in the recent surge of collective struggles.[13] Instead, it has been the urban poor and the organised working class who have been leading the charge.

A second major difference is that the struggles in South Africa have been much more fragmented. Not only have the struggles of the urban poor been isolated from one another, largely taking place within individual township communities, but they have also largely taken place separately from the struggles of organised workers. Compared with the more visible sites of global protest, contemporary resistance in South Africa has thus tended to be smaller, shorter, and more decentralized. There has yet to be a major protest where tens of thousands of people converge in a single centralized location over a period of weeks or longer. There is no parallel in South Africa to the iconic public spaces of

Southern resistance in critical perspective 5

resistance that have become household names in recent years: Tahrir Square (Egypt), Zucotti Park (United States), Puerta del Sol (Spain), Independence Square (Ukraine), Gezi Park (Turkey).

Third, protesters in South Africa draw from a different set of repertoires than their global counterparts. Cross-national linkages are a distinctive feature of the current global protest wave, and protesters are often quite well aware of what is happening in other parts of the globe. They are drawing inspiration from one another and communicating through various forms of cyber-technology. Yet there is little evidence that this cross-pollination has had more than a limited amount of penetration into South Africa (though see discussion of Occupy Umlazi in Chapter 5, by Lodge and Mottiar). Whereas the Egyptian Revolution was a primary reference point for the *indignados* in Spain and the Occupy activists in the United States, the anti-apartheid struggles of the 1980s are a much more significant reference point for protests in South Africa. This raises the question: Do the current struggles in South Africa resonate more with the cultures of the liberation struggle than they do with the new global culture of protest? Are the two necessarily different, or may they be mutually reinforcing?

If there are important differences between resistance in South Africa and the more visible examples of global protest, there are also important resonances. These include: a critical orientation towards representative democracy and especially the corruption of formal democratic institutions; the prominence of the youth and their use of social media; and experimentation with alternative forms of organisation and participatory forms of decision-making. Perhaps most importantly, contemporary resistance in South Africa is similarly underpinned by the spectre of economic insecurity. As Guy Standing notes, the current protest wave in the North is, at least partially, a product of the reorganisation of global capitalism around flexible and precarious forms of work.[14] A similar pattern is evident in South Africa, where collective action goes hand-in-hand with daily struggles in the face of widespread poverty and unemployment. Yet the particular forms of insecurity, and the political contexts in which they occur, are very different than those confronted in the Global North. While collective resistance in South Africa does share common features with resistance in the North, then, it often takes on particular South African forms. This volume aims to identify, unpack, and theorize those forms.

Antecedents of South African resistance in global perspective

It is impossible to understand contemporary resistance in South Africa outside of the history of its democratic transition. The struggles of today are deeply shaped by both memories of the apartheid regime and the movements that brought it down. They are also shaped by earlier waves of struggle within the post-apartheid period, which opened space for critical narratives and laid a foundation for new patterns of resistance. These waves of struggle, from the anti-apartheid struggle of the 1980s to the first wave of popular struggles in the post-apartheid period, parallel resistance that was occurring at a global level. Tracing these parallels is

6 *Marcel Paret*

useful, not only for making sense of current protest in South Africa, but also for linking it to the new global protest.

Organised around an ideology of white supremacy rooted in Afrikaner nationalism, apartheid was 'the most comprehensive racist regime meant to be a permanent structure that the world has ever seen.'[15] Perhaps most important for our purposes here, it also gave rise to one of the most vibrant periods of resistance the world has ever seen. Following a period of brutal repression and quiet in the 1960s, resistance began to re-emerge in the 1970s, most notably in the form of the 1973 strike wave and the 1976 uprising by youth in Soweto. By the 1980s struggles were proliferating in various forms, from workplace strikes to township boycotts and protests to armed insurrections to the creation of new resistance-oriented organisations. These struggles often revolved around 'bread and butter' issues such as wages, rents, and transport costs. But they fed into, and in turn energized, the broader struggle against apartheid. Animated by the common vision of a democratic, post-apartheid society, a characteristic feature of resistance during this period was the convergence and mutual coordination of struggles in workplaces and communities.[16]

The anti-apartheid struggle also represented the fusion of at least three separate global trends of resistance. First, it reflected the wave of decolonization that began to spread across Africa from the 1950s and reached many southern African countries in the 1970s. South Africa officially became a republic in 1961, but apartheid maintained many key features of African colonial rule.[17] In this sense it was the last holdout of colonialism and overt 'racial dictatorship',[18] which partially explains why the liberation movement was so vibrant. Second, the struggles of the 1980s paralleled the emergence of poverty-fuelled urban unrest throughout the Global South.[19] Indeed, the very same conditions of urbanization, unemployment, and poverty that lie beneath current protests had become prevalent in the final years of apartheid, and were a major impetus for resistance. Third, the involvement of black trade unions in the liberation struggle reflected a wider trend whereby the relocation of manufacturing capital into the developing world – most notably in South Africa, Brazil, and South Korea – sparked both the growth of new unions, and their engagement in broader democratic struggles.[20]

Combined with a growing movement from abroad, this confluence of resistance led to the crumbling of the apartheid regime. Its final demise was marked by the first democratic election in 1994, which brought the ANC to power with Nelson Mandela as the president. The post-apartheid transition infused South African society with a sense of optimism and hope. Speaking to this hope, the ANC's 1994 campaign slogan (which it still retains) promised 'a better life for all.' It follows that the period immediately after 1994 was one of relative calm, especially when contrasted with the tumultuous 1980s and early 1990s. This does not, however, mean that resistance and contention disappeared entirely. Instead it was funnelled into the dominant organisations of the liberation struggle – the ANC, the South African Communist Party, the Congress of South African Trade Unions (COSATU), and the South African National Civic Organisation (SANCO) – which would come to be known as the 'Alliance'. Yet to a certain degree these

Southern resistance in critical perspective 7

organisations began to dismantle the organs of 'people's power' that had been forged in the 1980s.[21] Having successfully toppled apartheid and installed a new state, many activists began to turn to their energy towards governance rather than resistance.

But the contradictions of post-apartheid capitalism were too significant to be contained. If the democratic transition had created new political freedoms, the lack of any substantial economic transformation meant that many South Africans continued to live in poverty. With the elimination of the pass laws, this poverty was increasingly relocated from the rural areas to the peri-urban periphery, including both formal townships and informal settlements. Post-apartheid poverty is underpinned by a high unemployment rate – hovering around 35 percent if 'discouraged work-seekers' are included – combined with the rise of part-time, temporary, informal, and other forms of precarious and low-wage work. It is exacerbated further by the privatisation of public goods such as water and electricity.

In the late 1990s these conditions gave rise to an upsurge in township-based struggles, often around evictions and water and electricity cut-offs.[22] Across the country these struggles became the basis for the formation of new organisations that would come to be known as the 'new social movements'. They were 'new' in the sense that they developed in the post-apartheid period, and thus were not part of the Alliance, even if they were often spearheaded by anti-apartheid activists and in some cases even initiated by Alliance partners. The most prominent among them were the Anti-Privatisation Forum (APF), Landless People's Movement, Anti-Eviction Campaign, Concerned Citizens Forum, and Treatment Action Campaign, most of which had a number of locally based affiliates. These organisations drew from and stoked the energy of resistance that was beginning to emerge on the ground. They were very critical of the ruling party and the 'neoliberal' trajectory of the ANC-led post-apartheid state, and called for a more radical program of public service delivery and redistribution to the poor.

The emergence of the new social movements in South Africa paralleled the rise of the Anti-Globalisation Movement or Global Justice Movement (AGM/GJM), whose iconic struggles included the 1999 Battle in Seattle and other protests against the IMF, WTO, and World Bank. This protest movement grew out of earlier resistance against structural adjustment policies in Africa and the Global South more generally.[23] Further, some of South Africa's social movements (e.g. the Soweto Electricity Crisis Committee, an affiliate of the APF), became prominent pillars of the AGM/GJM's 'movement of movements.'[24] Following from this global connection, it makes sense that two of their most important formative moments were during international conferences: the World Conference Against Racism in Durban, and the World Summit on Sustainable Development (WSSD) in Johannesburg, during which the new movements mobilized a massive march of 25,000 people against neoliberal-oriented development.[25] The new movements also participated in the World Social Forum, which became one of the most visible expressions of the AGM/GJM.

The heyday of the new social movements in South Africa was relatively short, peaking in 2002 with the WSSD march. Some of the movements remained

8 *Marcel Paret*

prevalent for several years afterwards. The Anti-Privatisation Forum, for example, did not officially collapse until 2010.[26] Further, many of the local, community-based affiliates – often referred to as 'concerned residents committees' and 'crisis committees' – remain alive, albeit as weakened shadows of their former selves. Yet by 2005 the social movements as a whole were clearly in a state of decline.[27] This decline paralleled, and was reinforced by, the decline of the AGM/GJM on a global scale. Just as the South African movements were beginning to disappear, so were the protests against the IMF, WTO, and World Bank.

Yet despite their limited duration, the new social movements in South Africa had a profound impact on the country. To a certain extent they put popular resistance back on the map, stepping into the void created by the massive demobilization of popular forces after 1994. As Dale McKinley, a long-time activist with the Anti-Privatisation Forum, reflected on the significance of that particular movement organisation:

> The APF's relevance stemmed from the reality of the ANC state's betrayal of the broad working class (i.e. inclusive of the underemployed and unemployed) . . . its role was to (partially) fill the organisational and political/ideological vacuum that had been created, so as to offer a new avenue for the voices and struggles of the poor and a means to impact on the most basic needs of the poor majority through mass mobilisation/action, organisational coherence, political engagement, educational initiatives and the creation of a new consciousness of the possibilities of radical change.[28]

It must be acknowledged that in the early 2000s, despite the persistence of widespread economic hardship, popular resistance and critiques of state policy were commonly discredited as being at odds with the continuation of the liberation movement. Along these lines the new social movements were often criticized by the Alliance organisations for being 'ultra-left' and counter-revolutionary. While this certainly proved to be difficult terrain for collective resistance, this earlier wave of struggle 'broke the ice' by giving some legitimacy to critiques of the state and the ruling party. Although they climaxed relatively early, therefore, the new social movements established a legacy of resistance that would continue long after their popularity had waned.

South Africa's contentious democracy

Just as the social movements were beginning to experience a period of decline in the middle of the 2000s, a new wave of struggle was emerging. This included an outbreak of community protests around issues of 'service delivery', which represented a somewhat new form of resistance. But it also included a continuation, and to some extent an amplification, of militancy by organised and semi-organised workers. Although these struggles began in the mid-2000s, they accelerated especially after 2009. This momentum parallels the spread of global protest in the wake of the 2008 global financial crisis.

Southern resistance in critical perspective 9

Beginning in late 2004 a series of community-based protests around public 'service delivery' issues began to spread across the country.[29] The protests are popularly referred to as 'service delivery' protests because they commonly place demands on various levels of government for the provision of resources and services such as houses, water, electricity, roads, streetlights, proper toilets, and refuse removal. According to mainstream news reports, an average of 238 such protests occurred per year between 2005 and 2014. They have also increased steadily: Between 2005 and 2008 there was an average of 10 protests per month; between 2009 and 2014 the monthly average jumped to 26.[30] Because these figures only capture protests reported in the media, they represent a lower bound on the actual number of protests. Police incident reports suggest that the true numbers are significantly higher.

The recent wave of community protests resembles the earlier wave of social movements in that it is rooted in the country's poverty-stricken townships and informal settlements. Community protests also express similar demands – issues of 'service delivery', for example, were central for the social movements – though they tend to revolve more around the immediate needs of community members, and less around broader demands for structural transformation. The key difference, however, is that community protests are more loosely organised and only partially, if at all, connected to formal organisations. It is in this sense that Gillian Hart refers to them as 'movements beyond movements.'[31] This fluidity reflects greater and more widespread discontent and resistance, which the social movements were unable to incorporate. It also feeds into the militancy of the protests, which often result in road barricades and property destruction.[32]

Paralleling this upsurge in communities, there has also been a consistent wave of resistance within workplaces. South Africa has one of the highest levels of strike activity in the world, ranking fourth in terms of working days lost per 1,000 workers for the period from 1999 and 2008.[33] According to official statistics provided by the South African Department of Labour, between 2005 and 2013 there was an average of 82 strike actions and 5.2 million working days lost per year.[34] Some of the largest strikes have taken place in the public sector, with major work stoppages including teachers, nurses, and others in 2007 and 2010. But industrial actions have also been prevalent in the private sector, particularly in the mining, manufacturing, and transport industries.

Workplace militancy has perhaps been more traditional in the sense that it is often led by unions. But even here collective organisation has begun to emerge outside the boundaries of formal organisation. It is worth noting, for example, that 45 percent, 52 percent, and 48 percent of industrial actions in the years 2012, 2013, and 2014, respectively, were 'unprotected', meaning that they took place outside of formal collective bargaining institutions.[35] Evidence also exists that union leaders are facing growing pressure from below. Analysing the massive 2007 and 2010 public sector strikes, for example, Ceruti shows how the impetus for collective action shifted: Whereas in 2007 the union leadership was the driving force, in 2010 the leadership essentially had the strike pushed onto them by the militancy of the members.[36] The uprising at Marikana, as well as the subsequent

10 *Marcel Paret*

farmworker uprising in the Western Cape, epitomized these trends, with militancy from below spilling over into informal organisation and action.

To begin to make sense of this widespread resistance, it must be situated against the backdrop of the declining hegemony of the ruling party, the African National Congress (ANC). Electoral support for the ANC grew during the first decade of post-apartheid democracy, increasing from 63 percent in 1994 to 70 percent in 2004, but it began to wane in the second decade, dipping back down to 62 percent by 2014. The ruling party now faces an increasingly formidable opposition, both from the Democratic Alliance, which is gradually shedding its image as a party only for white voters, and from the Economic Freedom Fighters, a popular new party founded in 2013 by expelled former members of the ANC Youth League.[37]

On top of these challenges, the ANC's key Alliance partner, COSATU, has been wracked by internal divisions which centre precisely over how organised workers should relate to the ruling party. The voices most critical of the ANC – NUMSA, the largest affiliate, and Zwelinzima Vavi, the former General Secretary – were expelled from the federation in 2014–2015, and have been promoting oppositional politics and structures. Other COSATU affiliates, such as the NUM, the South African Transport and Allied Workers Union (SATAWU), and the South African Municipal Workers Union (SAMWU) have experienced splits or widespread disaffection to non-COSATU unions. In short, while the ANC-led Alliance remains dominant, that dominance is increasingly insecure.

This volume aims to unpack the politics of resistance, in both communities and workplaces, in this period of declining ANC hegemony. What are the class dynamics at work, and how do they shape the motivations, aims, and organisation of protesters? How does this resistance relate to the post-apartheid state, the ANC, and party politics more generally? What is the relationship between formal and informal approaches to organizing? How has widespread resistance influenced or reshaped the organised Left? In addressing these questions we develop a perspective on contemporary global resistance that is firmly rooted in the experiences of the Global South.

Southern perspectives and critical theory

Processes of knowledge production mirror the social structures in which they occur. One such structure is the division between the advanced economies of the Global North and the peripheral economies of the Global South. Mirroring the colonial legacy of the divide and the persistent unequal development it represents, social science hierarchies tend to value and reward knowledge produced in the North more than knowledge produced in the South. This hierarchy is evident, for example, in where the most prestigious and most cited academic journals and scholars are situated.

In her book, *Southern Theory*, Raewyn Connell aims to disrupt this privileged position of the North with respect to knowledge production.[38] Taking aim at the canon of sociological theory – Marx, Weber, Durkheim, Coleman, Giddens,

Southern resistance in critical perspective 11

Bourdieu – she argues that it ignores both the experiences of people in the Global South as well as their intellectual production. In her view, sociological theory is Northern Theory, produced in the North about people in the North, and presents Northern experiences as universal. In response she calls for the democratization of knowledge production through the development of Southern Theory, which would be produced by scholars from the South and pertain to Southern experiences. Towards this end she aims to construct a new canon of sociological theory based on theorists from Iran, Argentina, Brazil, Mexico, India, Benin, and South Africa.

To a certain degree the study of social movements has fallen into the trap that Connell highlights. The dominant political process and resource mobilization perspectives, for example, were largely built around studies of North America and Europe.[39] Scholarship rooted in the South has been less central to the generation of social movement theory. But this does not mean that the Global South has been free of social movements, or that they have been ignored entirely by the academy. Indeed, there is a growing body of scholarship on social movements in Africa, Asia, Latin America, and the Middle East.[40] This volume thus contributes to a growing trend of developing social movement theory from the South.

Of course, the Southern Theory project has its own complications and limitations. Perhaps most importantly, it contains the risk of homogenizing knowledge production on both sides of the North/South divide. On the one hand it may undermine the critical side of Northern theory, however marginal it may be, and also gloss over crucial political and economic differences between developed countries. On the other hand the notion of Southern Theory may downplay important divisions and inequalities within the South. Not only are there vast economic, political, and cultural differences between and within countries in the South, but this diversity is overlaid with varied access to the North. Just as there are scholars from the North who maintain a deep engagement with the South, including both theoretical engagement and lived experience, there are many scholars in the South – including some in Connell's chosen canon – who are trained in, live in, or maintain close ties with the academies of the North.

For these various reasons, Burawoy advocates for an approach based not on Southern Theory but on Traveling Theory – an idea borrowed from Edward Said – which refers to the way in which social science knowledge traverses the North/South divide.[41] He argues that the meaning of social theory is transformed when it travels, often in subversive ways. He thus concludes: 'There is no meaningful Northern theory insulated from Southern theory, but only theory that circulates between North and South – and the best critical theory transforms itself as it traverses the globe, turning itself against itself.'[42] This approach perhaps underestimates the hegemonic role of the North in global knowledge production. But it resembles Connell's approach in the sense that it requires a democratisation of knowledge production, with scholarship rooted in the South playing an important role in the development of theory. In contrast to Connell, however, it also suggests that we should welcome the cross-pollination of theory across the North/South divide, reconstructing it along the way and pushing it in critical directions.

12 *Marcel Paret*

The contributions of this volume may be understood as a mixture of Southern theory, traveling theory, and critical theory. In making sense of the South African case, several authors engage and critique the traditional social movement theory of the North (see especially Runciman, Chapter 3). But more centrally the contributions have been inspired by a recent interest in bringing Marxism and capitalism back in to the study of social movements and contentious politics.[43] At the root of this resurgent interest in Marxism and capitalism is a call to situate protests and social movements within their broader historical and political economic contexts. This includes an emphasis on class structure and class struggle, which are themes that run throughout the current volume. Towards this end, the figures of both Marx and Polanyi loom large. Whereas Marx understood class struggles as emanating from exploitation at the point of production, for Polanyi they are rather a response to experiences of marketization and commodification. Whereas some contributions here point to a shift from Marx to Polanyi, with the latter assuming greater significance in the contemporary period (Burawoy, Chapter 2, Levenson, Chapter 6), others suggest that both are needed to make sense of current resistance (Webster and Ludwig, Chapter 9).

A renewed focus on political economy also calls for greater attention to the political content of resistance, which is a central focus of this volume. This dimension has often been neglected in social movement studies, in favour of explaining the emergence and success of movements.[44] In uncovering this political dimension, our analysis brings a host of new scholars and concepts to bear on the study of collective resistance – from Gramsci's notion of organic intellectuals (Sinwell, Chapter 10), to Auyero's analysis of patronage politics (Mukwedeya and Ndlovu, Chapter 7, and Dawson, Chapter 8), to Chatterjee's concept of political society (Paret, Chapter 4, Levenson, Chapter 6). These tools are useful for making sense of a postcolonial context where party politics, under ANC hegemony, remain incredibly crucial (Runciman, Chapter 3).

These theoretical interventions force the question of the *political* significance of resistance, and in particular, the extent to which it challenges or reinforces the status quo (on this question, see especially Lodge and Mottiar, Chapter 5, and Nieftagodien, Chapter 11). In South Africa, the results are mixed. Whereas current protest movements are certainly making waves and raising attention, thus far they have largely failed to destabilise the political and economic order that has dominated since the democratic transition in 1994. Attending to these nuances generates new perspectives on the politics of global resistance, particularly in the South.

In making these contributions to social movement theory, we also build on a rich history of South African scholarship on social movements, including a host of influential volumes that are referenced throughout the current volume.[45] These volumes illustrate the vibrancy of knowledge production within and about South Africa, though they are only rarely recognized and cited outside of the country. This lack of recognition stems partially from the limited attention that they give to the global context and resistance happening elsewhere. These previous volumes were also largely concerned with an earlier wave of struggles that began in the

The political terrain of current South African struggle

late 1990s, coalesced around the so-called new social movements, and peaked in the early 2000s. In contrast, we focus here on the struggles that accelerated after 2008, becoming visible to the world through the Marikana massacre, and we situate them within the context of proliferating global resistance.

The political terrain of current South African struggle

Marking a subtle shift from social movement organisations to the political contexts in which resistance takes place, this volume focuses on what may be understood as *terrains of struggle*. By this we mean particular political, economic, and cultural formations in which struggles emerge and develop. This does not mean we abandon the study of formal organizations, which remain quite important. Rather, it means that we situate them in relation to capitalism and class dynamics, including especially the rise of precarious and informal work, as well as unemployment. It also means developing a critical analysis of the state, which is especially significant in the context of South Africa's democratic transition. Finally, this approach allows for an analysis of different forms of organisation, both formal and informal, and their interaction with each other.

The volume is organised around the political formation of resistance on five different, yet overlapping, terrains of struggle. We begin with *global formations*, which focus on the diffusion of common conditions and practices across countries. Drawing on Polanyi's theory of the double movement, Michael Burawoy argues that global protest may be understood as societal responses to the ravages of marketization, from the devastation of land and the insecurity associated with flexible labour, to the anarchy of financial speculation and the commodification of knowledge. He also posits that these Polanyian 'countermovements' tend to take common forms, with critiques of representative democracy giving way to experiments with direct democracy, and an emphasis on occupying public space leading to tense interactions with law enforcement agents. These provocations are the starting point for Carin Runciman's chapter, which argues that movement research should focus less attention on formal organisations. She concludes that Burawoy's analysis largely applies to the South African context, but that it does not account for the significance of the ANC, thus suggesting the need to extend the Polanyian framework to incorporate issues of governance and party politics.

This task is taken up in the second section on *community formations*, which pertain to the ongoing and loosely organised struggles within impoverished townships and informal settlements. Drawing a common thread through the works of Frantz Fanon, Mahmood Mamdani, and Partha Chatterjee, Marcel Paret's chapter develops a theoretical approach to protest from spaces of political exclusion and economic marginality. This approach illuminates three key features of current protest: their location on terrains of governmentality, their organisation around recognition and community, and their strategic operation within a grey zone of illegality. Drawing on a series of Durban-based case studies, Tom Lodge and Shauna Mottiar examine the complicated political consequences of these struggles from spaces of exclusion. While concluding that communities are not 'anti-systemic',

14   *Marcel Paret*

they nonetheless uncover a deep commitment to democratic politics that could result in significant future challenges. Following on this theme, Zachary Levenson examines the case of a successful social movement in Cape Town, the Housing Assembly. Reinforcing Burawoy's emphasis on anti-commodification struggles, Levenson shows how focusing on the market, rather than the state, enables community members to overcome the fragmentation and underlying competition of community struggles.

Our third terrain of struggle is composed of *local state formations*, which are deeply entangled with community formations, but extend deeper into local party politics and municipal bureaucracies. Focusing on the case of Buffalo City (East London) municipality in the Eastern Cape, Tatenda Mukwedeya and Hlengiwe Ndlovu show how community protests become ensnarled in party politics through both the imposition of party leaders, who seek to use community mobilisation for political gain, and the invitation of community activists, who reach out to parties for assistance with their struggles. They argue that the mobilisations remain important expressions of widespread dissatisfaction, but that their entanglement with party politics ends up depoliticising community grievances. Hannah Dawson examines similar dynamics within the Zandspruit informal settlement just north of Johannesburg, with a particular focus on the perspectives of unemployed youth. But in contrast to Mukwedeya and Ndlovu, who illustrate how community-driven protest politics become incorporated into party politics, Dawson shows how factionalism within ANC may instigate community mobilisation. Though initially party-driven, however, the mobilisation nonetheless takes on a life of its own, with frustrated residents pushing for change that extends beyond the party and into the community.

Fourth, we turn to *labour formations*, including both municipal service workers as well as the Marikana mineworkers. Edward Webster and Carmen Ludwig trace the trajectory of struggles by the South African Municipal Workers Union (SAMWU), from the anti-apartheid movement, to the emergence of post-apartheid resistance with the new social movements, to the struggles of the contemporary period. They show how municipal workers adapted to the changing terrain of struggle – including both shifting political relationships and the casualization of work – by leveraging different forms of power, and eventually, organising around opposition to corruption and demanding permanent jobs for all workers. Whereas this innovation was driven largely by the union leadership, Luke Sinwell's chapter illustrates that the 2012 uprising by Lonmin mineworkers (at Marikana) was largely driven by workers from below. Tracing the formation of the independent worker committees and their R12,500 monthly wage demand, he emphasises how 'organic' intellectuals were able to effectively articulate the material conditions of the mines and communicate them to other workers.

These various formations of resistance, especially the uprising at Marikana but also the many other struggles within workplaces and communities, had a profound impact on the broader South African political context, including the organised Left. In the final section we turn to *Left formations*. Noor Nieftagodien examines the reorganization of the South African Left after Marikana, including the formation of the EFF and the tensions within COSATU, as well as the recent moves by NUMSA to establish a United Front of progressive forces and explore the possibilities of a Movement for Socialism.

Taken together these chapters provide a thorough investigation of the politics of protest in contemporary South Africa. They cover a wide range of areas, from Johannesburg to Cape Town to Durban to the Eastern Cape. They also combine theoretical innovation with rich empirical data, in many cases collected through extended ethnographic fieldwork. In doing so, they make a valuable contribution to the current study of global protest. Perhaps most importantly, they provide a perspective from the Global South, from one of its most restless countries. From the events at Marikana, to the daily protests in the townships and shack settlements, to the ongoing transformations of the labour movement, South Africa is fertile ground for making sense of resistance in the current era of global capitalism.

Notes

1 I extend a special thanks to Marcelle Dawson, Sarita Gaytan, Peter Alexander, and my co-editors, Carin Runciman and Luke Sinwell, for providing valuable feedback on previous versions of this chapter.
2 Peter Alexander, Luke Sinwell, Thapelo Lekgowa, Botsang Mmope, and Bongani Xezwi, *Marikana: A View from the Mountain and a Case to Answer* (Auckland Park: Jacana, 2012).
3 National Union of Metalworkers of South Africa (NUMSA), *NUMSA Special National Congress, December 17 to 20, 2013, Declaration*, December 20, 2013, accessed October 24, 2014, http://www.numsa.org.za/wp-content/uploads/2013/12/SNC-Declaration-final-copy.pdf.
4 Marcel Paret, Luke Sinwell, and Bridget Ndibongo, 'Are the Red Berets the Calm Before a Real Leftist Storm?' *Mail & Guardian*, May 16–22, 2014, p. 12.
5 Various, *Western Cape Agriculture Takes a Formal Decision to Come Out in Support of Du Doorns Strike*, November 12, 2012, accessed August 22, 2014, http://cosatu.org.za/show.php?ID=6684.
6 Marcel Paret and Carin Runciman, 'The 2009+ South African Protest Wave,' *WorkingUSA: The Journal of Labor and Society* 19, 3, 301–319 (2016).
7 Peter Alexander, 'A Massive Rebellion of the Poor,' *Mail & Guardian*, April 13, 2012, accessed April 17, 2012, http://mg.co.za/article/2012-04-13-a-massive-rebellion-of-the-poor.
8 Mike Davis, 'Spring Confronts Winter,' *New Left Review* 72 (2011): 5–15
9 Mohammed A. Bamyeh, 'The Global Culture of Protest,' *Contexts* 11 (2012).
10 Kees Biekart and Alan Fowler, 'Transforming Activisms 2010+: Exploring Ways and Waves,' *Development and Change* 44 (2013): 527–8.
11 Clive Gabay, 'Who's Heard of the African Spring?' *Open Democracy*, July 25, 2012, accessed October 24, 2014, https://www.opendemocracy.net/clive-gabay/who%E2%80%99s-heard-of-%E2%80%98african-spring%E2%80%99.
12 Paul Mason, *Why It's Kicking Off Everywhere: The New Global Revolutions* (London: Verso, 2012), 72.
13 In 2015 and early 2016, a series of student protests exploded across the country. These protests were perhaps more similar to the uprisings seen elsewhere, particularly in terms of the participation of educated youth. But they also tended to be more localized at specific universities. How the student movement will relate to the more sustained

16   *Marcel Paret*

resistance in communities and workplaces remains to be seen. See Paret and Runciman, 'The 2009+ South African Protest Wave.'

14 Guy Standing, *A Precariat Charter: From Denizens to Citizens* (London: Bloomsbury, 2014).

15 George M. Fredrickson, *Racism: A Short History* (Princeton: Princeton University Press, 2003), 133.

16 Gay Seidman, *Manufacturing Militance: Workers' Movements in Brazil and South Africa, 1970–1985* (Berkeley: University of California Press, 1994); Edward Webster, 'The Rise of Social Movement Unionism: The Two Faces of the Black Trade Union Movement in South Africa,' in *State, Resistance and Change in South Africa*, ed. Philip Frankel, Noam Pines, and Mark Swilling (London: Croom Helm, 1988).

17 Mahmood Mamdani, *Citizen and Subject: Decentralized Despotism and the Legacy of Late Colonialism* (Princeton: Princeton University Press, 1996).

18 Howard Winant, *The World Is a Ghetto: Race and Democracy Since World War II* (New York: Basic Books, 2001).

19 John Walton and David Seddon, *Free Markets and Food Riots: The Politics of Global Adjustment* (Oxford: Blackwell, 1994).

20 Seidman, *Manufacturing Militance*; Beverly Silver, *Forces of Labor: Workers' Movements and Globalization since 1870* (Cambridge: Cambridge University Press, 2003), 43–7, 54–64.

21 Michael Neocosmos, 'From People's Politics to State Politics: Aspects of National Liberation in South Africa,' in *The Politics of Opposition in Contemporary Africa*, ed. Adebayo O. Olukoshi (Uppsala: NAI, 1998).

22 Ashwin Desai, *We Are the Poors: Community Struggles in Post-Apartheid South Africa* (New York: Monthly Review Press, 2002).

23 Jackie Smith, 'Globalizing Resistance: The Battle of Seattle and the Future of Social Movements,' *Mobilization* 6 (2001): 1–19.

24 Tom Mertes, *A Movement of Movements: Is Another World Really Possible?* (London: Verso, 2004).

25 Prishani Naidoo and Ahmed Veriava, 'Re-membering Movements: Trade Unions and New Social Movements in Neoliberal South Africa,' in *From Local Processes to Global Forces* (Durban: Centre for Civil Society Research Reports Vol. 1, 2005).

26 Dale McKinley, *Transition's Child: The Anti-Privatization Forum* (Braamfontein: The South African History Archive, 2012).

27 Oupa Lehulere, 'The New Social Movements, COSATU, and the "New UDF",' *Khanya: A Journal for Activists* 11 (2005); Carin Runciman, 'The Decline of the Anti-Privatisation Forum in the Midst of South Africa's "Rebellion of the Poor",' *Current Sociology* 63 (2015): 961–79.

28 McKinley, *Transition's Child*, 19.

29 Doreen Atkinson, 'Taking to the Streets: Has Developmental Local Government Failed in South Africa?' in *State of the Nation: South Africa 2007*, ed. Sakhela Buhlungu, John Daniel, Roger Southall, and Jessica Lutchman (Pretoria: HSRC Press, 2007), 54–8; Susan Booysen, 'With the Ballot and the Brick: The Politics of Attaining Service Delivery,' *Progress in Development Studies* 7 (2007): 23–5; Peter Alexander, 'Rebellion of the Poor: South Africa's Service Delivery Protests – A Preliminary Analysis,' *Review of African Political Economy* 37 (2010): 25–40.

30 Paret and Runciman, 'The 2009+ South African Protest Wave.'

31 Gillian Hart, *Rethinking the South African Crisis: Nationalism, Populism, Hegemony* (Athens: University of Georgia Press, 2013).

32 Marcel Paret, 'Violence and Democracy in South Africa's Community Protests,' *Review of African Political Economy* 42 (2015).

33 Haroon Bhorat and David Tseng, 'South Africa's Strike Data Revisited,' *Brookings*, April 2, 2014, accessed August 22, 2014, http://www.brookings.edu/blogs/africa-in-focus/posts/2014/03/31-south-africa-strikes-bhorat.

Southern resistance in critical perspective   17

34 South Africa Department of Labour, *Annual Industrial Action Report* (Pretoria: Department of Labour, 2003–2014).
35 Ibid.
36 Claire Ceruti, 'The Hidden Element of the 2010 Public Sector Strike,' *Review of African Political Economy* 38 (2012): 151–7.
37 Marcel Paret, 'Contested ANC Hegemony in the Urban Townships: Evidence from the 2014 South African Election,' *African Affairs* 115, 460, 419–442 (2016).
38 Raewyn Connel, *Southern Theory: Social Science and the Global Dynamics of Knowledge* (Cambridge: Polity, 2007).
39 Doug McAdam, John D. McCarthy, and Mayer N. Zald, *Comparative Perspectives on Social Movements: Political Opportunities, Mobilizing Structures, and Cultural Framings* (Cambridge: Cambridge University Press, 1996).
40 Sara C. Motta and Alf Nilsen, *Social Movements in the Global South: Dispossession, Development and Resistance* (New York: Palgrave MacMillan, 2011); Joel Beinin and Frederic Vairel, *Social Movements, Mobilization, and Contestation in the Middle East and North Africa* (Redwood City: Stanford University Press, 2011).
41 Michael Burawoy, 'Traveling Theory,' in *Conversations with Bourdieu: The Johannesburg Moment*, ed. Michael Burawoy and Karl von Holdt (Johannesburg: Wits University Press, 2012).
42 Ibid., 217–18.
43 Colin Barker, Laurence Cox, John Krinsky, and Alf Gunvald Nilsen, *Marxism and Social Movements* (Leiden: Brill, 2013); Laurence Cox and Alf Gunder Nilsen, *We Make Our Own History: Marxism and Social Movements in the Twilight of Neoliberalism* (London: Pluto Press, 2014); Donatella della Porta, *Social Movements in Times of Austerity: Bringing Capitalism Back into Protest Analysis* (Cambridge: Polity, 2015).
44 Andrew Walder, 'Political Sociology and Social Movements,' *Annual Review of Sociology* 35 (2009): 393–412.
45 Nigel Gibson, *Challenging Hegemony: Social Movements and the Quest for a New Humanism in South Africa* (Trenton, NJ: Africa World Press, 2006); Richard Ballard, Adam Habib, and Imraan Valodia, *Voices of Protest: Social Movements in Post-Apartheid South Africa* (Scottsville: University of KwaZulu Natal Press, 2006); William Beinart and Marcelle C. Dawson, *Popular Politics and Resistance Movements in South Africa* (Johannesburg: Wits University Press, 2010); Marcelle C. Dawson and Luke Sinwell, *Contesting Transformation: Popular Politics and Resistance Movements in South Africa* (London: Pluto Press, 2012).

Part I
Global formations

2 Social movements in the neoliberal age

Michael Burawoy[1]

South Africa stands at the crossroads of two types of social movements – movements based on unequal inclusion in the major institutions of society and movements based on forcible exclusion from those institutions. This book offers case studies of the included – largely the well-established labor movement that exercises its power through the resources at its disposal and the dependence of capital and state on labor – but also of the excluded, typically protests against service-delivery deficiencies (electricity, water, healthcare, sanitation, etc.) that often resort to violence precisely because they have few resources to mobilize.

We might say that post-apartheid South Africa, having been born with expectations of inclusion, is increasingly the terrain of movements based on the excluded. The Marikana massacre of 2012 represents a turning point from one to the other – a strike by miners for a living wage is treated by the state as an insurgent revolt of the outsider. Earlier the appearance of xenophobic violence against immigrants in 2008 was another expression of a politics of precarity. The challenge to the ruling alliance – the formation of the United Front and the populist appeal of the party of the Economic Freedom Fighters – similarly reflects a turn toward a politics of exclusion. The move from inclusion to exclusion is a political shift in the relations between state and society as Marcel Paret describes in this volume (Chapter 3) and elsewhere.[2]

The transition so vividly being played out in South Africa reflects a much broader shift in the world beyond – from struggles of the included to struggles of the excluded, from Marx to Fanon; or to use Guy Standing's formulation, from the proletariat to a precariat; or in Partha Chatterjee's conceptualization, from the struggles in civil society to those of political society.[3] There is a certain ambiguity in Chatterjee's account as to whether the struggles of political society are distinctive of the global South, but others, such as Jean and John Comaroff are more forthright. They argue that the legacies of colonialism have made the South more vulnerable to the assault of 'neoliberalism', so that new modes of mobilization in the South are running ahead of the North, or as Jan Breman writes, the West is following the rest.[4] They are reversing the modernization teleology in which all things progressive were supposed to emanate from the North – now it is the South that is taking the lead as the 'hyperbolic prefiguration of its [north's] future-in-the-making.'[5] The South and North are such heterogeneous categories that it is difficult

22   Michael Burawoy

to make claims that one is following the other. Nevertheless, it can indeed be said that many countries of the North are heading in a southerly direction as they face the erosions of civil rights and workplace protections – protections that never existed in the South and where many novel experiments in market containment are now being developed, especially in semi-peripheral countries such as South Africa, Brazil, and India.

Rather than replace one teleology with another, I argue that we have to think of capitalism driving marketization across the globe, with very varying effects in different countries and regions, depending on the nexus of political, economic, and social structures. Nevertheless, the global wave of movements that began in 2011 and fizzled out two years later does reflect a broad but uneven shift towards exclusionary politics. I describe such exclusionary politics by reference to the rise of marketization – often summarily and inadequately labeled as neoliberalism – that lies behind a distinctive set of social movement repertoires found in both the North and the South. These movement repertoires call for a new theory of social protest that connects them to marketization.

As many others have done, I turn to Karl Polanyi's *The Great Transformation* to theorize social movements from the standpoint of marketization, more specifically as a response to the lived experience of commodification but also a response to the obverse process of ex-commodification, the expulsion from the market.[6] In this way I situate social movements in relation to the development of capitalism, expressing itself in what I call third-wave marketization. Finally, I turn to the place of sociology within this context – a field of study that is also under threat of commodification and, even worse, expulsion from commodification, that is, ex-commodification, whose survival will depend upon organizing itself as a social movement. Here, too, South Africa has been leading the way.

From marketization to exclusionary politics

If one is looking for innovative social movements from the South, then Latin America should be our first port of call. For many years much of the subcontinent was ruled by military dictatorship. The transition to democracy was a major and indisputable advance, but it has not fulfilled its promises, not least because the fall of political dictatorship was followed by another dictatorship, the dictatorship of the market through structural adjustment. In its wake came wave upon wave of injustice and inequality that have inspired Latin Americans, sociologists among them, to battle for a deeper democracy. We see this, for example, in the schemes of participatory budgeting in Brazil and elsewhere, in the piquatero movement and factory occupations in Argentina, in the ethnic democracy of Bolivia, and in the student movement of Chile. There has been a relentless struggle to counter market fundamentalism with new forms of participatory democracy, many of these movements have been inspired by those who have been dispossessed by – often state-sponsored – marketization.[7]

This Latin American history of the past 30 years has been replayed in concentrated form but in different registers across the world. The silent encroachment of markets instigated the Arab Uprisings.[8] It began with the self-immolation of Mohamed Bouazizi in Tunisia on December 17, 2010, that sparked uprisings across the region in Tunisia, Egypt, Yemen, Libya, Syria, and Bahrain. Calling for 'bread, freedom and social justice' these uprisings may have been revolutionary in their demands but they have not delivered the outcomes they sought. All eyes were fixed on Egypt, where national rebellion gave rise to a frail democracy that was then hijacked by the military. Difficult though it has been to dislodge dictatorships, the real problems only began after their dissolution.

In part inspired by these movements, protest by the indignados of Southern Europe have stood up to the regimes of austerity, imposed by ruling parties aided and abetted by regional and international financial agencies. In 2011 and 2012 we witnessed a wave of remarkable protests allied to trade unions in Portugal and to more anarchist politics in Spain as well as to the growing strength of Podemos, to Grillo's populism in Italy and to a massive General Strike in Greece, leading to the rise of Syriza but also the neo-fascist Golden Dawn – all different responses to economic insecurity, unemployment, debt, and dispossession. Thus, we see in Southern Europe the shift from movements secure in their inclusion to movements precarious in their exclusion.

The Occupy Movement followed a similar pattern. Lodged in public spaces it targeted the 1% that runs the world economy as the dispossessing other. The movement began in Zuccotti Park, targeting Wall Street, the home of finance capital, and spread across the United States, travelled to Europe, Latin America, and Asia. Once again, the driving force is not a mobilization from within major institutions but from outside against those institutions. Moving farther afield, in India, for example, peasantries fought against their dispossession by the introduction of Special Economic Zones, collusive arrangements between finance capital and the Indian state.[9] Many of these projects now lie moribund. In China today the engine of growth is moving from the flood of cheap migrant labor into the towns to land appropriation and real estate speculation for the urbanization of rural areas.[10] Again protests, perhaps less advertised, are spreading across rural China even if so far they have not been very effective in arresting the formation of a rentier class. Similar struggles are familiar in Latin America, where the expansion of international mining has not only displaced populations but also polluted water and air.

We must also pay attention to the student movement, most spectacularly emanating from Chile, that has been struggling against the marketization of education at all levels. Chile has vast disparities of wealth, and students are at the vanguard of protests in a society throttled by accumulating private debt. We saw similar struggles in England, where students faced soaring fees, but also spreading across Europe as financialization and regulation begin to corrode what were once strongholds of public education. Students, once the pride and joy of the nation's future, suddenly find themselves fighting for their survival, turning them from citizens to consumers, corrupting the meaning of public education.

Not all social movements can be so easily connected to forces of marketization. Social movements in Russia and its former tributaries in Central and Eastern Europe, having been liberated from the pathologies of administered economies,

24 *Michael Burawoy*

retain a faith in markets. There, movements focus on political authoritarianism. Yet even here the effects of marketization might be seen as propelling many of the rightist movements. They point to a swing away from more emancipatory movements to right-wing populist movements not just in the former Soviet bloc but across Europe and indeed across the global South.

Can we say that the wave and counter-wave of social movements have anything in common that would justify talking about them as an expression of a particular historical epoch? Can we detect any convergent set of repertoires that allow us to talk of a common wave of protest? Or should they be considered in isolation, reflective only of local or national rather than the global context? I first identify a set of repertoires that many of the movements share and then try to link them to the rise of marketization, an uneven process that spans the globe.

Common political repertoires

These new social movements of exclusion may be marked by their economic origins – responses to different forms and dimensions of marketization – but they gain expression and consciousness in the political arena. Let us consider some of the features they share.

First, they share what differentiates them. They all have a national specificity, whether it be a struggle against dictatorship, against austerity, or against the privatization of education. They are framed by national political terrains, which exhibit regional patterns – Southern Europe, Middle East, Latin America, South-East Asia, and Africa. Yet, at the same time, these movements are also globally connected whether through social media or traveling ambassadors. Movements have become an inspiration for each other even if their frame of reference is usually national.

Second, they derive from a common inspiration, the idea that electoral democracy has been hijacked by capitalism, or more specifically, finance capital. Governments are beholden to finance capital, which effectively paralyzes electoral democracy – capitalist in content and democratic in form. In Zygmunt Bauman's terms there is a separation of power and politics, so that power is concentrated in the hands of the capital-state nexus, while electoral politics is reduced to an ineffectual ritual.[11]

Third, the movements reject formal democracy to adopt direct democracy, sometimes called 'prefigurative politics' that involve horizontal connections as much as vertical struggles. The General Assemblies of participatory democracy have been the cellular foundation of many of these movements. The challenge, then, is to bring unity and broader vision to these autonomous, and often separatist, struggles. They have had varying success in connecting themselves to wider publics in more than ephemeral moments.

Fourth, while much has been made of virtual connections, these make concrete real space more rather than less necessary. To be effective, virtual communications requires its complement – the assembly points of public space, Zuccotti Park in New York, Catalunya Square in Barcelona, Tahrir Square in Cairo, Taksim

Social movements in the neoliberal age 25

Square in Ankara, etc. These assembly points were crucial to establish dense and creative communities, and the planning of new and novel actions. Social media become an auxiliary, if essential, tool of communication.

Finally and fifth, the occupation of public spaces has made the social movements vulnerable to a severe repressive backlash from police, often, but not always, backed up by the military. This repression is consistent with the destruction of the public more generally and the valorization of the private, but it has prompted a continuing cat and mouse game between movements and police, involving targeted repression and preemptive neutralization as well as naked coercion.[12] These movements have enormous staying power. They are a form of 'liquid protest' that disappears here only to reappear elsewhere. We have to look at them as part of a connected global movement, connected by social media that provide the vehicle for continual reorganization and flexibility. Fear of coercion has been replaced by despair and anger.

I agree with Carin Runciman's discussion in this volume that South Africa represents such a shift toward a movement of the excluded. Ostensibly the strike of the Lonmin miners was a strike of the employed and the included but it quickly turned into a struggle of the excluded. It was a specifically national strike framed by national political context. The striking Lonmin miners rejected their union and increasingly the ANC, convinced that capital and the state collaborated in their violent defeat. They formed a cohesive movement that definitely inspired struggles in other sectors of the economy, although there is little evidence that the struggles in South Africa were connected to struggles beyond. For the Marikana workers, geographical assembly points were more crucial than social media. At the same time the focus on physical location reflects and deepens their isolation from the wider society. Finally, the Marikana killings represent the prototype of the deployment of naked coercion, but also the way such ham-fisted techniques can actually galvanize public support for a social movement.

The conjecture of this paper is that these social movements which are *represented and represent* themselves as the revolt of the excluded can, indeed, be *explained* in terms of a differentiated response to marketization that has become a defining feature of our era. We need, in other words, a new sociology *of* movements that attends not only to the political repertoires they deploy but also to the pressures of marketization to which they are a response. Second, such a sociology should advance a unifying vision *for* these movements, a vision they so badly need that knits them together in a common project. Finally, third, sociology is itself subject to pressures of commodification and ex-commodification. As social scientists we have to drop the pretense that we are outside society, and explicitly recognize that we are part of the world we study and have no alternative but to take a stand. If we do not, sociology will become irrelevant and dissolve. Just as it is disrupting society, so marketization is also undermining the conditions of our own existence through the spread of poorly paid contingent faculty, expansion of on-line education and vocational degrees, and the rise of consumerized education. We need to connect sociology to its potential allies beyond the university before it is too late – *sociology becomes a social movement*. We take up each of these tasks in turn.

26   *Michael Burawoy*

Sociology of social movements

In the past 25 years, social movement and protest research has become one of the major subfields of sociology. The literature is large and diverse, but it is fair to say that the field's defining concepts – resources, organization, political opportunity, and framing, among others – seem to be less relevant for understanding movements of exclusion. It is worth noting that recent trends indicate that more of the field's practitioners recognize the theoretical limitations of these concepts. First, there was the dynamics of contention perspective that rejected the goal of a comprehensive theory as unachievable.[13] Second, there is a recent trend that stresses relational elements of movement development, mitigating grand theoretical designs by playing close attention to context and the full repertoire of actors.[14] Third, some have called to reintroduce political economy and Marxist concepts into the analysis,[15] which have been conspicuous by their absence in the field.

Just as James McCarthy and Mayer Zald[16] saw the turbulent 1960s as teeming with grievances, so now we see the world is teeming with social movements of the excluded that fall outside the field's theories of the past 25 years. The problem is not the existence of social movements but their temporality which can be understood only by exploring their origins and their context. We need to turn to the society from which they emanate; we need to (re)turn to theories of collective action that see them as rooted in the wider society. Thus, Alain Touraine and his collaborators insisted on rooting 'new social movements' of the 1960s and 1970s in post-industrial society, giving movements the possibility of fabricating their own worlds.[17] These were movements that transcended the pursuit of material interests characteristic of the old social movements (specifically the labor movement).

The 'new' social movements of today, however, have to grapple not with postindustrialism but with the devastation of society wrought by market fundamentalism, which affects the whole planet and not just particular societies, although their expression is usually inflected through a national sieve. To understand the connection between today's social movements and unregulated marketization I propose to turn to Karl Polanyi's *The Great Transformation*.

Written in 1944, explaining the continued existence of capitalism but without denying its problematic character, *The Great Transformation* can be considered a revision of *The Communist Manifesto* written a century earlier.[18] Polanyi argues that the experience of commodification is more profound and immediate than the experience of exploitation, which as Marx himself argued was hidden from those who were supposed to rebel against it. In effect Polanyi takes Marx's theory of commodity fetishism, namely that market exchange obscures its ties to production, more seriously than Marx who thinks such illusions will dissolve in class struggle. For Polanyi, the source of resistance lies in the experience of the market rather than production. The expansion of the unregulated market threatens to destroy society which reacts in self-defense, what he calls the counter-movement against the market.

Social movements in the neoliberal age 27

One of the virtues of Polanyi's theory, like Marx's, is that it links the micro-experience of people to the world systemic movements of capitalism through a series of mediating levels. The lynchpin of the connection lies in the idea of the fictitious commodity – a factor of production which when subject to unregulated exchange loses its use value. For Polanyi labor is but one such fictitious commodity; the others are land and money. Today these factors of production are subject to an unprecedented commodification that even Polanyi never anticipated.

When labor is subject to unregulated exchange, that is, when it is commodified, when it is hired and fired at will with no protection, when the wage falls below the cost of the reproduction of labor power and when the laborer cannot develop the tacit skills necessary for any production, so the use value of labor also falls:

> For the alleged commodity 'labor power' cannot be shoved about, used indiscriminately, or even left unused, without affecting also the human individual who happens to be the bearer of this peculiar commodity. In disposing of a man's labor power the system would, incidentally, dispose of the physical, psychological, and moral entity 'man' attached to that tag. Robbed of the protective covering of cultural institutions, human beings would perish from the effects of social exposure; they would die as the victims of acute social dislocation through vice, perversion, crime, and starvation.[19]

The issue, therefore, is not exploitation but commodification. Indeed, as Guy Standing has eloquently demonstrated, the problem today is the disappearance of guaranteed exploitation, and in its place the rise of precarity, not just within the proletariat but climbing up the skill hierarchy.[20] Precarity is part of the lived experience behind so many contemporary movements – from the Arab Uprisings to the Indignados, from the Occupy Movement to Student movements – but also, just as clearly behind so many of the movements in South Africa.

Thus, today's movements of the excluded have to grapple with the dispossession from access to alternative means of subsistence, that is, the elimination of social supports – including minimum wage legislation, unemployment compensation, and pensions but also access to land. Just as the separation of labor from land provides for the commodification of labor, so it also provides for the commodification of land, which according to Polanyi also threatens the viability of the human species. 'Nature would be reduced to its elements, neighborhoods and landscapes defiled, rivers polluted, military safety jeopardized, the power to produce food and raw materials destroyed.'[21]

> The economic argument could be easily expanded so as to include the conditions of safety and security attached to the integrity of the soil and its resources – such as the vigor and stamina of the population, the abundance of food supplies, the amount and character of defence materials, even the climate of the country which might suffer from the denudation of forests, from erosions and

28   *Michael Burawoy*

dust bowls, all of which, ultimately, depend upon the factor land, yet none of which respond to the supply-and-demand mechanism of the market.[22]

These prescient comments prefigure contemporary discussions about the plunder of nature, how the destructiveness of markets has led to a host of struggles, especially in the Global South, from landless movements in Latin America to popular insurgency against Special Economic Zones in India, protests against land speculation and expropriation in China. Throughout the world the mining of natural resources has generated militant opposition from communities whose livelihoods are threatened. It takes place within the urban context, too, against such processes as gentrification and the attempt to build global cities, both of which involve the expulsion of the marginal from their homes. We have to extend the commodification of land to the commodification of nature more broadly: the commodification of water that generated water wars in countries as far apart as South Africa and Bolivia, protest against market solutions to climate change, so-called carbon trading, and most recently against fossil fuel extraction through fracking.

Polanyi regarded money as a third fictitious commodity. For Polanyi money is what makes market exchange possible, but when it itself becomes the object of exchange, when the attempt is to make money from money then its use value as a medium of exchange is undermined. 'Finally, the market administration of purchasing power would periodically liquidate business enterprise, for shortages and surfeits of money would prove as disastrous to business as floods and droughts in primitive society.'[23] Polanyi was especially concerned that fixed exchange rates between currencies organized through the gold standard would create economic rigidities within national economies while going off the gold standard would create chaos and radical uncertainty. Today, we see how finance capital again becomes a prominent source of profit, making money from money, whether it be through micro-finance, whether it be loans to nation states, whether it be student loans or mortgages or credit cards. The extraordinary expansion of debt eventually and inevitably brings about bubbles and just as inevitably their popping. The creation of debt only further intensifies insecurity and immiseration, feeding protest across the globe. Indeed, loan sharks, even sponsored by the mining companies, were another major grievance of the Marikana miners.

There is a fourth fictitious commodity – knowledge – that Polanyi did not consider. The theorists of postindustrial society, preeminently Daniel Bell, recognized knowledge as an ever-more-important factor of production giving pride and place to the university as its center of production.[24] But Bell did not anticipate the way the production and dissemination of knowledge would be commodified, leading the university to sell its knowledge to the highest bidders, biasing research toward private rather than public interests, cultivating students as customers who pay ever-increasing fees for instrumentalized forms of knowledge. The university reorganizes itself as a corporation that maximizes profit not only through increasing revenues, but also cheapening and degrading its manpower by reducing tenured faculty, increasing the employment of low-paid adjunct faculty (which the university itself produces), and outsourcing services, all the while expanding its

Social movements in the neoliberal age 29

managerial and administrative ranks. The protests emanating from universities, from Chile to Quebec – be they from students or faculty – center on its privatization and the distortion of the production and dissemination of knowledge brought on by commodification.

Contemporary social movements, therefore, can be understood in terms of the creation of the fictitious commodity through different forms of *dispossession*, through the reduction of the fictitious commodity to an *object of exchange* that annihilates its commonly understood purpose, and through the new forms of *inequality* commodification produces. Any given movement may organize itself in the political realm, but its driving force lies in the experience of the *articulation of these different commodifications*. But marketization entails not just commodification but ex-commodification, the expulsion of potential commodities from the market. Whether this be labor, money, nature, or knowledge the other side of commodification is waste, which itself stirs up so many protests. When labor can no longer sell its labor power, when money is no longer of use value, when nature is destroyed, this also propels collective reaction. There is no one-to-one relation between social movement and a given fictitious commodity, but each movement is the product of the relation among fictitious commodifications and real ex-commodifications, both being the result of the wider and deeper expansion of the market. This is a general theory that insists on the particularity of social movements, which makes any sort of unity across movements difficult to achieve.

The wave of protests that have arisen to challenge this round of marketization does not, at least as yet, add up to a Polanyian counter-movement that would contain or reverse marketization. For that, there needs to be a far greater self-consciousness and vision among the participants of the connections among their movements and their roots in marketization. Such a consciousness requires not just a sociology *of* social movements but a sociology *for* social movements.

A sociology for social movements

Touraine's theory of social movements was also a theory *for* social movements.[25] At the center of his recast sociological theory were social movements, making history themselves, what he called 'historicity'. The sociologist was no longer outside society, studying its inherent laws of change, but inside society heightening the self-consciousness of movements in the fashioning of history. This reflected a period – post-industrialism – in which there was confidence in human agency to direct history whether via the state or civil society. There was an underlying optimism that capitalism could somehow be tamed and directed to human ends. That has all disappeared. We are now living in an era in which markets run amok, devastating all that stands in their way. A sociology for social movements must begin by understanding this period of unconstrained marketization.

We need, therefore, to situate Polanyi's fictitious commodities within a wider framework of the history of capitalism. The essence of *The Great Transformation* lies in an argument about the dangers of the expansion of the market, namely that it leads to a reaction from society that can be of a progressive character (social democracy, New Deal) but also of a reactionary character – fascism and Stalinism.[26] Thus, Polanyi's history has one long expansion of the market, starting at the end of the eighteenth century, destroying society along the way but also leading to a defense of society, secured through a counter-movement directed by states that regulate the market, specifically arising in response to the economic crisis of the 1930s – states that include regimes of social democracy and New Deal as well as fascism and Stalinism. Polanyi could not imagine humanity would dare to risk another round of market fundamentalism. Yet, that is just what happened, starting in the middle 1970s, developing on a global scale, leaving few spaces of the planet unaffected. The rising concern with globalization expresses the global reach of markets.

But this is not capitalism's first wave of marketization as is often implied by the use of the term 'neoliberalism'. Indeed, examining Polanyi's own history suggests it is not even the second but the third wave. Where he saw a singular wave spreading over a century and a half, we can now discern two – one that advanced through the first half of the nineteenth century and was turned back by the labor movement in the second half, and a second wave that advanced after World War I and was reversed by state regulation in the 1930s extending into the 1970s, which in turn was succeeded by a third wave of marketization that has yet to be contained. These waves of marketization become deeper over time as their scale increases, but they also involve different combinations of the fictitious commodities. The counter-movement to first-wave marketization in the nineteenth

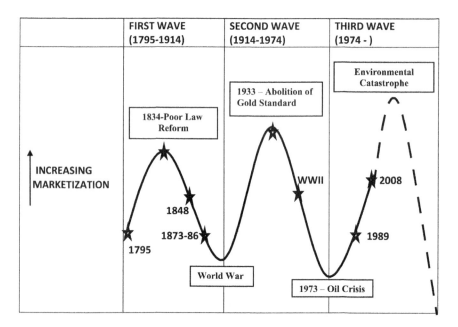

Figure 2.1 Three waves of marketization and their counter-movements

Social movements in the neoliberal age 31

century was dominated by the struggle to decommodify labor. In England (about which Polanyi writes) this assumed the form of the factory movement, cooperatives, Owenism, trade union formation, and the Labour Party. The local struggles spread, melded together, and compelled changes in state policy.

The success of labor struggles in the nineteenth century led to a crisis of capitalism, resolved through imperialist strategies and World War I, followed by an offensive from capital, leading to the _recommodification_ of labor. The assault of the market spread to the loosening of constraints on international trade through currencies pegged to the gold standard that, in turn, led to uncontrollable inflation and the renewal of class struggles. The upshot was a variety of regimes that sought to regulate markets through the extension of social rights as well as labor rights.

These regimes – whether social democratic, fascist, or Soviet – lasted until the middle 1970s at which time they faced a renewed and mounting assault from capital not only against the protections labor had won for itself but also against state regulation of finance, marked by the end of Bretton Woods. Indeed, we can see how the offensive against labor across the planet, but especially in the North, led to a crisis of overproduction that did not lead to a renewed Keynesian politics but to the financialization of the economy via the creation of new moneys that could be extended to individuals in the form of credit (credit cards, student loans, and, above all, sub-prime mortgages), but also to enterprises and countries generating unprecedented levels of debt. The bubble burst when the debtors – whether individuals, enterprises, or countries – could no longer deliver on their interest payments. There were few limits to what finance capital could commodify – from minerals to water, from land to air – creating the environmental catastrophe that the planet now faces. The solution to create new markets in the rights to pollute and destroy the atmosphere – the so-called carbon markets – has not proven to be a solution but a way of making money from the deepening ecological crisis.[27]

Third-wave marketization has gone far deeper than second-wave marketization in the commodification of labor, nature, and money. Moreover, to turn something into a commodity requires first that it be disembedded from its social and political moorings. Labor has to be dispossessed from its supports in the state, peasants have to be dispossessed from access to their land, people have to be dispossessed of access to their own body (so that their organs can be sold). This dispossession requires, in short, the escalation of violence perpetrated by states on behalf of capital, and direct deployment of violence by capital. Violence is at the heart of third-wave marketization in a way that Polanyi never anticipated.

Moreover, Polanyi did not and could not have anticipated a fourth fictitious commodity – knowledge. Today what used to be a public good – knowledge produced, for example, in the university was available to all – is fast becoming a private good. The production and dissemination of knowledge in the university has been commodified as a result of the forcible withdrawal of public funding. With important exceptions in such countries as China, India, and Brazil – and even here the situation is changing – the university has had to become self-financing by selling the knowledge it produces to industry (the growth of the collaboration of bio-medical sciences and pharmaceuticals), by seeking funds from donors and

32   *Michael Burawoy*

alumni, and above all by an exponential increase in student fees. The major universities around the world are sacrificing their accountability to local and national interests as they are subject to world ranking systems that force them to follow the standards of the richest universities in the United States. This program of rationalization brands the university as worthy or not of investment, working hand in glove with the commodification of the production and dissemination of knowledge which, in turn, is the source of new strategies for the commodification of labor, nature, and finance.

This Polanyian analysis faces a number of challenges. First, it is a perspective from the North. Polanyi has little to say about the world beyond Europe and the United States, except for the interesting description of colonialism in South Africa which he presents as an extreme destruction of society through commodification. What he misses, of course, is the importance of indirect rule, the development of labor reserves and what was effectively a cheap labor policy that set *limits* on the commodification of labor, if not its exploitation. Omitted is the crucial role South Africa and other parts of the colonial and dependent world played in the global economy, in sustaining Northern capitalisms. A revision of our Polanyian theory would require looking at the South African economic history from the standpoint of the three waves of marketization. Broadly speaking one can indeed say that the first wave of marketization focused on the development of South African mining; the second wave saw the superimposition and rising of dominance of manufacturing and new forms of commodification of land and labor – commodification that would experience a reversal in the form of apartheid. In the 1980s the third wave of marketization arrived with the apartheid state opening up the African labor market and challenging the protections of white labor. But it was the post-apartheid state, jettisoning the ANC's more socialist leanings, that became an agent of third-wave marketization. Indeed, democratization became a vehicle of loosening up and expanding markets in labor, land, water, and housing – although these processes should not be exaggerated as the South African state has made considerable efforts to provide welfare through social grants and housing schemes. In the area of higher education – a continuing strength of South Africa – there are pressures toward privatization, raising fees, outsourcing, and so on. Third-wave marketization is, indeed, sweeping the world but we have to also think of the *interdependence* of its different expressions in different countries and how in turn these different expressions give rise to reactive social movements.

The second problem of the Polanyian scheme is its inability to explain marketization itself. For him the rise of industrial civilization is coterminous with marketization and for Polanyi the future faces two alternatives: fascism or socialism. His account of the genesis of marketization in Britain stresses the role of ideas – the ideas of political economists, appalled by the Speenhamland system that created local subsidies for labor and thereby set up barriers to the development of a national labor market. However, once one recognizes the recurrent waves of marketization, then one has to begin to link them to the dynamics of capitalism – how marketization is a response to crises of accumulation, both crises of profitability and crises of overproduction.[28] The profitability crisis of the 1970s led to the expansion of the market through the commodification of labor, money, nature, and knowledge,

Social movements in the neoliberal age 33

a combination that varies over time and space. If the upswing of marketization is driven by the endogenous logic of capital, then there is no such endogenous logic to the countermovement, which is governed by subjective factors. Marketization certainly generates multiple reactive movements, but when and how they will add up to a counter-movement depends on the balance of social forces. For that we need to develop a sociology that establishes their inter-connection – a sociology built on the relation between crises of capitalist accumulation and market expansion. What I have offered here are the building blocks of such a theory – the specificity of third-wave marketization as the underlying cause of social movements, and third-wave marketization understood as the articulation of four fictitious commodities – labor, nature, finance, and knowledge. The possibility of a counter-movement has to take into account the forces that are propelling marketization.

Sociology as social movement

In underlining the fourth fictitious commodity – knowledge – I am pointing to the transformation of the conditions of production of knowledge. What relative autonomy the university possesses is rapidly evaporating in the face of its privatization. The pressures are visible here in South Africa where the university system has managed to maintain its integrity, but in much of the continent universities are becoming fee-paying vocational schools. To the extent that research continues it moves into policy units and think tanks. The academy is no longer outside society, an objective platform from which to study society as an external object of examination. The market has invaded this once-sacred terrain. Those disciplines that are best able to exploit market opportunities are the ones to benefit – the biomedical sciences, engineering, law, and business schools – and they become the more powerful influences within the university at the potential cost of the social sciences and humanities whose existence is under threat.

The social sciences, however, do not form a homogeneous block. Ironically, economics has created the ideological justification of market fundamentalism – the very force that is destroying the university as an arena for the independent pursuit of knowledge. Political science, concerned with political order, now aspires to be an extension of economics, reflecting the increasingly collusive relation between markets (and especially finance capital) and nation states. Of course, there are dissidents within both fields, and they play an important role, but the dominant tendency is the endorsement of market fundamentalism through the embrace of utilitarianism. Sociology, too, has endured efforts to turn it into a branch of economics, but the anti-utilitarian tradition within sociology from Marx, Weber, and Durkheim all the way to Parsons, Bourdieu, feminism, and postcolonial theory are so well entrenched that economic models have made few inroads.

Nor is this surprising since sociology was born with civil society – an arena of institutions, organizations, and movements that are neither part of the state nor part of the economy. But we should be careful not to romanticize civil society as some coherent, solidary whole as though it were free of exclusions, dominations, and fragmentations. It is Janus faced – it can aid the expansion of the market and state, but it can also obstruct or, at least, contain their expansion. This is

34   *Michael Burawoy*

where sociology is situated – its distinctive standpoint is civil society with all its divisions – examining the economy and state from the perspective of their consequences for civil society as well as the ways in which civil society supports the economy and the state. Like civil society, sociology looks two ways. On the one side it examines the social conditions of the existence of markets and states. On the other side, along with such neighboring disciplines as anthropology and geography, it studies and condemns the unregulated expansion of the state-market nexus with its destruction of civil society.

In the context of the rationalization and commercialization of the university, sociology is the one discipline whose standpoint, viz. civil society, behooves it to cultivate a community of critical discourse about the very nature of the modern university, but also conduct a conversation with publics beyond the university, making it accountable to those publics without losing its commitment to its scientific research programs. South African sociology has always stood at the forefront of such critical engagement, developing ties to civil society, pursuing questions generated by those ties, yet at the same time sustaining an autonomy and independence, essential to the development of research programs. The distinctiveness of South Africa's contribution to sociological analysis can be found not so much in the jettisoning of Northern sociology but in transforming it, hybridizing it, provincializing it, and reversing it, and above all making it accountable to local publics without losing its global referents. I'm thinking here of such institutions as SWOP (now called the Society, Work and Development Institute) at the University of the Witwatersrand that celebrated its thirtieth anniversary in 2015, or the Centre for Sociological Research at the University of Johannesburg, and most significantly the newly created National Institute of Humanities and Social Sciences whose architects and leaders have been sociologists.

As the membrane separating the university from society becomes ever thinner, failure to counter-balance the privatization of the university will end with the destruction of the university as we know it. It is in this sense that we must think of sociology as a social movement as well as scientific discipline, calling for a critical engagement with the world around. To sustain this dual and contradictory role, the discipline must develop its own mechanisms for internal dialogue, mechanisms that appear at the local level within the university, and at a national level but most importantly at a global level. Building such a global sociology requires the development of a global infrastructure that fosters dialogue and outreach, that produces a third-wave sociology to meet the theoretical and practical challenges of third-wave marketization, and to halt the Third World War that is being waged on communities across the planet.

Notes

1   I'd like to thank Marcel Paret both for his unflagging criticisms of this paper and for teaching me much about the politics of precarity. Thanks also to an anonymous reviewer who went through the text with meticulous care, correcting misstatements and adding others that I have adopted.

2   Marcel Paret, 'Precarious Class Formations in the United States and South Africa,' *International Labour and Working Class History* 89 (2016): 84–106.

Social movements in the neoliberal age   35

3 Frantz Fanon, *The Wretched of the Earth* (New York: Grove Press, 1963 [1961]); Guy Standing, *The Precariat: The New Dangerous Class* (London: Bloomsbury Academic, 2011); Partha Chatterjee, *The Politics of the Governed* (New York: Columbia University Press, 2004).

4 Jean Comaroff and John Comaroff, *Theory from the South* (Boulder, CO: Paradigm Publishers, 2012); Jan Breman, 'A Bogus Concept?' *New Left Review* 84 (2013): 130–8.

5 Comaroff and Comaroff, *Theory from the South*, 19.

6 Karl Polanyi, *The Great Transformation: The Political and Economic Origins of Our Time* (Boston: Beacon Press, 2001 [1944]).

7 Here I have been influenced by the research of Gabe Hetland's and his PhD dissertation *Making Democracy Real: Participatory Governance in Urban Latin America* (University of California, Berkeley, 2015).

8 See Adam Hanieh, *Lineages of Revolt* (Chicago: Haymarket Books, 2015).

9 Here I have been influenced by the research and dissertation of Michael Levien, *Regimes of Dispossession: Special Economic Zones and the Political Economy of Land in India* (Berkeley: University of California, 2013).

10 Here I have been influenced by the research and dissertation of Julia Chuang, *The Changing Foundations of Chinese Development: From Low-Cost Labor to Land Dispossession* (Berkeley: University of California, 2014).

11 Zygmunt Bauman, *Liquid Modernity* (Cambridge: Polity Press, 2000).

12 See Laleh Behbehanian, *Preemption of Resistance: Occupy Oakland and the Evolution of State Power* (PhD dissertation, University of California, Berkeley, 2016).

13 Doug McAdam, *Sidney Tarrow and Charles Tilly, Dynamics of Contention* (Cambridge: Cambridge University Press, 2001); Doug McAdam, and Sidney Tarrow, 'Introduction: *Dynamics of Contention* Ten Years On,' *Mobilization* 16 (2011): 1–10.

14 Charles Tilly, *Contentious Performances* (Cambridge: University of Cambridge Press, 2008).

15 Laurence Cox and Alf Nilsen, *We Make Our Own History: Marxism and Social Movements in the Twilight of Neoliberalism* (London: Pluto Press, 2014).

16 Jon McCarthy and Mayer Zald, 'Resource Mobilization and Social Movements: A Partial Theory,' *American Journal of Sociology* 82 (1972).

17 Alain Touraine, *Return of the Actor* (Minneapolis: University of Minnesota Press, 1988).

18 Polanyi, *The Great Transformation*; Karl Marx and Frederick Engels, *The Communist Manifesto* (London: Verso, 1998).

19 Polanyi, *The Great Transformation*, 76.

20 Standing, *The Precariat*.

21 Polanyi, *The Great Transformation*, 76.

22 Ibid., 193.

23 Ibid., 76.

24 Daniel Bell, *The Coming of Post-Industrial Society* (New York: Basic Books, 1976).

25 Touraine, *Return of the Actor*.

26 Polanyi, *The Great Transformation*.

27 Here I have learned much from Herbert Docena's PhD dissertation, *Passive Revolution on the World Stage: The Political Origins of Climate Change* (University of California, Berkeley, 2016).

28 Here I have been influenced by theory of long waves or Kondratieff waves. See, for example, Ernest Mandel, *Long Waves of Capitalist Development* (London: Verso, 1995). This theory of waves also broadly fit with the waves of inequality discovered by Thomas Piketty, *Capital in the Twenty-First Century* (Cambridge, MA: Harvard University Press, 2014).

3 South African social movements in the neoliberal age

Carin Runciman

Burawoy's thesis (Chapter 2) follows a small but growing critique of the mainstream study of social movements that advocates for the reintroduction of political economy into their analysis.[1] This chapter contributes to this emerging perspective and responds to Burawoy's thesis in three ways. First, it questions what is conventionally defined as a social movement. If we are to bring 'political economy back in'[2] to the study of social movements, then I argue we also need to rethink the basis upon which social movements are conventionally defined. Drawing upon the work of Laurence Cox and Alf Gunvald Nilsen, the chapter proposes an alternative conceptualisation of social movements that views them not as a particular organisational form, a perspective common in mainstream social movement theory, but as a praxis resulting from the material realities of everyday life.[3] Second, the chapter assesses to what extent Burawoy's global analysis of contemporary social movements applies to the South African context. The South African case, I shall argue, provides an insight into the two types of movement identified by Burawoy, movements of unequal inclusion and movements of exclusion. By analysing the common repertoires of struggle identified by Burawoy, this chapter examines the continuities and discontinuities between South Africa and the global protest wave. Finally, the chapter examines some of the critical tensions that emerge from attempts to forge a 'sociology *for* society' that Burawoy advocates.[4] A discussion of the role of intellectuals in movements is particularly pertinent to South Africa and has been the subject of recent debates drawing critical attention to dimensions of power, race and class.

Defining social movements

Social movements are commonly discussed and analysed without specific attention to understanding and defining what a social movement is. While there is no agreed definition of the term 'social movement', what is commonly understood today as a social movement, at least within sociological literature, was largely shaped by post-1960 forms of mobilisation emanating predominately from the United States and Western Europe.[5] As Burawoy highlights (Chapter 2), social movement theory from the United States has often been used as a general theory of movements across space and time, concealing how this theory is rooted often within the particularities of the civil rights movement. I argue that this has introduced an organisational bias within the study of social movements, and narrowed the vision of what is understood as a social movement. This has particular consequences for the analysis of movements in the Global South, which often do not correspond to the semi-professionalised movements of the Global North.

Opp provides a useful overview of the various ways in which the concept 'social movement' has been defined and used.[6] Surveying the literature, he concludes that a social movement can be defined as 'a collectivity of actors who want to achieve their goal or goals by influencing the decisions of a target.'[7] In elaborating this definition, Opp highlights two features which are commonly associated with social movements. First, the concept of a social movement generally refers to 'some degree of formal organisation', thus social movement scholars frequently study social movement organisations, although there is no agreed definition of what makes a social movement organisation.[8] Second, Opp notes that size is frequently mentioned as a defining element of a social movement. He argues that social movements are considered to comprise large numbers of people and groups, but that what constitutes 'large' is largely left undefined. Opp's synthesis of the literature does exclude certain important aspects, such as collective identity, which have been key to the definition of social movements for some scholars. However, the aim here is not to critique Opp in particular but to highlight the centrality of organisation to the study of social movements.

For those studying the South African context, such a definition of social movement poses problems. As Paret highlights (Chapter 1), much of the recent protest activity in South Africa has occurred outside the organisational form that would conventionally be understood as a social movement. Furthermore, although in recent years protest has become almost a daily occurrence (see Figure 3.1), these protests are fragmented organisationally and politically from one another and have yet to coalesce into a unified movement (see Lodge and Mottiar, Chapter 5).

An alternative analytical frame may be to focus not on social movements, but rather 'cycles of protest'.[9] Tarrow characterises cycles of protest as consisting of five features: 'heightened conflict, geographic and sectoral diffusion, the appearance of new organisation and the appropriation of old ones, the creation of new "master frames" of meaning, and the invention of new forms of collective action.'[10] However, this framework shares a similar organisational bias and furthermore, neglects an understanding of contemporary dynamics of capitalism. For Tarrow, the industrialised working class is central to the geographicical and sectoral diffusion outlined as a central feature of a cycle of protest. He writes:

> particular groups recur with regularity in the vanguard of waves of social protest (e.g., miners, students), but they are frequently joined during the peak of the cycle by groups that are not generally known for their insurgent tendencies (e.g., peasants, workers in small industry, white collar workers).[11]

However, in an era of neoliberal capitalist relations and significant class restructuring, in South Africa and elsewhere, the unemployed have frequently been at the

38 *Carin Runciman*

forefront of protest activity. If we want to 'bring capitalism back in', and situate the social movements of the neoliberal age in their historical, social, economic and political context, then we need to re-think what is conventionally understood as a social movement.

Laurence Cox and Alf Gunvald Nilsen have over numerous years been elaborating a Marxist theory of social movements.[12] As a starting point they take a fundamentally different position on what constitutes a social movement than what is commonly found in conventional social movement literature. Rather than viewing social movements as 'collective actors seeking inclusion into a political market',[13] Cox and Nilsen propose that movements are 'materially *situated* in the everyday reality of people's lives – needs, experience, relationships, praxis – and are better understood as extensions of this than as a subset of the political system.'[14] For them, social movements are thus defined as:

> *a process in which a specific social group develops a collective project of skilled activities centred on a rationality – a particular way of making sense of and relating to the social world – that tries to change or maintain a dominant structure of entrenched needs and capacities, in part or whole.*[15]

Thus, social movements are products of the social articulation of 'conflictual encounters between dominant and subaltern social groups'.[16] This enables an analysis of social movements that not only recognises the mobilisation of subaltern groups, but also highlights the ways in which dominant groups mobilise 'social movements from above'.[17] This definition of social movements recognises that parameters such as organisational form and collective identity are products of the intersections between the historical, material, social and political. In sum, what this approach advocates for scholars to do is overcome traditional disciplinary divisions as to how different modes of mobilisation are studied, for instance, labour movements are commonly analysed separately from social movements. This means that social movements should not be studied through a static, abstract and predetermined frame of analysis, but rather be understood as products of particular materially grounded contexts. However, this does not mean reducing the study of social movements to an economic reading. Analysing the Lesbian, Gay and Transgender (LGBT) movement, Hetland and Goodwin demonstrate how the analysis of class and political economy can develop perspectives on issues such as collective identity.[18] To further substantiate the value of this approach and its relation to Burawoy's thesis, the rest of this chapter develops this analysis in relation to the South African context.

South African social movements in the neoliberal age

Burawoy (Chapter 2) frames his discussion of social movements in a neoliberal age around two axes, 'movements based on unequal inclusion' and 'movements based on forcible exclusion.' Whereas the former stem from the precarity of the employed, and often unionised, workers, the latter is driven by the unemployed.

South African social movements 39

What connects the two movements is the experience of marketization, both in a global and a national context.

Burawoy bases his analysis of the neoliberal age on the work of Karl Polanyi. He argues that social movements should be understood through the lens of four fictitious commodities: labour, land, money and knowledge, the latter being an innovation made by Burawoy. Taking a Polanyian perspective, Burawoy argues that resistance is generated through the experience of the market, thus 'any given movement may organise itself in the political realm, but its driving force lies in the experience of the *articulation of these different commodifications.*' There is not room here to offer a detailed critique of Polanyi, and such analysis can be found elsewhere.[19] Instead, I shall develop Burawoy's analysis to trace how commodification and marketization have shaped South African movements.

South Africa certainly shares many of the features of marketization that are commonly found across the globe. In the post-apartheid era the numbers of precariously employed, under-employed and unemployed have increased. The expanded definition of unemployed (which includes discouraged job seekers) hovers close to 40 percent, while for those in work some estimates claim that at least half the workforce is employed in casual or temporary jobs.[20] Post-apartheid the economy has increasingly financialised, with the financial sector's share of the economy growing from 6.5 percent in 1994 to 20 percent in 2009.[21] The impact of the commodification of nature through cost-recovery measures for services such as water has also been an important aspect of the post-apartheid landscape.

It is important to note, however, that the post-apartheid period has not seen a relentless march of marketization. Unlike many of its counterparts in the North, South Africa has seen an increase in social spending. This is perhaps most evident in the provision of social grants, which increased from a total of R18 billion (2 percent of GDP) in 2000/01, to R94 billion (3.5 percent of GDP) in 2009/2010.[22] While social grants have played an important role in decreasing poverty in South Africa, more than half of the population still survives on less than R779 ($67) a month, or R26 ($2.20) per day.[23]

The trajectory of movements in post-apartheid South Africa can be mapped against these patterns of marketization. The resurgence of social movements and protest in the post-apartheid period was closely associated with what is widely regarded as a neoliberal turn of the African National Congress (ANC) government, as encapsulated by the introduction of the Growth Employment and Redistribution (GEAR) policy in 1996. The subsequent processes of cost-recovery and moves to privatise public services significantly affected the lives of poor, predominately Black, working classes. Between 1995 to 2001 unemployment increased by 2 million, 10 million households were disconnected from water and electricity, and 2 million people were evicted from their homes.[24] This was far from the 'better life for all' that the ANC consistently promised in its electoral campaigns.

The subsequent response to GEAR has been viewed as a split between the 'traditional' Left – represented by the Congress of South African Trade Unions (COSATU) and the South African Communist Party (SACP) – and what may

40   Carin Runciman

be understood as the 'new' Left, characterised by the range of social movement organisations and community-based organisations that emerged in the wake of post-apartheid marketization.[25] While the analysis of the so-called 'new social movements' has tended to dominate discussion and debates, it must be noted that the period has not been devoid of the mobilisation of workers within COSATU-aligned unions. Public sector workers, for example, embarked on two significant strikes in 2007 and 2010.[26] The split in the 'Left' is not only reflective of political differences, but also of the way in which marketization has reshaped the working class during the first two decades of South Africa's democracy.

Von Holdt and Webster use the image of an onion to describe how the working class in South Africa has been restructured into a small core of permanently employed workers and a much larger group of precariously employed, under-employed and unemployed.[27] The restructuring of the working class has fueled struggles based on both 'unequal inclusion' and 'forcible exclusion' (Burawoy, Chapter 2). While Burawoy draws attention to the idea of 'precarity' as a central driving force behind new movements, it is important to be attendant to differences between the Global South and the Global North. While in the North, precarity is often discussed as a feature of both working- and middle-class lives, encapsulated in the idea of the 'graduate with no future',[28] in the South relations of precarity are more widespread and primarily experienced by the working class.[29] Developing an analysis of how precarity is experienced in the South, the next section examines contemporary protest in South Africa.

South Africa's rebellion of the poor

Peter Alexander uses the term 'rebellion of the poor' to describe the wave of 'service delivery' protests which have been growing since 2004.[30] While there is debate as to how protest should be documented in South Africa, a range of different data sources clearly illustrate that protest in South Africa has been increasing.[31] Figure 3.1 presents data on protest captured from media reports by the Rebellion of the Poor protest monitor based at the University of Johannesburg. As the chart shows, protest has been increasing since 2004, with at least one protest a day occurring in 2012.

Protests that characterise this so-called rebellion tend to focus on a range of 'service delivery' issues, such as the provision of housing, water and electricity. They generally emanate from poorer sections of townships or informal settlements. As other scholars have noted, the characterisation of this wave of protest as mere 'service delivery' protests serves to obscure the politics which underlie them.[32] Paret (Chapter 1) highlights that, while the demands of protestors often centre on demands for basic services, they also simultaneously raise critiques about the quality of post-apartheid democracy. Protests take many forms. Oftentimes protestors march to the local municipality, the focus of much protest activity in South Africa, to hand over a memorandum of grievances. Increasingly, protestors have embarked on more disruptive and even violent action, including the barricading of roads, the burning down of local amenities such as clinics, and even

South African social movements 41

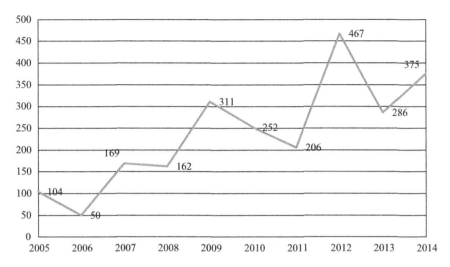

Figure 3.1 Community protests in South Africa, 2005–2014
Source: Rebellion of the Poor database

attacks on foreign-owned shops. Indeed the violence which seems to characterise South African protests has been the subject of intense debates.[33]

One of the difficulties researchers face in analysing this protest wave is the fragmented nature of these protests. Mottiar and Bond argue that protests are 'often geographically and politically isolated from each other, lack an ideological orientation and have no common programmes or bridging organizational strategies.'[34] The seeming lack of clear strategic and political orientation has led some commentators to characterise the protests as 'popcorn' protests, reflecting the way they seemingly spring out of nowhere but just as rapidly subside.[35] But the use of such terminology is problematic, as it belies the complex dynamics of protest that are mostly hidden from public view. Of particular importance are the numerous attempts that communities make to engage local government, often before any disruptive or violent activity, and the multiple rounds of community meetings that usually precede a protest. As Sinwell observes, a further weakness of scholarly analysis is the assumption that protests and social movements are essentially counter-hegemonic in nature.[36] Indeed, while the often disruptive and violent nature of protests may seem rebellious, other commentators highlight the continued dominance and persistently high levels of support enjoyed by the ruling party, the ANC.[37] In addition to this, a range of commentators have highlighted how protests are often underpinned by patronage politics from below and thus reflect an entanglement with the ANC, rather than a rejection of it.[38] While the political nature of protests may often be messy and contradictory, by returning to Burawoy's analysis we may see their common roots in conditions of precarity. As Burawoy highlights, while these struggles may take different forms, have

42   *Carin Runciman*

different goals and differing politics, they are connected through the way in which they express the materially situated lived experiences of marketization.

Common political repertoires: the South African case

Burawoy (Chapter 2) argues that the commonalities of marketization across the world have, in response, produced common political repertoires which, although national in their specificities, are globally connected. He defines five common political repertoires. First, he argues that movements are globally connected through social media or 'travelling ambassadors', which provide inspiration and link disparate struggles. Second, there is a generalised critique within such mobilisations that 'electoral democracy has been hijacked by capitalism'. Third, movements reject formal democracy in favour of direct democracy. Fourth, although social media and other virtual connections are important, they do not replace physical assemblies. Fifth, the occupation of public spaces is frequently met with violent repression from the police.

While Burawoy makes general examples to substantiate his typology, it has not yet been systematically applied to a national context. The following discussion uses Burawoy's common repertoires of struggle to analyse the South African case, drawing commonalities and differences between South Africa and the typology outlined by Burawoy. Although Burawoy discusses these repertoires as pertinent to both movements of unequal inclusion and exclusion, I largely limit my analysis here to movements of exclusion.

Virtual connections

The first feature Burawoy identifies attends to how specific struggles in different nation states are globally connected through social media and other forms of electronic communication. While the use of Facebook, Twitter and other forms of digital communication has been prominent in mobilisation in other parts of the world, in Southern (and Northern) movements of exclusion and precarity, a stratification by access of communication technologies is common. Recent protest activity in South Africa has largely occurred 'off the grid'. In 2007 only 7.3 percent of the population had access to the internet at home.[39] By 2013 this had risen, with 40.9 percent of the population able access to the internet, most of whom access the internet through cell phones.[40] Although growing, less than half of the population has access to the internet, and this figure would presumably be much lower within poor communities. This limits the ability of activists within poor working-class communities to make the global connections Burawoy highlights.

Even in the few instances where movements have made use of websites – organisations such as Abhahli baseMjondolo have both a website and Facebook account – questions arise as to who controls the content. It is commonly middle-class activists with access and technical skills who edit and update the content of such sites. This introduces significant power dynamics in shaping the public platforms of movements, particularly for an international audience, something that former Abhahli activist Bandile Mdlalose draws attention to in her account of the organsiation.[41] Therefore, although such technologies may provide points of connection between South African movements and the world, these points of connection are mediated by material relations, a point that is underdeveloped in Burawoy's thesis.[42]

Electoral democracy

The second dimension is that current movements share a view that electoral democracy has been hijacked by capitalism. Discussing the Occupy movement, Pickerill and Krinsky argue that the 2008 financial crisis created a 'tipping point in which the unfairness of bank bailouts juxtaposed against rising personal poverty triggered a moment of clarity of the absurdity of the current economic and political system.'[43] In South Africa, the global financial crisis did not generate the same kind of political 'tipping point' but it arguably did intensify the unfolding wave of community protests witnessed across the country (see Figure 3.1). In part this can be explained by the form the economic crisis took in South Africa. While the South African government did not have to bailout the financial sector, the country did experience the loss of 870,000 jobs in 2009 alone as a result of the crisis.[44] Despite the differences in how the crisis unfolded, the critique of democracy has been a salient feature of this movement.

A common theme that arises in discussions with protestors and activists is a sense of exclusion from South Africa's post-apartheid democracy. Commonly when democracy is discussed it is deeply entwined with a discussion of socioeconomic rights. Indeed, within southern Africa, South Africans exhibit the greatest awareness of the concept of democracy, but are much more likely to emphasise the realisation of socio-economic outcomes as crucial to democracy.[45] This focus on socio-economic outcomes is perhaps unsurprising given the historical experience of apartheid in which an exclusionary concept of citizenship was constructed around racially stratified rights to housing, services and employment, creating vast racialised inequalities.[46]

The fact that inequality has increased under a democratic regime frequently elicits comparisons between the apartheid past and the democratic present. This is reflected in numerous discussions with activists and illustrated here in an interview with Mandla, an activist from Soweto below. He explains:

> Before 1994 there was [sic] problems which differ from the problems that we are facing now. Before 1994 what I would say is that people were working and the price and the cost of living was low . . . after 1994 people were liberated from oppression, not from the economy. Everything was privatised and people could not afford to buy bread . . . Apartheid is gone and the new government is in but people cannot afford to run their life. That's where we think people have been sold to capitalism because there is no difference from the previous government and the present government, it seems as if they have changed the jockey and put another jockey on the horse.[47]

44   Carin Runciman

What Mandla expresses here through the idea of not being able to buy bread – that the material experiences of working-class Black South Africans are often worse now than under apartheid – has been common in my experiences talking with activists. That Mandla chooses to use bread as an example reflects not only the fact that it is a daily staple, but also that it is one of the commodities for which the apartheid regime regulated prices. The price of bread thus provides a direct and immediate example of how the forces of deregulation and commodification, unleashed in the transition to democracy, are experienced in everyday life. Crucially, Mandla recognises that the democratic transition of 1994 marked political liberation but not economic liberation. The critique of post-apartheid democracy, advanced by activists such as Mandla, has its roots in the anti-apartheid movement, in which a range of civic organisations and trade unions were orientated towards Left politics and socialist politics.[48] As a result, rather than being consigned to the 'dustbin of history', socialist ideas have continued to enjoy huge support in South Africa.[49] Thus, Mandla recognises the continuation of exploitative economic practices as the root of his problems. Mandla's interpretation is not necessarily widespread across the movement, as discussed previously. Recent mobilisations have often been diffuse in their political orientations, and Sinwell has cautioned against an over-optimistic reading of their counter-hegemonic potential.[50] While not all activists may be able to point to capitalism as the root cause of their problems, the material experiences of everyday life inform a deep sense that 'democracy is only for the rich.'[51]

While movements in South Africa may share a critique of democracy, it is debatable the extent to which electoral politics in South Africa has been 'reduced to an ineffectual ritual' in the eyes of the movement (Burawoy, Chapter 2). The continuing dominance of the ANC at the ballot box would suggest that despite widespread protest there is still a significant endorsement of the ANC's politics. This idea has been encapsulated in Susan Booysen's 'ballot and the brick' thesis. Booysen argues that protests form part of a 'dual repertoire', which poor communities use to fight for service delivery between elections, while remaining loyal to the party of liberation at election time.[52] However, some scholars have highlighted evidence to suggest a weakening of the ANC's political hegemony.[53] Voter turnout has declined rapidly over the 20 years of South Africa's democracy, from a high of 86 percent in 1994 to 57 percent in 2014. This means that in 2014, only 36.4 percent of the eligible voting-age population actually voted for the ANC. In Gauteng, a province with one of the highest rates of protest, this figure was lower still, with only 32.1 percent of the eligible voting-age population voting for the ANC.[54]

While voter registration and turnout may be decreasing in South Africa, an increasing number of community organisations and social movement organisations appear to be turning towards, rather than away, from electoral democracy as a mobilisation strategy. The Operation Khanyisa Movement, formed by the Soweto Electricity Crisis Committee, has since 2006 contested local government elections, and has a representative within the City of Johannesburg metropolitan municipality. Similarly, after a series of protests in Balfour in 2009, the Socialist Civic Movement emerged to win seats in the 2011 local government elections.[55]

Most recently the Bushbuckridge Residents Association contested and won seats in the 2011 local government elections and the 2014 provincial elections. Furthermore, within the United Front being led by the National Union of Metalworkers South Africa (NUMSA), many community-based organisations and Left political groupings have argued in favour of nominating candidates for the 2016 local elections.[56]

While the current protest movement may be critical of electoral democracy, this has not led to a withdrawal from this space of political contestation. In large part this can be explained by the fact that the right to vote for the majority was secured little more than 20 years ago. However, even in the North a total rejection of electoral politics has not occurred, as Syriza in Greece and Podemos in Spain both have important links to social movements. While the current protest movement in both the North and the South may be critical of electoral democracy, this has not led to a total withdrawal from this space of political contestation, as Burawoy contends.

Direct democracy

The third feature documented by Burawoy, that movements of the current period employ direct democracy in their mobilisation, is worthy of further examination. The ethos of deliberative participatory democracy is that all people should be able to express their views in an environment that facilitates participation and attempts to repress inequalities of power between individuals and organisations. Innovations within the internal democracy of movements seemed particularly apparent within the Occupy movement, where mass assemblies employed various techniques to encourage broad participation. Such styles of internal organising may appear new but, as Polletta highlights, the lineages of these forms of direct democracy can be traced as far back as to the eighteenth-century Quaker movement.[57] While these approaches may not be novel, they are distinctive, Polletta argues. In particular, she draws attention to the fact that in an age of social media the idea of 'participation' has become far more widely diffused across society, and that this influenced the internal culture of the Occupy movement.

In South Africa, the legacies of apartheid geography have meant that protest has not coalesced into the large public gatherings seen elsewhere. However, the organisation of protests frequently emanates from open and public community meetings in which issues are discussed, and mandates are given to community leaders based on the majority decision. This represents a form of direct democracy. However, the internal cultural repertoires of such meetings are distinct from that of the Occupy movement; for instance, the use of hand signals is rare. To understand this it is important to ground our understanding of the internal cultural repertoires of a movement within its historical context.

The civic movement that emerged in the 1980s played a crucial role in the struggle against apartheid, linking struggles around 'bread and butter' issues such as rent increases to the broader political context and opposition to the apartheid regime. Given the political context, an open and mass character to internal deliberations was clearly impossible but the civic movement created structures that

46 *Carin Runciman*

attempted to encourage democratic processes and ensure that the mandates of communities were followed. Although the structure of civics varied, they were commonly composed of street or yard committees, which then nominated leaders to represent them on a larger block committee. Representatives from the block committees then formed the area committee, which served as the executive leadership for the civic as a whole. This multi-layered leadership structure was also important in ensuring that activists could work somewhat autonomously from the other leadership structures, which counteracted the ability of the security forces to quash the movement through the arrest of high-profile leaders.[58] This tradition of cadre activism continues into the present day.

While open and public community meetings may often give the appearance of deliberative democracy, as Rebecca Pointer notes in her analysis of the Anti-Eviction Campaign, before meetings a small group of activists may meet to determine the agenda and, in some cases, largely determine the decisions that will be taken at the meeting. As Pointer highlights, these meetings often reproduced gendered exclusions.[59] Within my own research within the Anti-Privatisation Forum (APF), I often observed practices in which decisions made by a small group of activists were endorsed rather than debated within community meetings.[60] However, such practices, which may appear to be anti-democratic, had a high degree of popular legitimacy stemming as they do from the entrenched culture of cadre activism (but see Lodge and Mottiar, Chapter 5 for a differing perspective). This introduces a tension into understanding the practices of direct democracy, which may, at times, simultaneously be anti-democratic as well as popularly legitimate.

What this discussion highlights is that direct democracy should not be taken for granted, or assumed without critical interrogation. In the long-standing democracies of the Global North, the internal repertoires of movements have been shaped by an environment in which protest was, to a degree, tolerated. But in countries with authoritarian pasts, such as South Africa, the historical cultures of struggle continue to inform the present, creating forms of 'direct democracy' that look different to those employed elsewhere. Thus the analysis of direct democracy needs to be attentive to how practices differ over space and time.

Occupying public spaces and police repression

The final feature, the occupation of public spaces and police repression, are particularly pertinent to South Africa. As already noted, protest in South Africa has not been characterised by the large assemblies in central public places that have become emblematic in other parts of the world (see also Paret, Chapter 1). While protestors in South Africa may not have assembled in central public spaces of cities, the occupation of both public and private space has been a common repertoire of action. Road blockades of main arterial roads and highways is a common protest tactic. Furthermore, the occupation of private space frequently occurs through the occupation of land and the establishment of new informal settlements (Levenson, Chapter 6). While the kinds of spaces and the forms of their occupation may differ in South Africa, there is a shared experience of police repression.

As Wood highlights, the strategies of protest policing must be understood in relation to the political, social and economic forces of marketization on police organisations.[61] Across the world, policing and the policing of protest has increasingly become more militarized, and made more extensive use of intelligence gathering.[62] South Africa is no exception, with military-style ranks being introduced in 2010, as just one example.

While the Public Order Policing unit (the most common police unit to respond to protest in South Africa) is supposed to employ a logic of 'crowd management' in policing protest, recent experiences highlight the extent to which police seemingly resort to the use of force, commonly rubber bullets, tear gas and even, on occasion, live ammunition to disperse protestors. As a result, between 2004 and 2014, at least 42 people were killed by police during protests, excluding those killed at Marikana.[63] In addition to this, the state frequently attempts to circumvent the right to protest, and in the process increasingly criminalises protestors. A number of documented cases of state surveillance of activists have also occurred.[64]

A sociology for social movements?

Burawoy's intervention into the field of social movement studies does not just advocate a reframing for how social movements should be analysed, but also calls for a new mode of knowledge production. He argues that one of the challenges for a global sociology is to 'construct a sociology *for* society'.[65] This argument advances Burawoy's previous calls for public sociology.[66] In brief, Burawoy argues that 'public sociology aims to enrich debate about moral and political issues by infusing them with sociological theory and research.'[67] Burawoy (Chapter 2) notes that, compared with other parts of the world, South Africa 'has always stood at the forefront of such critical engagement.' While the particular history of South African sociology, shaped as it was by the struggle against apartheid, may have created a sociology more engaged with the public outside of the academy compared to its US counterpart, the shape of that engagement requires further critical interrogation.

While South African sociologists may be more engaged with civil society than in other parts of the world, the discipline is still caught in global modes of knowledge production that frequently do not speak to the theoretical, tactical and political questions that face social movements. Therefore, the way in which knowledge is constructed for and about mobilisation requires a fundamental rethinking, as others have argued.[68] Furthermore, particularly in the South African context, there are important dimensions of 'race', class and gender in the process of knowledge production that need to be addressed. The role of predominantly White intellectuals in Black organisations and movements has been something which has been debated for a long time in South Africa as well as other parts of the world.[69] Recently these debates resurfaced over an article written by Bandile Mdlalose, a Black female activist, in *Politikon*.[70] Critics of the article claimed her account did not meet the standard academic conventions by not providing references, for instance. This was countered by a number of other scholars who noted the

48   *Carin Runciman*

hypocrisy of a situation in which academics quoting an activist's account is given legitimacy, but seemingly not when activists write their own account.[71] The resultant debate has re-focused a critical and necessary interrogation of the relationship between sociology and movements.

As Tittle has argued, the danger in Burawoy's position is that it elevates the role and influence of sociologists, and in so doing may 'embrace a form of inequality that in other contexts Burawoy would probably abhor.'[72] These kinds of power dynamics are particularly sensitive in the South African context. Protest and movements are largely, but not exclusively, driven by the Black working classes. The academy, however, remains largely White and middle class structurally and culturally, especially at the senior levels. Indeed the structure of the South African academy and the curriculum it teaches formed part of the central focus of the #FeesMustFall student movement that erupted in 2015 and into 2016, with calls for the decolonisation of knowledge. As scholars working in the South African academy and scholars working with movements, we must be attentive to these power dynamics.

Conclusion

This chapter has responded to Burawoy's intervention into social movement studies, which has advocated for the reintroduction of political economy into the field. Taking this challenge seriously, this chapter has argued that the foundational concept, the social movement, needs to be reconceptualised in such a way as to incorporate the material basis of mobilisation. In so doing, the field can overcome the organisational bias that I have argued has shaped social movement scholarship. Developing this analysis, the chapter has drawn upon Burawoy's thesis to analyse how the forces of marketization have driven both movements of unequal inclusion and forcible exclusion in South Africa.

A main feature of Burawoy's thesis is to argue that the global countermovement to marketization has produced five common political repertoires which, although national in their specificities, are globally connected. The chapter noted many commonalities between the repertoires employed in South Africa and elsewhere, particularly in the occupation of space and the experience of police repression. However, it has also drawn attention to the ways in which the analysis of common political repertoires may become overextended if not rooted in the intersections between marketization, inequality and past mobilisations of particular national contexts. To that end, the chapter has also highlighted three areas of weakness within Burawoy's thesis. One, the South African case highlights that the use of social media is not widespread across the world. Two, while there is a shared critique of electoral democracy, this has not led to outright rejection of electoral politics in either the South or the North. Three, what direct democracy looks like is shaped by historical circumstances. The history of cadre activism that continues into the present plays a significant role in shaping the internal culture of South African movements.

South African social movements 49

Finally, this chapter has considered how Burawoy's intervention into the field of social movement studies necessitates not only a change in the way movements have been conventionally analysed, but also the mode in which knowledge is produced for and about movements. The student movement in South Africa has recently called for the 'decolonisation' of knowledge, a call which academics must take seriously, especially those working with movements. What is needed is not just a sociology which attempts to infuse public debates with sociological knowledge but a public sociology that also considers and re-considers how knowledge is produced with and on movements.

Notes

1 Colin Barker, Laurence Cox, John Krinsky, and Alf Gunvald Nilsen, *Marxism and Social Movements* (Leiden: Brill, 2013); Laurence Cox and Alf Gunvald Nilsen, *We Make Our Own History: Marxism and Social Movements in the Twilight of Neoliberalism* (London: Pluto Press, 2014).
2 Gabriel Hetland and Jeff Goodwin, 'The Strange Disappearance of Capitalism from Social Movement Studies,' in *Marxism and Social Movements*, ed. Colin Barker, Laurence Cox, John Krinsky, and Alf Gunvald Nilsen (Leiden: Brill, 2013).
3 Cox and Nilsen, *We Make Our Own History*.
4 Michael Burawoy, 'Facing an Unequal World,' *Current Sociology* 63 (2015): 29.
5 Graeme Chesters and Ian Welsh, *Social Movements: The Key Questions* (Oxon: Routledge, 2011).
6 Karl-Dieter Opp, *Theories of Political Protest and Social Movements: A Multidisciplinary Introduction, Critique, and Synthesis* (London: Routledge, 2009).
7 Ibid., 40.
8 Ibid., 41.
9 Sidney G.Tarrow, *Power in Movement: Social Movements and Contentious Politics* (Cambridge: Cambridge University Press, 2011).
10 Ibid., 133.
11 Ibid.
12 Cox and Nilsen, *We Make Our Own History*.
13 Alberto Melucci, *Nomads of the Present: Social Movements and Individual Needs in Contemporary Society* (London: Hutchinson Radius, 1989), 23.
14 Cox and Nilsen, *We Make Our Own History*, 56, emphasis in the original.
15 Ibid., 57, emphasis in the original.
16 Ibid.
17 Ibid.
18 Hetland and Goodwin, *The Strange Disappearance*.
19 See Chris Hann and Keith Hart, *Market and Society: The Great Transformation Today* (Cambridge: Cambridge University Press, 2009); Nancy Fraser, 'Can Society Be Commodities All the Way Down? Post-Polanyian Reflections on Capitalist Crisis,' *Economy and Society* 43 (2014): 541–558.
20 Hein Marais, *South Africa Pushed to the Limit: The Political Economy of Change* (London: Zed Books, 2011), 177.
21 Ibid., 130.
22 Ibid., 238.
23 Statistics South Africa, 'Methodological Report on Rebasing of National Poverty Lines and Development of Pilot Provincial Poverty Lines,' accessed February 13, 2015, http://beta2.statssa.gov.za/publications/Report-03–10–11/Report-03–10–11.pdf.

50 *Carin Runciman*

24 Nigel G. Gibson, 'Poor People's Movements in South Africa – The Anti-Eviction Campaign in Mandela Park: A Critical Discussion,' *Journal of Asian and African Studies* 39 (2004).

25 Dale T. McKinley, 'The Crisis of the Left in Contemporary South Africa,' in *Contesting Transformation: Popular Resistance in Twenty-First Century South Africa*, ed. Marcelle C. Dawson and Luke Sinwell (London: Pluto Press, 2012).

26 Claire Ceruti, 'Unfolding Contradictions in the "Zuma Movement": The Alliance in the Public Sector Strikes of 2007 and 2010,' in *Contesting Transformation: Popular Resistance in Twenty-First Century South Africa*, ed. Marcelle C. Dawson and Luke Sinwell (London: Pluto Press, 2012).

27 Karl Von Holdt and Edward Webster, 'Work Restructuring and the Crisis of Social Reproduction: A Southern Perspective,' in *Beyond the Apartheid Workplace: Studies in Transition*, ed. Edward Webster and Karl Von Holdt (Scottsville: University of KwaZulu-Natal Press, 2005).

28 Paul Mason, *Why It's Kicking Off Everywhere: The New Global Revolutions* (London: Verso, 2012).

29 Jan Bremen, 'A Bogus Concept,' *New Left Review* 84 (2013); Ronaldo Munck, 'The Precariat: A View from the South,' *Third World Quarterly* 34 (2013); Marcel Paret, 'Politics of Solidarity and Agency in an Age of Precarity,' *Global Labour Journal* 7, 2, (2016).

30 Peter Alexander, 'Rebellion of the Poor: South Africa's Service Delivery Protests – A Preliminary Analysis,' *Review of African Political Economy* 37 (2010): 25–40.

31 Peter Alexander, Carin Runciman, and Trevor Ngwane, *Community Protests 2004–2013: Some Research Findings*, Media briefing, Johannesburg, February 12, 2014; Derick Powell, Michael O'Donovan, and Jaap De Visser, *Civic Protests Barometer: 2007–2014* (Cape Town: Dullah Omar Institute), accessed May 18, 2016, http://dullahomarinstitute.org.za/news/south-africa2019s-violent-protests-reach-the-all-time-high-2013-mlgi-report; Carin Runciman, Peter Alexander, Mahlatse Rampedi, Boikanyo Moloto, Boitumelo Maruping, Eunice Khumalo, and Sehlaphi Sibanda, *Counting Police Recorded Protests: Estimates Based on South African Police Service Data* (Johannesburg: University of Johannesburg, 2016).

32 Peter Alexander, Carin Runciman, and Trevor Ngwane, 'Growing Civil Unrest Shows Yearning for Accountability,' *Business Day*, March 7, 2014, accessed February 12, 2015, http://www.bdlive.co.za/opinion/2014/03/07/growing-civil-unrest-shows-yearning-for-accountability; Paret, *Introduction*.

33 Karl Von Holdt and Peter Alexander, 'Collective Violence, Community Protest and Xenophobia,' *South African Review of Sociology* 43 (2012); Karl Von Holdt, 'On Violent Democracy,' *The Sociological Review* 62 (2014); Marcel Paret, 'Violence and Democracy in South Africa's Community Protests,' *Review of African Political Economy* 42 (2015).

34 Shauna Mottiar and Patrick Bond, 'The Politics of Discontent and Social Protest in Durban,' *Politikon* 39 (2012): 316. See also Lodge and Mottair, Chapter 5.

35 Shauna Mottiar, 'From "Popcorn" to "Occupy": Protest in Durban, South Africa,' *Development and Change* 44 (2013): 603–619.

36 Luke Sinwell, 'Is "Another World" Really Possible? Re-Examining Counter-Hegemonic Forces in Post-Apartheid South Africa,' *Review of African Political Economy* 38 (2011): 61–76.

37 Susan Booysen, 'With the Ballot and the Brick: The Politics of Attaining Service Delivery,' *Progress in Development Studies* 7 (2007); Susan Booysen, 'The Ballot and the Brick – Enduring Under Duress,' in *Local Elections in South Africa: Parties, People, Politics*, ed. Susan Booysen (Bloemfontein: Sun Media, 2012).

38 Malose Langaand Karl Von Holdt, 'Insurgent Citizenship, Class Formation and the Dual Nature of a Community Protest: A Case Study of 'Kungcatsha,' in *Contesting Transformation: Popular Resistance in Twenty-First Century South Africa*, ed. Marcelle C. Dawson and Luke Sinwell (London: Pluto Press, 2012); Hannah Dawson,

'Patronage from Below: Political Unrest in an Informal Settlement in South Africa,' *African Affairs* 113 (2014).

39 Statistics South Africa, *Community Survey 2007*, accessed February 13, 2015, http://beta2.statssa.gov.za/?page_id=3920.

40 Statistics South Africa, *General Household Survey: 2013*, accessed February 13, 2015, http://beta2.statssa.gov.za/publications/P0318/P03182013.pdf.

41 Bandile Mdlalose, 'The Rise and Fall of Abahlali Base Mjondolo, a South African Social Movement,' *Politikon* 41 (2014): 345–353.

42 See also Lodge and Mottiar, Chapter 5.

43 Jenny Pickerill and John Krinsky, 'Why Does Occupy Matter?' *Social Movement Studies* 11 (2012): 279–287.

44 Marais, *South Africa Pushed to the Limit*, 178.

45 Robert Mattes, Yul Derek Davids, and Cherrel Africa, *Views of Democracy in South Africa and the Region: Trends and Comparisons* (Cape Town: Afrobarometer, 2000), accessed July 23, 2015, http://afrobarometer.org/sites/default/files/publications/Working%20paper/AfropaperNo8_0.pdf.

46 Faranak Miraftab and Shana Wills, 'Insurgency and Spaces of Active Citizenship: The Story of Western Cape Anti-Eviction Campaign in South Africa,' *Journal of Planning Education and Research* 25 (2005): 200–217.

47 This interview was conducted January 25, 2010 as part of my doctoral research on the Anti-Privatisation Forum. See Carin Runciman, *Mobilisation and Insurgent Citizenship of the Anti-Privatisation Forum, South Africa: An Ethnographic Study* (Unpublished PhD thesis, University of Glasgow, 2012).

48 Moses Mayekiso, *Township Politics: Civic Struggles for a New South Africa* (New York: Monthly Review Press, 1996); Elke Zuern, *The Politics of Necessity: Community Organizing and Democracy in South Africa* (Madison: University of Wisconsin Press, 2011).

49 Jane Duncan, 'The Enduring Appeal of Socialist Ideas,' accessed January 20, 2015, http://sacsis.org.za/site/article/1881.

50 Sinwell, 'Is Another World Possible.'

51 Mandla Tshabala, Interview, January 25, 2010.

52 Booysen, 'With the Ballot and the Brick,' 22.

53 Marcel Paret, 'Contested ANC Hegemony in the Urban Townships: Evidence from the 2014 South African Election,' *African Affairs* (forthcoming); Carin Runciman, 'The "Ballot and the Brick": Protest, Voting and Non-Voting in Post-Apartheid South Africa,' *Journal of Contemporary African Studies* 115 (2016): 419–442.

54 Collette Schulz-Herzenberg, *Voter Participation in the South African Elections of 2014* (Pretoria: Institute for Security Studies), accessed October 9, 2014, http://www.issafrica.org/publications/policy-brief/voter-participation-in-the-south-african-elections-of-2014.

55 Peter Alexander and Peter Pfaffe, 'Social Relationships to the Means and Ends of Protest in South Africa's Ongoing Rebellion of the Poor: The Balfour Insurrections,' *Social Movement Studies* 13 (2013): 204–221.

56 Personal communication.

57 Francesca Polletta, 'Participatory Democracy's Moment,' *Journal of International Affairs* 68 (2014).

58 Mark Swilling, 'Civic Associations in South Africa,' *Urban Forum* 4 (1993).

59 Rebecca Pointer, 'Questioning the Representation of South Africa's "New Social Movements": A Case Study of the Mandela Park Anti-Eviction Campaign,' *Journal of Asian and African Studies* 39 (2004).

60 Runciman, *Mobilisation and Insurgent Citizenship*.

61 Lesley J. Wood, *Crisis and Control: The Militarization of Protest Policing* (London: Pluto Press, 2014).

62 See Donatella Della Porta, Abby Peterson, and Herbert Reiter, *The Policing of Transnational Protest* (Aldershot: Ashgate, 2006); Wood, *Crisis and Control*.

52   *Carin Runciman*

63   Alexander et al., *Community Protests*.
64   Jane Duncan, *The Rise of the Securocrats: The Case of South Africa* (Auckland Park: Jacana Media, 2015); Michael Clark, *An Anatomy of Dissent and Repression: The Criminal Justice System and the 2011 Thembelihle Protest* (Johannesburg: SERI, 2014); Right2Know, *Big Brother Exposed: Stories of South Africa's Intelligence Structures Monitoring and Harassing Activist Movements*, accessed August 10, 2015, http://bigbrother.r2k.org.za/wp-content/uploads/Big-Brother-Exposed-R2K-handbook-on-surveillance-web.pdf.
65   Burawoy, 'Facing an Unequal World,' 29.
66   Michael Burawoy, 'Public Sociologies: Contradictions, Dilemmas, and Possibilities,' *Social Forces* 82 (2004); Michael Burawoy, 'For Public Sociology,' *American Sociological Review* 70 (2005).
67   Burawoy, 'Public Sociologies,' 1603.
68   Douglas Bevington and Chris Dixon, 'Movement-Relevant Theory: Rethinking Social Movement Scholarship and Activism,' *Social Movement Studies* 4 (2005).
69   Mondli Hlatshwayo, 'White Power and Privilege in Academic and Intellectual Spaces of South Africa: The Need for Sober Reflection,' *Politikon* 42 (2015).
70   Mdlalose, 'The Rise and Fall.'
71   Patrick Bond, 'The Intellectual Meets the South African Social Movement: A Code of Conduct Is Overdue, When Researching Such a Conflict-Rich Society,' *Politikon* 42 (2015); Steven Friedman, 'Letter for Concern by Steven Friedman and Signatories,' *Politikon* 42 (2015).
72   Charles R. Tittle, 'The Arrogance of Public Sociology,' *Social Forces* 82 (2004).

Part II

Community formations

4 Postcolonial politics
Theorizing protest from spaces of exclusion

Marcel Paret[1]

Despite the remarkable growth and progress of social movement scholarship since the 1970s, two recent critiques point to major gaps in the field. One critique comes from Walder, who argues that because of an overwhelming focus on mobilization – how and why movements emerge, develop, and succeed – social movement scholars have largely failed to examine the political orientations of social movements, and especially the way in which they are shaped by social structures.[2] A second, and related, critique by Hetland and Goodwin, argues that social movement scholars have increasingly failed to consider the relevance of capitalism and dynamics of class struggle.[3] Whereas the former critique calls for greater attention to the substantive content of contentious politics, the latter critique calls for situating contention within a broader political economic terrain.

This double challenge is especially germane to the project of building social movement theory from the global South, where the terrain of struggle differs dramatically from the Northern contexts of traditional social movement theory. The particular features of the Southern context include, at a political level, the history of colonial rule, liberation struggles, and postcolonial transitions, and at an economic level, dependency, poverty, and surplus labour. These are not simply opportunity structures that create openings for collective action. At a deeper level they are also social structures that influence collective experiences, interpretations, and political orientations. A theory of contentious politics in the global South must begin to wrestle with these connections.

This chapter aims to develop a theory of protest that is relevant for the postcolonial societies of the global South. It does so by identifying an excluded domain of society, which is marginalised in relation to both the economy and the state. The first half of the chapter develops a theoretical framework. I begin by unpacking two works by Frantz Fanon and Mahmood Mamdani, each of which leverages the urban/rural divide to theorise different segments of society, and then present Partha Chatterjee's contrast between civil society and political society as their synthesis. The second half of the chapter uses this theoretical foundation to illuminate key features of contemporary community protests in South Africa. The analysis contributes to social movement theory in general, and to an understanding of popular politics in South Africa in particular.

56   *Marcel Paret*

Postcolonial transitions: society and the urban/rural divide

As a starting point for a theory of postcolonial politics, I begin with two classic works: Frantz Fanon's *The Wretched of the Earth*, and Mahmood Mamdani's *Citizen and Subject*.[4] These books are similar in that they both develop theories of colonial society that are organised around the urban/rural divide. Both theorists also underscore a connection between forms of colonial society, the character of postcolonial transitions, and forms of postcolonial society. Fanon's analysis is primarily based on the national liberation struggle in Algeria, though he also references other cases throughout Africa and Latin America. Mamdani's analysis draws on a variety of cases from sub-Saharan Africa, with a sustained treatment of both Uganda and South Africa.

Each theorist points to a tension between politics rooted in the urban and politics rooted in the rural. But they approach this tension from very different angles. Fanon's analysis focuses on the relationship between society and economy, showing how the urban/rural divide manifests in an opposition between the national bourgeoisie and the peasantry. Mamdani focuses instead on the relationship between society and state, showing how the urban/rural divide manifests in an opposition between citizens and subjects. I take each in turn.

Fanon: society and economy

Fanon develops his analysis of decolonization through a contrast between the capitalism of the 'West' and the capitalism of the 'colonies'. In the former, he argues, the bourgeoisie is strong, capable of providing material concessions, and thus rules with confidence.[5] This leads to a vibrant civil society and the promotion of democracy: 'When the bourgeoisie is strong, when it can arrange everything and everybody to serve its power, it does not hesitate to affirm positively certain democratic ideas which claim to be universally applicable.'[6] In contrast, the bourgeoisie in the colonies is weak, unable to generate material concessions, and rules through repression and patronage.[7] Here capital must use 'moral power' rather than 'economic power', justifying its domination on the basis of national identity rather than material concessions.[8]

This situation of 'underdevelopment' lays the foundation for anti-colonial struggle, which for Fanon involves two simultaneous and interwoven movements: a struggle to expel the colonisers, and a struggle within the colonised group for leadership of the nation. He lays out two possible trajectories of decolonization, each one led by a different class alliance of the colonised with a different political orientation. One trajectory is led by an urban bloc, including the middle-class fractions of the colonised – intellectual elites, technicians, shopkeepers, teachers, civil servants – as well as the relatively small working class. This bloc aims to reconstitute capitalism by replacing the European colonisers with indigenous people as the national bourgeoisie. The other trajectory is led by a rural bloc, including the peasantry and a group of dissident intellectuals who have been expelled from the towns. This bloc seeks to transform the economy and society, redistributing wealth and implementing a radical democracy.

Postcolonial politics 57

This portrayal of anti-colonial struggles flips classic Marxist analysis on its head. For Marx the working class was the revolutionary agent of social transformation, and the peasantry a 'sack of potatoes' with little potential for collective organization. Fanon maintains this view in his analysis of developed countries. Here he views the peasantry as undisciplined, unorganised, individualistic, and reactionary,[9] while 'the working class has nothing to lose; it is they who in the long run have everything to gain.'[10] But his analysis of the underdeveloped world is the mirror opposite. In this context, he argues, the working class is a 'most pampered' and 'comfortably off fraction,' comprising 'also the "bourgeois" fraction of the colonised people.'[11] With 'everything to lose',[12] urban workers are 'individualistic' and align with the national bourgeoisie so as to maintain their privilege. Conversely, for Fanon the peasants are the revolutionary agents of colonial society. This is because they are 'outside the class system', and thus 'have nothing to lose and everything to gain.'[13] As a result, the peasantry are disciplined and altruistic, they stand with the community, and they are prepared for political struggle.[14]

In Fanon's analysis the lumpenproletariat, comprised of former peasants who roam the urban periphery in search of economic opportunity, are an important swing group that helps to determine which bloc will prevail. Contrasting further with Marx, he views the lumpenproletariat as centrally important and *potentially* revolutionary. But for him their historical role is undetermined. While they may be 'individualistic' and easily manipulated by elites,[15] they are also a 'fraction which has not yet succeeded in finding a bone to gnaw in the colonial system.' As a result, he argues, the lumpenproletariat 'constitutes one of the most spontaneous and the most radically revolutionary forces of a colonised people.'[16] If the peasantry can win them over, Fanon suggests, the lumpenproletariat enable the spread of revolutionary transformation by providing a crucial link to the urban areas.[17]

Fanon is particularly critical of the national bourgeois road to decolonisation, which serves the interests of the 'embryonic' working class but is useless from the perspective of national development: 'The national bourgeoisie, since it is strung up to defend its immediate interests, and sees no further than the end of its nose, reveals itself incapable of simply bringing national unity into being, or of building up the nation on a stable and productive basis.'[18] In this scenario, economic failure leads to a one-party dictatorship, repression, and tribalism, which are necessary for capital to secure domination and its own economic well-being.[19] Fanon is equally critical of the organised working class, who are 'the most faithful followers of the nationalist parties' and 'become candidates for governmental power.'[20] While they eventually recognise, in the postcolonial period, 'the objective necessity of a social program which will appeal to the nation as a whole', by this point they are too stale and too detached from revolutionary approaches to garner mass support.[21]

These portrayals of postcolonial society resonate with the 'new', democratic South Africa. The following are among the most obvious parallels: the persistence of one party rule; consistent use of the state as a tool of accumulation, such as through Black Economic Empowerment programs; the close ties between

58 *Marcel Paret*

organised labour and the state, due to the official alliance between the Congress of South African Trade Unions (COSATU) and the ruling African National Congress (ANC); and growing repression of protest activity. The heavy hand of the state was thrust into the public spotlight with the Marikana massacre, which left 34 workers dead at the hands of the police (see Chapter 1). But state repression has also become a persistent feature of community protests, with the police killing more than 50 protesters between 2004 and 2014.[22]

Highlighting how the failures of the national bourgeoisie lead to poverty and disaffection amongst the people,[23] Fanon anticipates the fierce combination of material deprivation and protest that has returned to South Africa in the post-apartheid period. He also explains how these dynamics interact with mass migration and urbanization: 'the mass of the country people with no one to lead them, uneducated and unsupported, turn their backs on the poorly laboured fields and flock towards the outer ring of suburbs, thus swelling out of all proportion the ranks of the lumpenproletariat. The moment for a fresh national crisis is not far off.'[24] This analysis resonates with the acceleration of urbanization in South Africa, including both 'internal' and cross-border migration, which has gone hand-in-hand with urban poverty and unemployment.[25]

Under the leadership of the national bourgeoisie, Fanon's analysis of postcolonial society is bleak. For the newly independent middle classes the main priority is to 'replace the foreigner' in politics and business, and the working classes and unemployed follow their lead. Struggles for economic survival thus turn into conflict around ethnic, religious, tribal, territorial, and national categories.[26] Emphasizing the prevalence of anti-foreigner hostility, his analysis bears a chilling resemblance to the 2008 xenophobic attacks in South Africa:

> From nationalism we have passed to ultra-nationalism, to chauvinism, and finally to racism. The foreigners are called on to leave; their shops are burned, their street stalls are wrecked . . . If the Europeans get in the way of the intellectuals and business bourgeoisie of the young nation, for the mass of the people in the towns competition is represented principally by Africans of another nation. . . . We observe a permanent seesaw between African unity, which fades quicker and quicker into the mists of oblivion, and a heartbreaking return to chauvinism in its most bitter and detestable form.[27]

If Fanon's analysis was prophetic about the 'pitfalls of national consciousness' under bourgeois leadership,[28] however, it leaves unexplored the potential of a renewed progressive politics in the postcolonial period. It thus begs the question: Where in postcolonial society, if anywhere, is the revolutionary potential of the peasantry? Does it follow the peasantry into the towns, making the impoverished urban masses the new revolutionary agent? In highlighting the struggles of the peasantry, Fanon's analysis lays a foundation for the study of protest from spaces of exclusion. In his case, this entails a radical politics of redistribution and democratization that emerges from the economic periphery. But exclusion is not only economic, it may also be political.

Mamdani: society and state

Mamdani and Fanon launch their analyses from very different vantage points. Fanon begins with the colonial class structure, and then understands society as emerging from this economic base. Mamdani instead takes the colonial state as the starting point, and understands society in relation to a particular form of governance or rule. He argues that colonial rule in Africa was organised around a 'bifurcated state', which operated through different forms of power in the urban and rural areas. Whereas the urban state was based on 'civil' power, organised around citizenship rights, the rural state was based on 'customary' power, organised around the administrative authority of tribal elites. This gives specificity to the classic notions of 'direct' and 'indirect' rule:

> Direct rule was the form of urban civil power. It was about the exclusion of natives from civil freedoms guaranteed to citizens in civil society. Indirect rule, however, signified a rural tribal authority. It was about incorporating natives into a state-enforced customary order. Reformulated, direct and indirect rule are better understood as variants of despotism: the former centralised, the latter decentralised . . . [Thus,] the colonial state was a double-sided affair. Its one side, the state that governed a racially defined citizenry, was bounded by the rule of law and an associated regime of rights. Its other side, the state that ruled over subjects, was a regime of extra-economic coercion and administrative driven justice.[29]

With this theoretical framework, apartheid in South Africa may be understood as an extreme version of African colonialism. It combined a centralised despotism in the urban areas, which used racial divisions to exclude Africans from basic citizenship rights, with a decentralised despotism in the rural areas, which used ethnic divisions to subject Africans to traditional-administrative authority. As the apartheid state clamped down on rural-to-urban migration, and forcibly relocated entire communities from the urban to rural areas, Africans were increasingly subject to the local authority of tribal chiefs.[30] But the division remained: The infamous Section 10 provision of the 1952 Native Laws Amendment Act exempted a small proportion of the urban African population from removal, while others lived in the urban areas illegally.[31]

This reading of apartheid differentiates between two different forms of state-society relation. Mamdani suggests that in the urban areas, Africans 'were exempt from the lash of customary law but not from modern, racially discriminatory civil legislation.'[32] Thus, while urban Africans were not 'exalted as rights-bearing citizens', they comprised a society that was deeply entangled with civil power and its regime of rights. In contrast, rural Africans related to the state not as second-class citizens with limited rights, but rather as subjects of local tribal authorities. For Mamdani this contrast lay beneath the brutal conflict that emerged on the Witwatersrand in the early 1990s. The conflict revolved around tension between township residents with urban residence rights, and migrant workers who lived in the hostels – in Mamdani's vocabulary, the 'rural in the urban.' The two groups

60   *Marcel Paret*

coalesced around different political formations: Township residents were organised through the ANC and its affiliated trade unions, which were grounded in the struggle for racial equality; and migrant workers were organised through the Inkatha Freedom Party, which was grounded in a commitment to traditional tribal authority.

Similar to Fanon, Mamdani suggests that the content of the postcolonial transition is contingent upon rural inclusion. Whereas for Fanon a democratic transition could only be led by the revolutionary peasantry, for Mamdani complete democratization requires a transformation of the customary order. Mamdani also mirrors Fanon's pessimistic analysis of urban-centered decolonization. But rather than the weakness and narrow orientation of the national bourgeoisie, for him the limits are rooted in the emphasis on civil power. Mamdani thus argues that the liberation struggle in South Africa, including the increasingly powerful black labour movement, was biased towards the urban areas and 'remained prisoners of a civil society–centered perspective.'[33] Leaving customary power intact, the liberation movement eventually patched up this conflict 'from above' by incorporating tribal leaders into the post-apartheid state:

> Without a presence in either the [rural] reserve or the [urban] hostel – and without a program for democratizing customary rule in either – the ANC could reach the rural only from above, through Native Authorities. . . . To defuse an intertribal collision, it settled for an intertribal alliance from above.[34]

Mamdani's analysis points to the persistent salience of ethnicity in the postcolonial period, as a result of a failure to democratise customary power. This salience appears, for example, in the ANC's growing reliance on an ethnic Zulu base from the late 2000s. Extending Mamdani's analysis, Neocosmos also shows how the urban bias, in combination with a growing emphasis on the state as the locus of politics and citizenship – as opposed to society and 'people's power' – led to renewed ethnic hostility in the post-apartheid period in the form of anti-foreigner xenophobia.[35]

Perhaps most important for our purposes, however, Mamdani's analysis raises the question of subjects in the postcolonial period. If Fanon compels us to ask what happens to the politics of the revolutionary peasantry, Mamdani compels us to ask: On what political terrain do subjects operate, particularly once they have migrated from rural areas to urban slums? His analysis of customary power points to two key features: the decentralization of power to local authorities, and an emphasis on administrative control rather than legal rights. If Fanon's excluded peasantry and lumpenproletariat occupy a space of resistance based on economic exclusion, Mamdani's terrain of decentralised administration may be understood as a space of resistance based on political exclusion. The following section aims to integrate these two perspectives.

Postcolonial politics 61

Political society as postcolonial exclusion

Fanon and Mamdani both theorise a political terrain of the excluded. For Fanon this terrain is defined by the economic periphery of the peasantry and lumpenproletariat, who stand in contrast to the economically privileged national bourgeoisie and working class. For Mamdani this terrain is defined by local administrative control over subjects, as opposed to the centralised regime of restricted rights enjoyed by (second-class) citizens. Partha Chatterjee's notion of political society may be understood as a synthesis of these two approaches.[36] Not only does political society denote an excluded domain of society, in contrast to an included domain that he refers to as civil society, but also it is linked to marginalised realms of both the economy and the state. In this sense it builds on the insights of both Fanon and Mamdani (see Table 4.1).

This theoretical extension is closely linked to a historical demographic shift. The late twentieth century was marked by massive rural-to-urban migration in the developing world of the global South. This large-scale human movement led to the growth of peri-urban slums, which are defined by poverty, underemployment, and informal economic activity.[37] In South Africa this process was facilitated by the elimination of apartheid-era restrictions on black movement, giving way to population growth within impoverished urban townships and an explosion of informal shack settlements. We may therefore say that Fanon's peasants and Mamdani's subjects have, over time, relocated from the rural to the urban. Both theorists anticipate this transition, but neither makes it central to their analysis. In contrast, the urban slum is the primary site for Chatterjee's political society.

Chatterjee's analysis emerges from a critique of classic notions of civil society, which he argues are grounded in the normative ideal of popular sovereignty. Comprised of individual citizens with equal access to rights, the legitimacy of civil society is based on the participation of citizens in decision-making, such as through voting and formal procedures of deliberation. While attractive in theory, for Chatterjee this view of society has limited relevance for 'most of the world', and particularly for those living in the global South. This is because most people are not treated by the state as proper rights-bearing citizens. As an 'actually existing form', he argues, civil society is 'demographically limited'.[38] In his analysis of

Table 4.1 Postcolonial politics: included society vs excluded society

	Included society	*Excluded society*
Fanon	National bourgeoisie, working class	Peasants, lumpenproletariat
Mamdani	(Second-class) citizens	Subjects
Chatterjee	Civil society	Political society

62 Marcel Paret

India, for example, civil society is limited to the middle classes and the elite, who have the resources necessary for participation.

In contrast, political society represents the domain of the excluded. Revolving around the urban poor, it includes those who do not possess the necessary resources to engage with the state in the way imagined by theorists of civil society:

> For the majority of people in postcolonial societies, the normative status of the virtuous citizen will remain infinitely deferred until such time as they can be provided with the basic material and cultural prerequisites of membership in civil society. Until the arrival of that liberal millennium, however, they can only deal with a governmental system with the resources they can muster in political society.[39]

The notion of political society is grounded in Foucault's analysis of governmentality, which refers to the way in which states manage populations.[40] Rather than ensuring equal rights and participation in sovereignty, governmentality is about weighing costs and benefits, surveying and surveillance, collecting information, and providing for the well-being and security of the population. Mirroring Mamdani's domain of decentralised despotism, political society relates to the state as subjects, not citizens.

Chatterjee links this distinction between civil society and political society to the formal and informal sectors of the economy, respectively.[41] As the hegemonic terrain of corporate capital, he argues that civil society is rooted in liberal notions of individualism, equal rights, and private property, and operates according to the logic of capital accumulation. Conversely, as the hegemonic terrain of non-corporate (informal) capital, political society operates according to the logic of livelihood realization, which requires reversing the negative effects of capital accumulation. Political society is thus bound to civil society through the process of capital accumulation, but also represents its critical opposite:

> As a matter of fact, it could even be said that the activities of political society in postcolonial countries represent a continuing critique of the paradoxical reality in all capitalist democracies of equal citizenship and majority rule, on the one hand, and the dominance of property and privilege, on the other.[42]

By offering a critique from the economic periphery, political society may be said to inhabit the legacy of Fanon's revolutionary peasantry. Chatterjee affirms, in fact, that demands from political society – for government provision of basic needs – are partly a response to the failure of capital-intensive economies to absorb the labour of dispossessed peasants.[43]

Though not limited to any specific part of the globe, Chatterjee implies that political society is especially prevalent in the global South for two inter-related reasons. First, because of the legacy of colonial rule there is a shorter history of civil and political rights. Whereas in the Western democracies the extension of

Postcolonial politics 63

civil and political rights preceded the onset of the welfare state and thus governmentality, in developing countries colonial populations were treated as subjects rather than citizens. Further, he argues, while liberation movements were animated by the promise of equal rights and citizenship, in practice this promise has been overwhelmed by the 'developmental state' and the empirical realities of providing security and welfare.[44] Second, the prevalence of political society in the global South stems from the prominence of surplus labour and the informal sector. These are certainly characteristic features of the South African economy, with its high level of structural unemployment. Attempts to generate subsistence within the informal sector are one response to situations of poverty and underdevelopment. Collective struggles on the terrain of political society are another.

Political society and community protests

The analysis of political society is relevant to contemporary struggles in South Africa. It is particularly useful for making sense of the protests that have been sweeping through the country's townships and informal shack settlements since the middle of the 2000s. According to major news outlets, between 2005 and 2014 there were more than 2,300 such protests nationwide, averaging nearly 20 protests per month. In the peak year of 2012 the figure reached an average high of 39 protests per month, or 1.3 protests per day.[45] These struggles are popularly known as 'service delivery' protests, but scholars and commentators have alternately described them as 'movements beyond movements',[46] 'collective violence',[47] protests for 'public service',[48] and a 'rebellion of the poor'.[49] Each label underscores a somewhat different characterization, but they are not necessarily contradictory. Indeed, they may be understood as different aspects of struggle on the terrain of political society.

To illuminate the connections between political society and community protests, the following analysis draws on more than two years of fieldwork in South Africa's Gauteng province between 2010 and 2014. As part of this research I conducted or oversaw 239 interviews with workers, community residents, and activists. I focus here on interviews conducted with protest leaders in two communities where protests occurred in 2013: Bekkersdal, a township on the West Rand with a mixture of both formal housing and informal shack settlements; and Motsoaledi, an informal shack settlement located within the townships of Soweto. I also draw from a database of community protests in Gauteng, constructed by scholars at the University of Johannesburg (hereafter 'UJ database').[50]

The concept of political society illuminates three key features of community protests. First, it highlights their *location on the terrain of governmentality*. Perhaps the most consistent feature of the protests is their orientation towards the state, and the local state in particular. According to the UJ database, for example, two thirds of community protests in Gauteng between 2004 and 2012 were directed at local government, and a quarter were directed towards either higher levels of government or government in general.[51] It is common, for example, for protesters to criticize the state for failing to meet the promises of the anti-apartheid

64 *Marcel Paret*

liberation struggle, including the ANC's consistent promise since 1994 to redistribute resources and secure a 'better life for all'.

Community protests appeal to the popular mandate of the state to provide for the well-being and security of the South African population, and particularly poor and working-class black citizens. The most common demands are for housing, water, and electricity, but other frequent demands include proper toilets, tar roads, and street lights; better refuse removal services; access to land; and improved health care. In common language and the public sphere, these various resources are loosely conceptualised as 'services' that should be 'delivered' by the state, thus giving rise to the popular 'service delivery' label. Protesters often demand 'service delivery' or 'development' in general, calling on the state to make some improvement – any improvement – in terms of meeting the basic needs of the community. As one protest leader in Bekkersdal put it: 'We are governed by the government. Now this whole thing, the blame and everything, it goes back to the government. Then the government will be able to categorise, in terms of their failures for service delivery upon this community.'[52]

These demands take place against a backdrop of poverty, fueled by unemployment and underemployment. The shortage of stable employment leaves community members to eke out a livelihood in any way they can, from survivalist activity to sharing at the household level to forms of non-wage servitude. In this context of material hardship, protesters call on the state to provide a certain level of social protection. When asked why protests had exploded in Bekkersdal in late 2013, one community member explained:

> You know, from the mere fact that people are unemployed. And they get this notion from local government, where from R200 your parents must now pay R1,900 [in gravesite fees]. It angers them, because they themselves are unemployed. And it angers them that there was money put to develop this community, for them to get employment, and they don't. So it means that people who are leading them are just people who want to loot from them, and not necessarily to develop them.[53]

The initial trigger for the Bekkersdal protests was the decision by the municipality to raise the standard fee for a local gravesite, to nearly ten times the previous rate. But with unemployment and poverty simmering, this issue blew the lid off a boiling pot of community frustrations, which ranged from the leaking sewerage to the failure of the municipality to provide jobs. A prominent young leader in her early 20s remarked:

> My demands specifically were: you can see I have a baby. Our kids cannot play, they are not safe. We needed our municipality to come and unblock the drains. Secondly, [the] unemployment rate. We needed them to do their job and employ youth. Thirdly, as they had promised to assist us with schools, we heard the money was out but the municipality, we hear, misused that money. So we thought if we speak our voice, we will be heard.[54]

Postcolonial politics 65

As these quotes begin to reveal, demands for state provision are frequently coupled with complaints about government corruption and maladministration. Protesters demand that public officials do their job so that they may appropriately provide services to poor communities. In this sense the notions of 'service delivery' and 'public service' are not opposing, but rather mutually reinforcing. The fact that residents often attribute their situation to poor governance also attests to the relevance of governmentality. Indeed, Chatterjee suggests that complaints about corruption often increase alongside demands for state provisions: 'people in India are vocal about the incompetence, corruption, and lack of integrity of politicians. . . . But the curious fact is that the expectations from government for the provision of various services has not diminished at all; rather, it has increased.'[55] The same would appear to be true for South Africa.

A second feature of community protests that is illuminated by the notion of political society is the *centrality of demands for community recognition*. In attempting to influence how they are governed, people must be able to identify themselves as worthy of governance. For Chatterjee this is done by forging 'communities', thus giving moral coherence to empirically defined groups:

> Populations respond to the regime of governmentality by seeking to constitute themselves as groups that deserve the attention of government. . . . They form associations to negotiate with governmental authorities and seek public support for their cause. Their political mobilization involves an effort to turn an empirically formed population group into a moral community. The force of this moral appeal usually hinges on the generally recognised obligation of government to provide for the poor and the underprivileged.[56]

In contrast to civil society, which revolves around a national community composed of theoretically homogeneous citizens, political society comprises a heterogeneous population that approaches the state as sub-national communities. This alternative understanding of community represents precisely the terrain where capital has limited penetration, and where demands for basic livelihood have particular legitimacy.[57]

This analysis resonates with the highly localised nature of community protests. While in some instances the protests do spread to nearby areas, they are frequently contained to a relatively small geographical area such as a particular section of a township or an informal shack settlement. It is especially common for protesters to make demands in the name of 'the community' as a whole, as illustrated by one protester in Bekkersdal: 'If I am fighting for service delivery, I am not fighting for me, I am fighting for the whole community. Everyone living in the community is community. So if one is going there, another there, then it is not working.'[58]

Not only does this comment emphasise the need for solidarity between members of the community, but it also aims to distance the protests from narrow efforts at personal gain. To be sure, there is almost always internal contestation (or at least suspicion) over which individuals or organizations will represent the community. But whoever does secure the leading voice must speak in the name of

66   *Marcel Paret*

'the community', or else risk criticism from either inside or outside. As part of this imposition of unity for the sake of moral power, it is common for residents to form associations and committees that eschew political parties, which have an air of particularism. A community leader in Bekkersdal described how this worked for the Greater Westonaria Concerned Residents' Association, which became the popular face of the community after the protests began:

> For example, within the leadership of this Concerned Residents' [Association] we are apolitical as a structure, but we have representatives from different political parties. We have also representatives of the ANC, variously, EFF, AZAPO, UDM. They are accommodated here as a mandate that comes from a public meeting to say that: if we want to push the struggle, this struggle cannot be pushed by a certain group or political party or a group of people, but we need to amalgamate as a community in concern.[59]

While the centrality of community may have a unifying thrust, it may also pit segments of the population against each other as they vie for state attention and access to finite resources. This competitive dimension is evident in the South African context, where protesting communities often contrast their plight with positive developments in nearby areas. A resident of Motsoaledi, an informal settlement in Soweto, captured this dynamic well when he explained why members of his community had decided to protest:

> Let me go back to this example . . . at home they know you love this watch, and they buy it for your brother, and your brother is younger than you. How would that make you feel? It is the same as Freedom Park. Freedom Park was our little brother. [It] came way after Motsoaledi. But look at it, everybody has houses . . . now they have proper sanitation, they have electricity, they have everything that we do not have, and actually it makes some of the people very angry . . . This is the first place that came before Freedom Park, before a couple of other places, but only to find those places have already been built. They have been developed, but Motsoaledi is still . . .[60]

This sentiment lay beneath a series of protests in Motsoaledi, climaxing in a major disruptive protest in April 2013 that included the burning of a KFC restaurant. The central focus of the protest was the demand for housing, with the understanding that this would also bring improved access to electricity, water, sanitation, and tar roads. These amenities had already been provided to nearby areas, and residents of Motsoaledi did not want to be left behind.

A third feature of community protests that is consistent with the notion of political society is their *strategic politics*. Collective struggles in political society often eschew existing laws and regulations, engaging in extra-legal tactics and calling on the state to make exceptions: 'These claims are irreducibly political. They could only be made on a political terrain, where rules may be bent or stretched, and not on the terrain of established law or administrative procedure.'[61] Chatterjee suggests that this strategic field of struggle is 'necessarily temporary and contextual', with one of the key features being the instability of community-based organization: 'such constructions [of community] are often fleeting and seldom acquire stable forms of political organization – another mark of their deviance from civil society.'[62]

This analysis resonates with community protests in South Africa, which often rest on rather fluid forms of political organization. A protest typically emerges after somebody has called a mass meeting, enabling community members to raise grievances, and it is collectively decided that a protest is needed to attract the attention of the state. These meetings may be quite democratic, with widespread participation and consensus-based decision-making. But they often lack formal organization, such as a constitution and elected leaders. Beyond this, communities may promote their cause by building connections with middle-class lawyers or activists, government bureaucrats, or political party agents – whoever may be helpful in shifting the levers of governmentality.

The fluid organization of community protests is closely linked to their tactics. Having exhausted formal legal channels with little success, protesting communities often turn to disruptive tactics such as barricading roads and destroying property.[63] Emblematic of political society, these approaches operate in a grey zone of informality and illegality, where disruptive or 'violent' tactics may be used strategically:

> When a situation has to be demonstrated as intolerable or outrageous, there is frequently a spectacular show of violence, usually involving the destruction of public property or attacks on government institutions or personnel. Violence here is not mindless or blind, but rather, even in its most passionate expressions, calculated to elicit the desired response from the government and the public.[64]

We have thus come back around, full circle, to where we began with Fanon. For him, the revolutionary potential of the peasantry was associated with a cathartic, unifying, and democratic use of violence.[65] A similar case may be made for community struggles in South Africa.[66]

Popular struggles in South Africa

This analysis relates to two outstanding puzzles regarding popular struggles in contemporary South Africa (further details are provided in Chapter 1). One puzzle is the general decline of the more formal social movements that emerged around 2000, such as the Anti-Privatisation Forum, which drew their base from poor township communities. Why have these movements not prospered in the context of widespread resistance from the very same types of communities? A second puzzle is the separation of labour struggles from community struggles, despite the fact that both have increased rapidly over the past several years. How can we make sense of this separation, especially given the legacy of labour-community

68   *Marcel Paret*

collaboration during the 1980s? These are huge questions, and it is not possible to fully address either one here. But I want to briefly underscore the possible relevance of political society for both.

One could reasonably argue that the primary function of the social movements was to bring together various community struggles, give them organizational coherence and ideological direction, and scale them upwards into a broader challenge to neoliberal capitalism. At least some of the movements sought a radical transformation of civil society around the ideal of socialism, including the removal of the ANC as the ruling party. Yet the extent to which this vision of transformation resonated on the ground was consistently unclear. This is captured well by two community activists who were affiliated with the APF, yet raised questions about its socialist and anti-ANC stance:

> You see these marches, people are not talking about socialism as an option so why impose ourselves . . . do we know what alternative people are looking for? We don't know. There has never been a single march where people had marched and said we want socialism.[67]
>
> [We are] not anti [-ANC] because we are watch dogs. Because they have promised, we make sure of the promises. . . . If they fail then you see us coming in consulting them, or marching, or do whatever. So we are just rectifying what they are not doing well.[68]

These reflections are more in line with political society. They are not about reorganizing the sociopolitical order, but rather manipulating it to meet basic livelihood needs. This raises the question of whether the social movements declined, and failed to link up with the new community protests, because they were ineffective on the terrain of political society.

A similar dynamic may be said to have emerged with respect to unions. Labour struggles around bread and butter issues, such as wages and benefits, are similar to struggles within political society in the sense that they revolve around meeting basic livelihood needs. Wildcat or 'unprotected' strikes, especially, are similar to community protests because of their informality and potential illegality. Yet while political society is about the relation between subjects and the state, worker strikes typically take aim at employers. To the extent that unions confront the state – such as by demanding minimum wage laws, or even an expansion of welfare provisions – they are often closer to the ideals of civil society. When workers in South Africa take to the street for one-day 'socioeconomic protests', for example, they often do so through legally sanctioned marches, and appeal to the broad rights of citizens. This is quite different from community protests, which typically present more narrow goals and often rely on illegal tactics.

What form of politics does connect with political society? For Chatterjee the answer is populism, which involves unifying 'the people' against those in power, and creating a 'relation of equivalence' between 'unfulfilled demands directed at an unresponsive governmental authority'.[69] He thus argues that 'populism *is* the *effective* form of democratic politics in the contemporary world.'[70]

There is some evidence in South Africa to support this claim, particularly with respect to political parties. In recent years the ruling party, the African National Congress (ANC), and its recently formed and quickly popular rival, the Economic Freedom Fighters (EFF), have been among the most effective organizations in terms of relating to protest-affected communities. Both parties offer expansive political platforms that address a wide range of demands presented by the poor black majority. The ANC continues to rely on its legacy as the party of national liberation, uniting the people in opposition to an often amorphous array of forces – domestic and international – which seek to derail its ongoing 'national democratic revolution'. Conversely, as a breakaway party from the ANC, the EFF unites the people around their frustration with the ruling party, and particularly its inability to deliver on the promises of the postcolonial transition. While largely operating as formal bureaucratic organisations within civil society, the success of both parties may be understood as reflecting, at least partially, their ability to appeal to popular energies emerging from within political society.

Conclusion

This analysis suggests that to understand contemporary patterns of resistance in South Africa – and the global South more generally – we must pay attention to both the political orientations of protest and their social structural roots. It highlights, in particular, the importance of society's more marginalized spaces – terrains of political and economic exclusion – where struggles revolve around governmentality, demands for community recognition, and a strategic politics that operates in a grey zone of legality. Not only does this approach reveal important dimensions of protest, but also it enables us to understand its relation to a broader field of popular struggle. For these reasons, studying the politics of protest from spaces of exclusion may prove to be especially fruitful for making sense of social movements in the current period.

Notes

1 I thank Prishani Naidoo, Claire Bénit-Gbaffou, Carin Runciman, and the editor of the *Mobilization* book series for helpful comments on previous versions, and for the feedback provided by participants in two Johannesburg events: a conference on Contentious Politics, Capitalism, and Social Movement Theory put on by the Centre for Social Change, and a seminar put on by the Center for Indian Studies in Africa.

2 Andrew Walder, 'Political Sociology and Social Movements,' *Annual Review of Sociology* 35 (2009).

3 Gabriel Hetland and Jeff Goodwin, 'The Strange Disappearance of Capitalism from Social Movement Studies,' in *Marxism and Social Movements*, ed. Colin Barker, Laurence Cox, John Krinsky, and Alf Gunvald Nilsen (Leiden: Brill, 2013).

4 Frantz Fanon, *The Wretched of the Earth* (New York: Grove Press, 1963); Mahmood Mamdani, *Citizen and Subject: Contemporary Africa and the Legacy of Late Colonialism* (Princeton: Princeton University Press, 1996).

5 Fanon, *The Wretched of the Earth*, 38, 166, 175, 180–1.

6 Ibid., 163.

70   *Marcel Paret*

7 Ibid., 164–83.
8 Ibid., 166.
9 Ibid., 111.
10 Ibid., 108–9.
11 Ibid., 108–11, 122.
12 Ibid., 109.
13 Ibid., 61.
14 Ibid., 61, 111–12, 114, 127–8, 131–3, 143.
15 Ibid., 111, 115, 136–7.
16 Ibid., 129.
17 Ibid., 128–9.
18 Ibid., 159.
19 Ibid., 164–9, 181–3.
20 Ibid., 109, 122.
21 Ibid., 120–3.
22 Peter Alexander, Carin Runciman, and Trevor Ngwane, *Community Protests 2004–2013: Some Research Findings*, Media briefing, Johannesburg, February 12, 2014.
23 Ibid., 167–9, 172–3, 182–3.
24 Ibid., 186.
25 Marcel Paret, 'Precarious Class Formations in the United States and South Africa,' *International Labour and Working Class History* 89 (2016).
26 Ibid., 155–64.
27 Ibid., 156–7.
28 Ibid., 148–205.
29 Mamdani, *Citizen and Subject*, 18–19.
30 Ibid., 100–2.
31 Marcel Paret, 'Apartheid Policing: Examining the US Migrant Labor System through a South African Lens,' *Citizenship Studies* 19 (2015).
32 Mamdani, *Citizen and Subject*, 19.
33 Ibid., 293.
34 Ibid., 293–4.
35 Michael Neocosmos, *From 'Foreign Natives' to 'Native Foreigners': Explaining Xenophobia in Post-Apartheid South Africa* (Dakar: CODESRIA, 2010).
36 Partha Chatterjee, *The Politics of the Governed: Reflections on Popular Politics in Most of the World* (New York: Columbia University Press, 2004); Partha Chatterjee, *Lineages of Political Society: Studies in Postcolonial Democracy* (New York: Columbia University Press, 2011).
37 Mike Davis, *Planet of Slums* (London: Verso, 2007).
38 Chatterjee, *Politics of the Governed*, 39.
39 Chatterjee, *Lineages of Political Society*, 206.
40 Michel Foucault, *Security, Territory, Population* (Basingstoke: Palgrave MacMillan, 2007).
41 Chatterjee, *Lineages of Political Society*, chapter 10.
42 Ibid., 231.
43 Ibid., 213–15.
44 Chatterjee, *Politics of the Governed*, 34–6.
45 Marcel Paret and Carin Runciman, 'The 2009+ South African Protest Wave,' *WorkingUSA: The Journal of Labor and Society* 19, 3, 301–319 (2016).
46 Gillian Hart, *Rethinking the South African Crisis: Nationalism, Populism, Hegemony* (Athens: University of Georgia Press, 2013).
47 Karl von Holdt, 'On Violent Democracy,' *The Sociological Review* 62 (2014).
48 Steven Friedman, 'People Are Demanding Public Service, Not Service Delivery,' *Business Day*, August 6, 2012, accessed July 7, 2015, http://www.bdlive.co.za/articles/2009/07/29/people-are-demanding-public-service-not-service-delivery.

49 Peter Alexander, 'Rebellion of the Poor: South Africa's Service Delivery Protests – A Preliminary Analysis,' *Review of African Political Economy* 37 (2010).
50 For details, see Alexander et al., *Community Protests*.
51 These figures exclude protests where the target is unknown, which is the case for 22 percent of the total.
52 Interview April 17, 2014.
53 Interview March 26, 2014.
54 Interview June 20, 2014.
55 Chatterjee, *Lineages of Political Society*, 73.
56 Ibid., 15.
57 Ibid., chapter 10.
58 Interview March 12, 2014.
59 Ibid.
60 Interview September 16, 2013.
61 Chatterjee, *Politics of the Governed*, 60.
62 Chatterjee, *Lineages of Political Society*, 23.
63 Marcel Paret, 'Violence and Democracy in South Africa's Community Protests,' *Review of African Political Economy* 42 (2015).
64 Chatterjee, *Lineages of Political Society*, 21.
65 Fanon, *The Wretched of the Earth*, 93–5.
66 Paret, 'Violence and Democracy.'
67 South African History Archive, The Anti-Privatisation Forum Collection, Collection 3290. March 30, 2010. File D2.2.5. Transcript of Interview with Sipho Magudulela.
68 South African History Archive, The Anti-Privatisation Forum Collection, Collection 3290. November 22, 2010. File D2.2.9. Transcript of Interview with Johannes Mokonyane.
69 Chatterjee, *Lineages of Political Society*, 141.
70 Ibid., 40, original emphasis.

5   South Africa 'unrest' or rebellion

A focus on Durban community protests

Tom Lodge and Shauna Mottiar

Rates of protest in South Africa are comparatively higher than those recorded for similar protests around the world.[1] Recent studies confirm a rise in 'community protest' since 2004[2] and a doubling of protests between 2009 and 2012.[3] A number of arguments have been put forward to explain the continuing protest. Susan Booysen[4] argues that protest is only ostensibly insurrectionary and not anti-systemic. It occurs mostly in areas where the ruling party African National Congress (ANC)'s 'service delivery' is better than average. Protest is considered effective because it elicits responses from government in the form of task teams, the dismissal of underperforming local authorities and undertakings to 'deliver'. In this way, responses to protest have ensured that the ANC continues to attract strong support in local elections. Peter Alexander suggests that the upsurge in 'service delivery' protest in 2009 was related to beliefs that the Zuma Administration would be more open to citizen grievances. In this setting government retained general legitimacy and still had 'scope for manoeuvre'.[5] Mottiar and Bond view protest as a form of political participation in which citizens find alternatives to poorly developed formal channels of access through 'inventing' their own spaces. However, they caution, 'protest repertoires are yet to be viewed as complementary to normal channels of political participation' by the authorities. Furthermore, protest has failed to generate a transformational agenda.[6]

An alternative understanding of protest centres on the process of building 'new social movements' that address general grievances but link them to wider systemic concerns. Kelly Rosenthal[7] has argued that the Soweto Electricity Crisis Committee (SECC) was a key site where alternatives to the 'dominant hegemony' were created. Similarly the Anti Privatisation Forum (APF) worked to unite local struggles to 'forge working class alternatives to capitalism'.[8] These studies take seriously the post-2000 gestation of issue-based social activism and argue that movements have the potential to channel widespread material grievances into opposition to the dominant ruling order. Not all supporters of these movements favour abandoning formal political channels however; the ANC's failures to alleviate poverty has created fresh space for radical politics, in the view of Dawson.[9] Contemporary protest then may represent a trajectory towards a new kind of politics, a 'new wave' that brings together a fresh configuration of class actors that seeks far more radical change than earlier phases of mass action.

South Africa 'unrest' or rebellion 73

This chapter considers whether protest in Durban presents a counter hegemonic challenge. It does so drawing from Durban case studies in Umlazi, Cato Manor and South Durban. The focus is on three questions: Are protestors connected, and if so, through which networks or modes of solidarity or sources of inspiration? Do protestors reject procedural channels – are they 'anti-system'? And, do protesters challenge existing political leadership?

Three Durban case studies

The chapter draws from three Durban protest case studies conducted over the past three years. The first is the Umlazi 'Occupy' of 2012 where a group of twelve 'Occupiers' as well as four Durban-based activists were each interviewed individually. The activists were associated with the Unemployed Peoples Movement (UPM), the Democratic Left Front (DLF) and the Centre for Civil Society (CCS). The Occupiers were recorded as 'anonymous' because of the threats faced by protestors in Umlazi in the face of police repression. The activists interviewed, however, gave their consent to be named. Located on Durban's south-west border, originally an Anglican mission reserve, from 1967 as a designated township, Durban's largest, Umlazi accommodated people relocated through apartheid clearances of the inner city. Politically relatively quiescent through the 1980s, the township would from 1990 become one of the major arenas of conflict between Inkatha-affiliated hostel dwellers and ANC-affiliated youth in neighbouring shanty settlements.[10]

The second case study is based on a sample of ten household interviews in a well-known Durban 'hotspot' for protest, Cato Manor (Ward 30). Residents and activists interviewed here remained anonymous again, because of fears faced by protesters in the light of police brutality. Cato Manor was one of the earliest sites of African urban settlement and an ANC stronghold from the 1950s through to the present. These interviews were drawn from Masxha, an RDP[11] settlement where residents access electricity and water services and from Greenland, a nearby informal settlement where water is accessed from standpipe and electricity through illegal connections. Three community activists were also interviewed.

The third case study is based on a sample of ten household interviews – conversations with individuals in the presence of other household members – in the South Durban basin where there has been sustained opposition to environmental degradation by petro-chemical industries in the area. Here respondents were drawn from Ward 68 specifically, flat dwellers in the historically 'Indian' area of Merebank and the 'Coloured'[12] area of Wentworth. All of the respondents were affected by petro-chemical pollution and oil spills. Two activists associated with the non-governmental organisation (NGO) the South Durban Community Environmental Alliance (SDCEA) were also interviewed. Again, all of the respondents were interviewed anonymously. A number of additional conversations were held later with activists from Abahlali baseMjondolo (Abahlali), the Right 2 Know Campaign and the CCS. All but one of these activists gave their consent to be named. The limitations of the methodology are acknowledged with regards to

74 *Tom Lodge and Shauna Mottiar*

the small sample sizes. Snowballing was employed rather than random sampling to ensure that field guides (who may have had specific associations with social movements or NGOs) would not direct the process. However, even with these small samples, in each vicinity the responses shared location-specific characteristics, suggesting they may reflect more widely shared perceptions.

Are protestors connected?

When Durban residents participate in protests against local living conditions, are they on a trajectory towards becoming a more sustained kind of oppositional movement? In other words, are protestors connected, and if so, through which networks or modes of solidarity or sources of inspiration? And do such networks and solidarities extend beyond the neighbourhoods in which they live?

The Umlazi occupiers present a very strong case of protest generating a structured movement. The 'Occupy' lasted more than a month in July 2012 during which local shack dwellers invaded the grounds of the local councillor's office. At any one time there were about 3,000 'Occupiers' of this space, for the most part Zakheleni shack settlement (Ward 88) residents with a record of 'doing things for themselves'.[13] Occupiers referred to decisions made at the 'Occupy' as being a 'community mandate'[14] and reflecting the 'voice of all community members'.[15] A prominent figure in the 'Occupy' was community activist and Zakheleni resident Bheki Buthelezi. Buthelezi represented both the Ward 88 Crisis Committee and the UPM even though activists were clear that 'UPM is not the leader (of the 'Occupy'), Ward 88 is the leader'.[16] During the 'Occupy', community mobilisations stemmed from regular community meetings at which 'collective decisions' were taken, 'there was no hierarchy' and 'nobody was above another' – 'decisions were made by the community'.[17] Other forms of mobilisation included advertisements about the 'Occupy' in the form of pamphlets and the announcing of the 'Occupy' site in the shack settlement using a loudspeaker. A UPM activist argued that building a movement requires patience and that struggle rooted in a community is the most legitimate kind of struggle. In this sense people most likely to join a protest action are those who become '*gatvol*' (fed up) and all the build-up results in protest/movement action which reflects 'their pain'; 'they own it'.[18]

The physical space of the 'Occupy' seemed to have much to do with respondents' understandings of their struggle: 'Every day more and more people would come to see what this is all about and join. If you had a cabbage at home you bring that to share – and everyone else brings what they have to eat'.[19] As opposed to a protest that lasted a couple of hours the 'Occupy' represented a space – 'the peoples office', set up in the ground opposite the councillor's office, where people could discuss views, struggles and demands and where they could bond as a community. Implicit in this last aspiration was a generalised perception that the ward councillor discriminated in her treatment of residents on the basis of their political affiliations or ethnicity or nationality; 'Occupy' is to work together in a community – no divisions' (Umlazi Occupier 7), 'We are the united residents of

Ward 88'[20] and 'We are united (for development) whether NFP, IFP, BCP, ANC or Zimbabwean – everyone here is part of us'.[21]

Despite this very evident consciousness of a solidarity that is grounded in a localised perception of community, as their choice of name suggests, the Umlazi occupiers borrowed rhetorically from the international 'occupy' movements of the previous year and may have been more deeply informed and inspired by external ideas. The 'Occupy' revealed a strong presence of civil society in the form of social movements UPM, DLF and Abahlali. Did the presence of social movements in Umlazi affect occupiers' shared ideas and meanings regarding their cause? At least three occupiers and an activist invoked a 'living like a chicken' metaphor to explain the reason for protest and for the 'Occupy': 'We are living like chickens; we have no roof, no food, sometimes, no dignity'.[22] A couple of occupiers did, however, make mention of being the '99% against the 1%'. This statement followed the rhetoric of the Wall Street 'Occupy', and Umlazi respondents explained that community leaders had arranged a screening for them of the documentary 'Occupy Wall Street' which they had found instructive on how international protests were waged. Occupiers also mentioned political education workshops focused on the political economy and global capitalism offered to them by the DLF. On the whole, though, the language they used suggests more local preoccupations.

What connects protestors in Cato Manor? Several of our informants suggested there was an identifiable group of 'active people' who 'gather others together and plan protest'.[23] Though the same informant believed that this 'community of active people' was 'made up of all kinds, educated, employed, nurses, teachers, men and women', two other residents suggested that 'most protestors are unemployed – those who are employed join later' (Respondents 3 and 4, Cato Manor). Activists themselves spoke about 'call[ing] meetings to discuss the issues that affect us', but they suggested that they made a deliberate choice to avoid the creation of any kind of standing organisational structure:

> There's no specific leader. At each meeting different volunteers will step forward to take on the various roles, [for example], communicating with everybody etc. So 'leaders' change from meeting to meeting. It's better this way also from the point of view of the police singling certain people out as 'protesters'.
>
> (Activists 2 and 3, Cato Manor).

The activists' aversion to hierarchical organisation is very similar to the collectivist ethos one encounters when speaking to the Umlazi Occupiers. Here the apparent absence of references to organised civil society groups other than the ANC in this vicinity is rather striking, even Abahlali, quite strongly established in other Cato Manor vicinities, appeared to have no purchase here. Despite the lack of activist associations, residents often spoke about a shared sense of common purpose; protest 'It's lead by us, community members and activists'.[24] As another resident insisted, 'All of us living here meet and decide to hold a protest'.[25] One

76   Tom Lodge and Shauna Mottiar

of the Cato Manor residents had also seen media images of the Occupy Wall Street protest but, unlike the Umlazi protestors, he was disinclined to draw from it any local salience: 'I've seen the Occupy Wall Street on TV but it doesn't help me – that's American'.[26] The most frequent evocations of struggles outside the immediate local setting were references to struggles in other Durban localities, and with respect to these, our informants were convinced that their example served as a catalyst for others: 'I think our protesting influenced other protest: Ward 1, Ward 11, Ward 87 and Ward 88. We've even influenced protest as far away as Inanda'.[27] Other communities were 'inspired' because 'we take a stand'.[28] Indeed, Cato Manor protestors actively sought to foster such connections: 'We also link with other communities about their protest.'[29]

In Umlazi and in Cato Manor, all the residents we spoke to were active and frequent protestors. In South Durban our snowball sample yielded only three informants who were willing to speak about protests on the basis of first-hand experience. All our respondents were well informed, though, about the recent history of local demonstrations against industrial pollution in their neighbourhood. The Merebank residents were especially disinclined to believe that protest could elicit positive changes, though: 'Is protest effective? No, it's not worth protesting. It never comes right.'[30] As one of the flat-dwellers explained to us: 'No one from here protests. Maybe at the shopping centre. But Engen doesn't affect us much. When there was an oil spill my washing wasn't affected because I didn't have anything on the line. Those who did were paid out by Engen though, so they do take responsibility when things happen.'[31] Engen is the main South African oil company, set up after Mobil divested itself of its local affiliate.

In Cato Manor 'everyone protests',[32] but not so in Merebank. In Merebank you cannot rely on other people, apparently: 'People will go with you and protest but something happens and they will say they weren't there.'[33] We should talk to the people across the road, in Wentworth, we were told, they were more likely to be engaged, '. . . the 'Coloureds' in Wentworth who are concerned with all the trucks, the smell and all that. They go on marches';[34] 'We don't protest; It's mostly the "Coloureds" in Wentworth who protest.'[35]

And indeed, when we crossed the road and asked Wentworth residents about whether they thought protest could be effective in obtaining improvements or concessions, their responses were mainly positive: 'Protest can be effective if carried out properly';[36] 'Protest works. Protest is good if you're honest and not just for yourself.'[37] Even so, the examples of successful actions that residents spoke about were activities described in the third person: undertaken by other people: 'They marched to Engen with placards, they toyi-toyed – but there was no violence. . . . There were people there from Clairwood, Isipingo, the Wentworth Development Forum (WDF), the Merebank Residents association, the Isipingo Residents Association and Desmond D'sa who chairs the WDF was also there.'[38]

Ostensibly, then this particular demonstration was a convincing show of orchestrated communal unity. Or was it? We asked who most of the protestors were. 'Probably people who care about the issues. While some people have an

South Africa 'unrest' or rebellion   77

idea of their rights, we've never had a "community protest", it's all issue related – like anti-drugs etc.'[39] The same informant made a direct comparison with Umlazi: 'People there – in Umlazi – are like minded and unified so they can protest effectively.' South Durban community leaders we spoke to confirmed what the interviews with residents suggested, that protest was largely the outcome of planned initiatives undertaken by activist agencies who could draw upon externally derived resources and action repertoires: 'SDCEA provides most of the funding, T-shirts, banners, etc. Earthlife provides information and research and so does the CCS.' The SDCEA plays an especially vital role:

> Protest is mainly planned. Take, for example, the last protest opposing plans for the port expansion and the increased number of trucks on the road: SDCEA mobilised Merebank and Clairwood communities with loud hailers and also used its email list to spread the word to other organisations such as Earthlife. They also provided transport for people to come to the protest – people from Wentworth, Merebank and Clairwood came by the busload. SDCEA also printed T-shirts for everyone which read 'We shall not be moved.' SDCEA also does the applying for permission to protest etc., all the logistics of protest.

Certain protests were indeed spontaneous, for example, when community members assembled outside the house of a prominent local drug dealer after he had shot a child, but on the whole, protest depended upon organised mobilization: 'I'm not sure there would be mobilization without SDCEA',[40] the leaders told us. In Merebank, especially, 'folk are inward and introverted; they don't want to get out there and fight the "bad" or "hopeless" causes.' And even when their efforts at local protest mobilization are successful, protest fails to empower people; 'the bonding that takes place during a protest is not taken home after the protest'.[41]

Connections among South Durban protesters were therefore largely externally networked compared with forms of communal agency apparent in Umlazi and Cato Manor where respondents stressed 'ownership' of their protest actions.

Do protestors reject procedural channels?

Is collective direct action a substitute for participation in the existing provisions for bringing issues and grievances to the attention of authority such as the local government ward committees? Are protestors withdrawing from formal political participation by abstaining from voting in elections or by ending any engagement with political parties?

In Umlazi, the month-long 'Occupy' attracted up to 3,000 people at a time and came to an agreement following occupiers' demands which included a disciplining of the ward councillor and a re-election of the ward committee. The new ward committee included a 60% representation of members of the Ward 88 Crisis Committee. Mottiar[42] has argued that Occupiers shifted from working within 'invented' spaces to working within 'invited' spaces, that is, moving from the

78 *Tom Lodge and Shauna Mottiar*

'people's office' into a ward committee which suggests that the 'Occupy' was not prompted by systemic disaffection and that 'the "common sense" of development' of occupiers was much the same as those envisioned by 'those in power'.[43] The shift also confirms that grassroots strategies are flexible, often utilizing formal as well as informal means of participation[44] or in this case, utilizing informal means of participation to secure access to formal means of participation.

The sequence of events suggests that occupiers did not reject procedural channels. This is borne out by the fact that before the 'Occupy' Zakheleni residents marched to the eThekwini (Durban) municipality and handed over a memorandum detailing their demands for better services and also demanding the resignation of their ward councillor on the grounds of failing to perform and a lack of accountability. The municipality did not, however, respond within the seven days stated in the memorandum. Activists also argued that they had made many attempts to engage with the ward councillor but to no avail. The ward councillor had further failed to hold ward meetings, thereby curtailing their participation at the local level even further.[45] Occupiers did not, however, give up at this stage. After four weeks of the occupation they succeeded in obtaining a meeting with the mayor, the ANC Branch Executive Committee, the Municipal Housing Portfolio Committee Chair and municipal officials at the city hall. On this occasion 'concessions were made by the municipality' and 'the community demanded, and won ward profiles, maps and documents with the most up to date data'.[46] Indeed, activist China Ngubane has described this meeting as a 'breakthrough' where a 'working relationship was established between the occupiers and their political representatives'.[47]

So, in Umlazi, the Occupiers succeeded in achieving better representation at the ward level and in any case, could access more senior officials at the town hall. A similar tactical fluidity was evident in the testimony we collected in Cato Manor. In the neighbourhoods in which we spoke to residents, we were told there were 'two camps', in contrast to the cohesion so evident at Zakheleni. A minority of residents were supporters of the existing ward councillor who had been imposed on the ward by the party leadership, whereas most people had supported another candidate. So in the case of the majority of residents, 'we don't go to ward meetings'. But, 'we do attend ANC regional and province meetings'.[48] No, we were told, people did not attend ward meetings, because this particular councillor was venal, however, 'if we had an honest councillor [we] would attend meetings'.[49] As it was, though, at ward meetings there was no room for dissenters. Even the activists would attend meetings 'if everybody in the ward was welcome or if those of us who happen not to support the councillor could even get into the venue'.[50]

Certain residents we interviewed clearly belonged to the ward councillor's camp, though. He believed that using sanctioned channels of access worked better than protest. 'General meetings and consultative meetings held by the ward councillor' were more likely to lead to the kinds of decisions that were followed by action, he insisted. On the other hand: 'Protest has no significance because no decisions are made and nothing will come of it.' [Instead] 'we should be persistent through the formal processes rather'.[51] One of the Greenland shack dwellers

South Africa 'unrest' or rebellion 79

concurred with this view, maintaining that 'following the political process is much better than protest'. He was indeed a member of the ANC and belonged to the ward committee, so, not surprisingly, he had 'to follow the process'. People must be patient, though, he said: 'You start with the local councillor; if this doesn't work you take it to the mayor, then the minister, then the public protector, you can go to the president himself after that but you can't by-pass the official process.'[52]

All the Greenland shack-dwellers we spoke with used procedural channels, at least as a first resort. Protest was not always the best option: 'the ward councillor [was] a good option too', another of the Greenland residents assured us.[53] In the older established neighbourhood of Masxha, however, people were less predisposed to enter the 'invited' space of procedural politics, for they had experienced too many disappointments: 'In meetings just a lot of promises are made – things will happen in 60 days, then 90 days. . .'.[54] Really, 'writing to the ANC gets you nowhere so protest shows them that we are angry'.[55] The Cato Manor activists seemed to express widely shared sentiment when they remarked that, 'Well, these [formal] methods would only work if there was justice.' Even so, as we will see, local voting behaviour suggests that Cato Manor residents are still making strong commitments to institutionalised political participation. Even amongst our most politically disaffected informants, the activists, their testimony suggests they would prefer the formal processes to work. 'We are not at all anti-system', they insisted.[56]

In South Durban, Merebank flat dwellers attended their apartment block's 'body corporate' sessions because these addressed the most immediate issues affecting them, but as regards ward meetings, 'No, they're doing nothing good.'[57] One resident 'used to go when the old councillor was here' but the new councillor 'stays in Wentworth', across the road and his more local predecessor 'was more accommodating'.[58] Not all councillors were unresponsive, though, 'Your councillor may or may not act to serve you; it depends what you are asking for.'[59] With only one exception, residents did not view protest as an effective alternative to raising issues at ward meetings or complaining to councillors. In one case, our respondent maintained that regarding protest, 'in a way it's good, because people get to say how they feel, express their opinions.'[60] Also, service provision was not so bad: 'There's no problem with services – if you pay your bills on time you'll have no problems.'[61] And, with respect to the industrial pollution, 'the councillors are working on it'.[62] In this ward, though the councillor was a member of the Democratic Alliance (DA), the main opposition party: 'The ANC representative doesn't ever come around to check on us.'[63] None of our Merebank respondents belonged to a political party and hence did not attend party meetings.

In Wentworth we encountered stronger convictions than in nearby Merebank about the effectiveness of protest when compared with the outcomes of using officially instituted channels: 'Protest at some times is better – they listen to you while in meetings they just talk.'[64] Yes, 'everybody should take the streets', another Wentworth resident observed.[65] Most of the Wentworth flat-dwellers we interviewed never attended ward meetings, 'and we have lots of ward committee meetings',[66] so this seems to have been a conscious choice. A respondent who

80　*Tom Lodge and Shauna Mottiar*

habitually attended ward meetings was by his own self-description, a 'heavy member' of a political party.[67] Significantly, of the Wentworth residents we encountered he was also the only one who was predisposed to assertively participate in protest activities.

In the case of the South Durban activists we spoke with, they had no reservations about using whatever channels were available. We asked them whether they understood protest as a rejection of formal methods of political participation – as an alternative to 'system' politics and received a firm answer: 'You should work at both at the same time.'[68] And, indeed, they conscientiously attended any public meetings arranged by municipal politicians: 'We go to meetings when we hear about them', though, they said, too often such events were poorly publicised even though, 'of course, we believe in using all methods'. Indeed, you needed to begin with the existing channels of representation: 'We'll write a letter or hand over a memo and if nothing comes of it *then* we protest: you can't just start protesting.'

The most basic element in citizen political participation is, of course, voting. Turnout data in elections are instructive. Most of the people we spoke with in Umlazi, Cato Manor and South Durban were habitual voters in local and national polls; only one told us that she 'had lost faith in elections' and in fact had never voted.[69] A comparison of voting patterns between the 2009 and 2014 national elections reveal that the percentage voter turnout in Cato Manor Ward 30 in two voting districts where respondents voted increased between 2009 and 2014 from 65% and 67% to 84% and 81%, respectively. The same trend was notable in Merebank and Wentworth (Ward 68) where voter turnout increased from 67% and 70% to 70% and 71%, respectively. However, the increase in voter turnout in South Durban was not as high as the increase in voter turnout in Cato Manor. Voter turnouts in Umlazi (surveyed across three voting districts in Ward 88 where respondents voted) reveal a mix; there was a drop in voter turnout in two voting districts from 89% and 84% to 77% and 74%, but a rise in the third voting district from 73% to 76%.[70]

To summarise then, our interviews indicated a varied propensity to use local procedural channels: willingness to use any fresh opportunities to take up positions in 'invited spaces' as these became available for Zakheleni residents, a feeling amongst most Cato Manor respondents that ward meetings were unwelcoming occasions, and in Merebank a general scepticism about the accessibility of local government. On the other hand, with one exception, all our respondents voted and in this they seem to have been typical.

Do protestors challenge existing political leadership?

An activist argued that the 'Occupy' was a space for the uniting of local struggles and a method allowing residents of Umlazi to consider the broader issues contributing to their poverty and inequality: 'You may have been given a piecemeal toilet but you're still unemployed.'[71] Despite these sentiments, however, none of the occupiers interviewed applied anti-systemic objections to the ruling ANC; they were quite clear on this: 'We are not against the ANC but poor service delivery

South Africa 'unrest' or rebellion 81

and municipalities not doing their jobs properly.'[72] 'We are not against the Council (eThekwini), only of what they did in our ward.'[73] Indeed, when the 'Occupy' ended, an Abahlali activist stated, 'We need more sustained struggles; Umlazi is now quiet but the land/house and employment issues are still there.'[74]

In the Cato Manor localities, from what respondents told us, their continuing support for the ruling party was not in question. 'We mobilise under the banner of the ANC despite protesting.'[75] In this historic heartland of the ANC's core support, 'We live the ANC, we were born ANC.'[76] No, really, 'we don't hate the ANC, but they must listen to us – they must not hide.'[77] Even the activists working for politically autonomous civil society groups seemed to have an unwavering sense of adherence to the organisation: 'We belong to the ANC, and we hope they will always lead us.'[78] Here, they assured us, 'there is no challenge to the ANC. We don't for example want the DA in power. We were born and bred ANC. We don't want another home, but change is needed.'[79] 'It's not ANC policies – it's people not doing their jobs properly' to blame for their discontents, they said.[80] Or maybe not: 'Some ANC policies need to be critiqued, so blame is at the national level, but the ANC's top-down approach is also to blame.'[81]

And this is the point. 'Belonging' to the ANC may not rule out the possibility of challenging leadership in profound ways. 'We don't hate the ANC, but they must learn to listen to us', declared one of the Cato Manor respondents.[82] The statement suggests a 'we' which is not quite 'living' in the ANC. And when they say 'we belong to the ANC' maybe what they are saying is that the ANC should belong to them and if it does not then it's 'top-down approach is to blame'. In Cato Manor, to think about replacing the ANC with a parliamentary alternative is implausible, but to think about a very different leadership, under different leaders, is not so difficult, especially in a province which led a successful party revolt against incumbent leadership not so long ago. 'We are about sober politics', one of the respondents assured us, 'we want equality.'[83] To use the conceptual language employed by Marcel Paret in his contribution to this volume (Chapter 4), these are the demands for communal recognition that are characteristic of what might be expected in the 'political society' inhabited by groups who are still in many senses excluded – and what these demands conceive of as recognition may require quite a different mode of leadership.

In Merebank and Wentworth the ANC is not locally dominant and in the ward in which our respondents lived, at different times both Inkatha Freedom Party (IFP) and DA-affiliated councillors had won local elections. In the Merebank flats, a resident believed, 'we support the ANC, but they just don't hear us.'[84] A sense of distance between themselves and political officials charged to represent them was very evident; it can be read in the observation already quoted in this chapter, that 'The ANC representative doesn't ever come around to check on us'.[85] Here it seems to be a distance that is extended by racial identity, a consideration to which we return in our concluding section. People were disinclined to protest, it was suggested, because any political assertion might attract unwelcome attention from political leaders. In a district targeted for industrial redevelopment: 'They want us to go and live with the black community in KwaMashu, [but] this is our

82   *Tom Lodge and Shauna Mottiar*

community here.'[86] None of the Merebank residents we encountered belonged to a political party, nor did they attend party meetings. One of them explained that they 'don't get involved in politics; they all promise things but it's false promises'.[87] Even so, with one exception, they dutifully voted, whenever the opportunity arose. Meanwhile in Wentworth, only one of the residents we interviewed belonged to a political party and he voted and attended branch meetings.[88] He and one other normally did vote in elections, and another was 'thinking about voting next year'.[89] Even those who were not habitual voters were quite certain that their electoral abstention was not an expression of political protest. That confident consciousness of collective agency that was so evident in the testimonies we collected in Cato Manor was conspicuously absent in these South Durban vicinities; what was needed was 'more people with steering capabilities'[90] but such capabilities were not present locally. Our respondents were not joiners, they didn't belong to trade unions for instance. As one noted, 'I've never been a member, I don't want to be marked person.'[91]

The activists who spoke to us in South Durban had a much stronger feeling of being part of a wider political movement. They agreed that the local kinds of mobilisation they were engaged in were certainly 'part of a broader political project challenging existing power relations' (the phraseology we used in our question). These community leaders were not ANC members, though one was considering joining the ANC Youth League, 'because the best way to make change is from the inside'.[92] When they abstained from voting, this was definitely as a consequence of political conviction. 'All parties are corrupt', one of them declared.[93] 'But politics is not really for me', the activist who was thinking of joining the ANC conceded. Despite their feeling of engagement in a broader political project, the local environment in which they were working was hardly the kind of setting that might generate profound political assertions. In Merebank, they maintained 'folk are inward and introverted'. To be sure, people might make different political choices, as is evident in elections, even if our respondents were probably mainly ANC supporters, but such decisions are hardly the promptings of ideologically motivated challenge to existing political leadership.

What do the election results tell us about political party support and loyalty? Results drawn from the past two national elections show that the ANC has begun losing support in Cato Manor Ward 30, gaining 80% and 89% of the vote in 2014 down from 88% and 95% in 2009 for the two voting districts surveyed. The trend is similar in the three voting districts surveyed for Ward 88 in Umlazi although the losses are not as significant: here the ANC's share of the vote dropped from 89%, 89% and 88% in 2009 to 87%, 89% (actual 88.81%) and 85% in 2014. Voting patterns in Ward 68 recorded a significant shift between 2009 and 2014, with the DA gaining ground in both Merebank and Wentworth. In Merebank the DA increased its share of the vote from 53% in 2009 to 82% in 2014, cutting into the IFP's 15% in 2009 (decreased to 1% in 2014). In Wentworth, likewise, it increased its share of the vote from 57% in 2009 to 71% in 2014. Here it seems to have drawn from the losses suffered by the Congress of the People (COPE), the Independent Democrats (ID) and the IFP.[94]

South Africa 'unrest' or rebellion   83

As the election results suggest, these protest movements are not animated by impulses to explicitly reject the ruling party's leadership, though clearly in the different settings in which we conducted our interviews there are quite sharp contrasts in the degree to which people feel an identification with the ANC. But respondents do expect different behaviour from leadership; in that sense the language of even the most loyal ANC supporters is critical and in their distinction between loyalty to a national leadership and rejection of its local representatives profound kinds of challenge may be implicit.

Protest in Durban: a counter-hegemonic challenge?

Umlazi and Cato Manor residents interviewed were much more predisposed to participate in confrontational kinds of protest than residents interviewed in the South Durban locations. The Merebank residents were especially disinclined to become actively engaged in protest, not least because they were worried about the consequences of attracting official attention. After all, the South Durban neighbourhoods are under threat because of proposals for industrial expansion.

Cato Manor residents in protesting seemed to be mobilised through informal networks rather than being prompted by any external direction from outside bodies – these appeared to be the main agencies in inspiring demonstrations in South Durban. The extent to which the residents themselves felt a sense of political efficacy was very striking in Cato Manor; much less so in South Durban. Most of the people we spoke with in both locations were habitual voters, though in Cato Manor residents were more likely to attend meetings and use any other procedural channels for political participation as well as being susceptible to direct action through protest. In contrast to most of the residents we interviewed in South Durban, Cato Manor residents felt a strong emotional loyalty to the ANC even though they were critical of its local leadership. Loyalty to the ANC was also evident among respondents in Umlazi even though during the Umlazi 'Occupy' there was space for other kinds of organised activism. In contrast to Cato Manor the presence of well organised civil society was very evident, in particular the social movement organisations UPM, DLF and Abahlali. The 'Occupy' was, however, described as a 'community mandate' and largely arising from and initiated by residents of Zakheleni despite the presence of various social movements and activists.

Of all the activists that we spoke with, these South Durban leaders were most predisposed to view their local struggles ideologically as part of a broader political project challenging existing relationships of power, responses to challenges that 'start higher up, as high as BRICS, but implemented lower down affecting everyone'. However, they were quick to remind us, here, in this locality, 'people here don't know about or understand the issues'. Of the three groups, the leaders of the South Durban protestors were most susceptible to outside sources but as external leaders themselves and not locally resident they had to work hard to foster the kind of 'do it yourself/own it' communal agency so apparent in Umlazi and Cato Manor.

84 *Tom Lodge and Shauna Mottiar*

How do we explain these differences among findings from our research sites? Cato Manor's 'action preparedness' may be a reflection of the solidarities and empathies that are fostered by a particular pattern of settlement. Distinctions between public and private space are looser in densely built RDP settlements as well as the shanty neighbourhoods of Cato Manor and Umlazi, and public spaces are important sites of sociability. Our respondents in South Durban, both in Merebank and in Wentworth, lived in two-storey apartment blocks, located in fenced compounds. Common spaces existed for parking and for hanging out washing, but residents seemed much more likely to spend time at home behind closed doors. This together with the social distinctions and divisions that are the effect of a more complex local class structure in the South Durban neighbourhoods might inhibit the kinds of confidently assertive communal identity evident in Cato Manor and Umlazi. Two additional differences set the South Durban experience apart from the protests in Cato Manor and Umlazi. In South Durban the communities in which we did our fieldwork were historically Indian and Coloured. Particularly with respect to the Indian respondents in Merebank a feeling of communal marginality seemed to reduce political self-confidence. Secondly, in South Durban, the main protagonists are environmental protestors on the one hand and big business on the other; the state and its officials remain on the sidelines in their encounters and this may limit the scope for civic activism leading to more profound kinds of political challenge. Spatial considerations were especially important in the Umlazi 'Occupy'. Aside from Occupiers setting up 'the people's office', the 'Occupy' space became known as a free space open to all where grievances were shared and ideas discussed. There was also a sense of resident or community 'bonding' and of fostering 'solidarity' and 'unity' among all ethnicities and political loyalties in the face of attempts by local authorities to cause divisions.

The most obvious difference, though, among our fieldwork sites, likely to influence local political behaviour in each, is the presence or absence of street-level political organisation. In Cato Manor and Umlazi the ANC's day-to-day presence was very evident from residents' habitual attendance at branch meetings and their consideration of themselves as active members of the organisation. In Merebank, political parties did not seem to have assertive local networks of support and ANC representatives, in the experience of our informants, were visitors, not neighbours, and infrequent ones at that. As noted previously, in any case, election results suggest that in this vicinity of South Durban, electoral support for the ANC is as patchy as other localities in KwaZulu-Natal, in which most residents are Indian or Coloured.

To be sure with respect to the Cato Manor residents that we spoke with, protest was certainly a part of the normal repertoire of political participation and it did not imply disengagement with formal channels of procedural democracy nor did it signal disaffection with the ANC. In Masxha and Greenland, militant street action, it seems, continues to function as a mechanism through which the ruling party can reconnect with its base support. It could still generate opportunities for the creation of 'mutual respect' between residents and officials 'with the ANC listening to us and hearing our problems'. As one of our informants recalled, protest could even on occasions elicit civility from the police. In Umlazi the 'Occupy' movement ended with the fulfilment of key demands and occupiers shifting from protest 'spaces' into formal 'spaces' of participation.

What do the three case studies suggest about the political trajectory of South African protest? Is protest a means through which the ruling party continues to regenerate its legitimacy? Is it from the point of view of its participants simply another channel through which concessions can be extracted from authority? The extent to which the ANC may be inclined to use demonstrations as opportunities for re-engagement through responding in a conciliatory fashion certainly varies, though. Abahlali's emergence, for example, was after the state condemned protestors as criminal. This reaction may reflect perceptions that have become more widespread among senior ANC leaders and top government officials. After an ANC-NEC meeting at the beginning of 2013, the ANC's secretary general announced that the ANC's executive was directing 'the state to find ways and implementable means . . . to deal with the twin phenomenon of violent strikes and violent community protests'. Head of the ANC's elections committee Ngoako Ramatholdi subsequently explained that what was needed was an 'iron fist' to deal with the 'seas of anarchy' generated by service delivery protests.[95] Such predispositions may be present within lower echelons of leadership. In Cato Manor, we were told the ward councillor 'called in' police from outside vicinities, Inanda and Mont Clair, to avoid deploying officers in home settings where they might sympathise with protestors.[96] Indeed Umlazi activists recorded a number of incidents of police brutality and intimidation in response to their demands before the 'Occupy'.[97] The rise in protests and in more violent public order policing[98] may signal a lessening in the likelihood of protestors engendering the kind of 'listening' reaction experienced by our Cato Manor respondents. This reduces opportunities for protestors 'to alternate the brick (protest) and the pro-ANC ballot',[99] weakening the mechanism through which the ANC renews its moral authority.

Most of the protesters we interviewed were clear that their actions were not 'anti-systemic', nor did they seek an alternative to the ruling party. However, they were emphatic that 'democracy' is rooted in accountability and transparency: 'sober politics' or 'the people's office'. This signals an entrenched understanding of democratic principles which are grounded in democratic values as opposed to merely a set of material benefits which could be extracted from democratic processes. Invoking of these values may yet pose challenges to top echelon members of the ruling party.

Notes

1 Peter Alexander, 'Rebellion of the Poor: South Africa's Service Delivery Protests – A Preliminary Analysis,' *Review of African Political Economy* 37 (2010): 27.

2 Peter Alexander, Carin Runciman, and Trevor Ngwane, *Community Protests 2004–2013: Some Research Findings*, Media briefing, Johannesburg, February 12, 2014.

3 Jane Duncan, 'The Politics of Counting Protests,' *Mail and Guardian*, April 14, 2014, accessed May 10, 2015, http://mg.co.za/article/2014-04-16-the-politics-of-counting-protests/.

86 *Tom Lodge and Shauna Mottiar*

4 Susan Booysen, *The African National Congress and the Regeneration of Political Power* (Johannesburg: Witwatersrand University Press, 2011).
5 Alexander, 'Rebellion of the Poor,' 2010.
6 Shauna Mottiar and Patrick Bond, 'The Politics of Discontent and Social Protest in Durban,' *Politikon* 39 (2012): 18–21.
7 Kelly Rosenthal, 'New Social Movements as Civil Society: The Case of Past and Present Soweto,' in *Popular Politics and Resistance Movements in South Africa*, ed. William Beinart and Marcelle Dawson (Johannesburg: Witwatersrand University Press, 2010).
8 Carin Runciman, 'The Decline of the Anti-Privatisation Forum in the Midst of South Africa's "Rebellion of the Poor",' *Current Sociology* 63, 7(2015): 961–979
9 Marcelle Dawson, 'The Cost of Belonging: Exploring Class and Citizenship in Soweto's Water War,' *Citizenship Studies* 14 (2010): 285.
10 Paulus Zulu, 'Durban Hostels and Political Violence Case Studies in KwaMashu and Umlazi,' *Transformation* 21 (1993): 1–23.
11 Between 1994 and 2001 more than one million low-cost houses eligible for government subsidies were built under the Reconstruction and Development Programme (RDP). The RDP was formulated to address socio-economic inequality, social service shortfalls and poverty at the time of South Africa's transition to democracy.
12 The term 'Coloured' was used during the apartheid era to denote people of mixed race. It is a term that is still used in South Africa for racial classification even though in many arenas it is considered derogatory and the term 'so-called Coloured' is favoured.
13 Interview, Ayanda Kota, UPM activist, August 8, 2012.
14 Interview, Respondent 8 Umlazi, August 22, 2012.
15 Interview, China Ngubane, CCS activist, August 22, 2012.
16 Ibid.
17 Ibid.
18 Interview, Ayanda Kota, UPM activist, August 8, 2012.
19 Interview, Respondent 4 Umlazi, August 22, 2012.
20 Interview, Respondent 5 Umlazi, August 22, 2012
21 Interview, Respondent 3 Umlazi, August 22, 2012.
22 Interview, Respondent 6 Umlazi, August 22, 2012.
23 Interview, Respondent 1 Cato Manor, September 26, 2013.
24 Interview, Respondent 3 Cato Manor, September 26, 2013.
25 Interview, Respondent 6 Cato Manor, September 26, 2013.
26 Interview, Respondent 3 Cato Manor, September 26, 2013.
27 Interview, Respondent 1 Cato Manor, September 26, 2013.
28 Interview, Respondent 9 Cato Manor, September 26, 2013.
29 Interview, Respondent 4 Cato Manor, September 26, 2013.
30 Interview, Respondent 4 Merebank, October 30, 2013.
31 Interview, Respondent 3 Merebank, October 30, 2013.
32 Interview, Respondent 9 Cato Manor, September 26, 2013.
33 Interview, Respondent 5 Merebank, October 30, 2013.
34 Interview, Respondent 2 Merebank, October 30, 2013.
35 Interview, Respondent 5 Merebank, October 30, 2013.
36 Interview, Respondent 7 Wentworth, October 30, 2013.
37 Interview, Respondent 8 Wentworth, October 30, 2013.
38 Interview, Respondent 6 Wentworth, October 30, 2013.
39 Interview, Respondent 7 Wentworth, October 30, 2013.
40 Group Interview, Activists 1 and 2 South Durban, October 30, 2013.
41 Ibid.
42 Shauna Mottiar, 'From "Popcorn" to "Occupy": Protest in Durban, South Africa,' *Development and Change* 44 (2013): 603–619.

South Africa 'unrest' or rebellion   87

43 Luke Sinwell, 'Is "another world" Really Possible? Re-Examining Counter-Hegemonic Forces in Post-Apartheid South Africa,' *Review of African Political Economy* 38 (2011): 66.
44 Faranak Miraftab, 'Invited and Invented Spaces of Participation: Neoliberal Citizenship and Feminists' Expanded Notion of Politics,' *Wagadu* 1 (2004): 1–7.
45 Mandy de Waal, 'Service Failure: Next Step the Dissent,' *Daily Maverick*, June 25, 2012, accessed June 1, 2015, http://www.dailymaverick.co.za/article/2012–06–25-service-failure-next-step-silence-the-dissent/.
46 China Ngubane, 'Occupying Umlazi: Hesitant Steps towards Political Ideology in the Durban Township,' *Politikon* 41(2014): 365.
47 Ibid.
48 Interview, Respondent 1 Cato Manor, September 26, 2013.
49 Interview, Respondent 3 Cato Manor, September 26, 2013.
50 Groups Interview, Activists 1 and 2 Cato Manor, September 26, 2013.
51 Interview, Respondent 2 Cato Manor, September 26, 2013.
52 Interview, Respondent 7 Cato Manor, September 26, 2013.
53 Interview, Respondent 8 Cato Manor, September 26, 2013.
54 Interview, Respondent 1 Cato Manor, September 26, 2013.
55 Interview, Respondent 4 Cato Manor, September 26, 2013.
56 Group Interview, Activists 2 and 3 Cato Manor, September 26, 2013.
57 Interview, Respondent 2 Merebank, October 30, 2013.
58 Interview, Respondent 4 Merebank, October 30, 2013.
59 Interview, Respondent 1 Merebank, October 30, 2013.
60 Interview, Respondent 5 Merebank, October 30, 2013.
61 Interview, Respondent 2 Merebank, October 30, 2013.
62 Interview, Respondent 3 Merebank, October 30, 2013.
63 Interview, Respondent 4 Merebank, October 30, 2013.
64 Interview, Respondent 6 Wentworth, October 30, 2013.
65 Interview, Respondent 7 Wentworth, October 30, 2013.
66 Interview, Respondent 9 Wentworth, October 30, 2013.
67 Interview, Respondent 1 Wentworth, October 30, 2013.
68 Group Interview, Activists 1 and 2 South Durban, October 30, 2013.
69 Interview, Respondent 1 Merebank, October 30, 2013.
70 'National and Provincial Election Results,' Electoral Commission of South Africa, accessed August 20, 2015, http://www.elections.org.za/content/Elections/National-and-provincial-elections-results/.
71 Interview, Ayanda Kota, UPM activist, August 8, 2012.
72 Interview, Respondent 7 Umlazi, August 22, 2012.
73 Interview, Respondent 4 Umlazi, August 22, 2012.
74 Interview, Abahlali activist, November 15, 2012.
75 Interview, Respondent 1 Cato Manor, September 26, 2013.
76 Interview, Respondent 4 Cato Manor, September 26, 2013.
77 Ibid.
78 Interview, Activist 1 Cato Manor, September 26, 2013.
79 Interview, Activist 2 Cato Manor, September 26, 2013.
80 Interview, Activist 1 Cato Manor, September 26, 2013.
81 Group Interview, Activists 2 and 3 Cato Manor, September 26, 2013.
82 Interview, Respondent 4 Cato Manor, September 26, 2013.
83 Interview, Respondent 1 Cato Manor, September 26, 2013.
84 Interview, Respondent 1 Merebank, October 30, 2013.
85 Interview, Respondent 4 Merebank, October 30, 2013.
86 Interview, Respondent 1 Merebank, October 30, 2013.
87 Interview, Respondent 5 Merebank, October 30, 2013.

88 Interview, Respondent 6 Wentworth, October 30, 2013.
89 Interview, Respondent 10 Wentworth, October 30, 2013.
90 Interview, Respondent 7 Wentworth, October 30, 2013.
91 Interview, Respondent 6 Wentworth, October 30, 2013.
92 Interview, Activist 1 South Durban, October 30, 2013.
93 Interview, Activist 2 South Durban, October 30, 2013.
94 'National and Provincial Elections,' 2014.
95 Johann Burger, 'Between a Rock and a Hard Place – Policing Public Violence in South Africa,' *ISS Today*, February 14, 2013, http://www.issafrica.org/iss-today.
96 Respondent 1 Cato Manor.
97 Ngubane, 'Occupying Umlazi.'
98 James Brent Styan, 'One Protestor Shot Dead Every Four Days,' *City Press*, February 6, 2014, accessed May 15, 2015, http://www.news24.com/Archives/City-Press/1-protester-shot-dead-every-4-days-20150429.
99 Booysen, *The African National Congress*, 485.

6 Social movements beyond incorporation

The case of the housing assembly in post-apartheid Cape Town

Zachary Levenson[1]

In 2009, housing activists from across the Cape Flats began meeting at a non-governmental organisation (NGO) in Salt River called the International Labour Research and Information Group (ILRIG). This was a direct outgrowth of an ILRIG-run community activist course, similar to those offered by various left NGOs in many South African cities, and soon began to operate under the moniker 'Housing Assembly'. Five years later, the Housing Assembly is a vibrant activist organisation, no longer simply a space for discussion, but an association that attempts to coordinate housing struggles across the City of Cape Town. After a number of its early recruits were involved in land occupations in Mitchell's Plain in 2011 and 2012, the group assumed a very different identity from that with which it began. Whereas it began as a haphazard talk shop for existing activists, it quickly grew into an expansive (and expanding) organisation with local branches in neighborhoods across the Cape Flats.

While the number of service delivery–related protests has steadily increased over the past decade,[2] the same period has witnessed the degeneration of existing social movement organisations. Cape Town's Anti-Eviction Campaign fragmented into competing factions, each claiming to represent the core organisation. Another housing social movement, Durban's Abahlali baseMjondolo, similarly experienced struggles between competing leaderships. Debates raged over the question of membership: Were formally affiliated residents actively involved or merely claimed on paper? The same dynamic was at work during the deterioration of the Anti-Privatization Forum: Political debates were limited to its leadership, whereas many affiliated community activists were unfamiliar with the organisation's politics.[3]

Few local uprisings have coalesced into social movement organisations, making the Housing Assembly anomalous in its ability to overcome the localism characterising the current round of service delivery struggles. It formally launched in late March 2014, despite operating quite actively for three years prior. As I observed it over 15 months of participant observation fieldwork in Cape Town (spanning a period of 3 years),[4] the Housing Assembly regularly facilitates critical discussions about the limits of existing social movement models and how to avoid their pitfalls. Rather than making direct demands on the local government, the organization pursued a strategy of decommodification, targeting the market rather

90 *Zachary Levenson*

than the state. The full decommodification of housing would mean direct access to houses and land without the mediation of markets; housing would be distributed in accordance with need, and decommodification would be achieved through direct occupation of land rather than negotiation with local government officials. The alternative – pressuring the state – characterises the majority of recent housing and service delivery–oriented social movements and protests in South Africa.

By centering its strategy on a coordination and defense of land occupations, the Housing Assembly recognises the limits to acting as a pressure group on the local government. In this chapter, I argue that targeting the market is beneficial to the organisational dynamics of social movements. This strategy emphasises the generalised nature of the post-apartheid housing crisis, overcoming state-imposed divisions among residents. Preexisting movements tended to organise on a parochial basis around specific housing identities: the shack dweller, the backyarder, the number on a waiting list, the recipient of crumbling state-provisioned housing, or the subject of perpetually delayed in situ upgrading. These categories are 'state-imposed' insofar as each residential group has historically negotiated with officials over specific housing policy issues relevant to their own respective situations. In other words, these divisions are a product of state mediation. Targeting the market rather than the state enables residents to organise collectively, overcoming these divisions.

Social movements and the politics of incorporation

A rich literature on post-apartheid social movements[5] has considered the role of organised struggles in relation to privatisation, but less so relative to democratisation and the changing role of the state in relation to popular demands. Only a handful of authors[6] attempt to think through the social role of movements both in the transition to democracy and afterward. Advocates of this latter approach characterise social movements as inherently orientated toward making demands on the state. In this telling, social movements are effective insofar as they render themselves legible to the state through formalisation. More generally, they are envisaged as voluntary associations incorporated into the local state through a process of devolution of decision-making.

As exemplified in recent books by Steven Robins[7] and Elke Zuern,[8] social movements can be understood as partners that bargain with the state to reach a consensus palatable to all stakeholders. For Robins, social movements that formally align with (or else become) NGOs are responsible forces of pressure from below on the state; all others are 'ultra-left',[9] dismissed as an aberration in these processes, and therefore inexplicable other than as deviations. By deploying an entirely external metric – that of incorporation – to define success, Robins misidentifies these movements' own criteria for being successful. In the terms of this chapter, he criticises decommodification movements for targeting the market rather than the state, even when this is precisely their aim.

Zuern provides a far more useful account. Rather than dismissing contentious political organisations as 'ultra-left' as does Robins, she 'challenges the

Social movements beyond incorporation 91

assumption that rights will evolve without political conflict'.[10] The material effect of struggle in this model is to diversify the base of political input into state administration, 'open[ing] the door to the creation of a more substantive democratic system'.[11] Thus her great merit is to shift from a purely procedural to a material conception of democracy,[12] but even in this reformulation, the focus remains on socio-economic rights rather than their concrete realisation. Social movements understood in this framework, while making material demands or otherwise, remain political pressure groups. Any possibility of other modes of struggle – above all, struggles that target not the state but the market – are excluded.

In an Indian context, Partha Chatterjee's analysis[13] of social struggles resonates closely with Robins and Zuern. He develops the concept of 'political society' to distinguish those residents who lie outside of the purview of the formal state from effective members of civil society, or rights-bearing citizens.[14] In this formulation, 'it is resistance that tests rather than overtly violates the limits of conventional political practice. In so doing, it sometimes manages to induce responses from governmental agencies that change the familiar forms of the conventional.'[15] Social struggles become part of a population's representation of itself as an intelligible community, rendering it legible to the state as a worthy recipient of service delivery, settlement upgrading, and the like. But if members of civil society ('citizens') are guaranteed certain rights, then the assurances of the law do not extend these guarantees to members of political society ('populations'). Rather, in comporting itself as an intelligible community, an informal settlement population competes with others over the limited resources of post-colonial delivery regimes. According to Chatterjee's formulation then, political society is not only inherently competitive, but also orientated toward the local state, wittingly or otherwise. All social struggles are reduced to a population's attempt to hail the delivery apparatus.

In this context, how should we understand the politics and potential trajectory of social movements such as the Housing Assembly? While the pressure group model is clearly one means of theorising the role of social movements in a transitional conjuncture, I argue that social movements do not exclusively target the state but may also target the market. Conceiving of social movements as political pressure groups cannot account for land occupations, illegal electricity reconnections, and other direct strategies of decommodification at the heart of the movements Robins dismisses as 'ultra-left'. There is now an enormous literature on urban social movements that address the market rather than the state in a Northern context,[16] but this framing is rarely applied in relation to struggles in Southern cities.

When constituted as organised social movements, anti-market struggles typically arise from cases in which the state is perceived to have failed to adequately ensure access to basic necessities. For example, Bond and McInnes describe the emergence of the Soweto Electricity Crisis Committee (SECC) as a direct consequence of the failure of the ruling African National Congress (ANC) to provide electricity connections.[17] The steady privatisation of electricity, and subsequently of water,[18] catalysed frustration with the state as a target of demands. Instead,

92   *Zachary Levenson*

residents took it upon themselves to illegally reestablish electricity connections. As Nilsen describes in the context of Indian social movements resisting the commodification of land, state power is conjunctural; only where negotiation with state actors 'bears fruits' is it logical to make demands.[19] The state may be engaged instrumentally by social movements, but this is only one of many possible strategies. Where such engagement fails, resisting commodification directly is a rational alternative.

Bond and McInnes conclude their account of the SECC with a turn toward Karl Polanyi's 'double movement', the theorist most often cited to explain the emergence of anti-commodification movements. The 'double movement' was Polanyi's attempt[20] to explain the emergence of decommodification movements. As excessive commodification of land, labor, and money begins to impede the very functioning of society, social actors increasingly struggle against the market. Michael Burawoy (Chapter 2) reworks this formulation to explain the emergence of a diversity of social movements. He argues that different forms of commodification generate different movement responses, and that in any given conjuncture, it is the 'articulation of these different commodifications' that allows us to understand these reactions. The use of Polanyi to explain decommodification struggles reads the *movement* in double movement and the *movement* in social movement as one and the same. But in concrete applications, Polanyi is useful for illustrating *that* movements arise in response to commodification, but less so for explaining *how* social movements contest commodification in practice.

My account of the Housing Assembly's emergence and genesis is a preliminary attempt to explain what it would look like in practice to target the market. The case of illegal electricity reconnections is instructive: Where the state proves to be an inefficient means for achieving decommodification, direct decommodification can be a viable alternative strategy. In this chapter, I argue that the Housing Assembly is charting a novel path for housing-oriented social movements in post-apartheid South Africa. Instead of limiting its repertoire to resisting evictions and demanding housing, the organisation frequently bypasses the state altogether by encouraging land occupations on private property as well as municipally owned land. Where the state proves to be an instrument incapable of actually delivering land or housing, direct seizure may be a viable option.

Housing crisis, organisation, and the politics of representation

After the slow dissipation of the Western Cape Anti-Eviction Campaign, Cape Town's most militant and successful citywide housing rights organisation, demand began to arise for an organ capable of transcending localised dissent and spontaneous service delivery protests. The earliest attendees of Housing Assembly meetings were largely seasoned activists from housing-orientated groups of various sizes. As the character of the organisation changed during the period 2011–13, new members were increasingly unaffiliated with any existing group. Many had been active in their local civic associations or the United Democratic Front in the

Social movements beyond incorporation 93

1980s, but few of the members drawn in after these initial meetings were themselves formally affiliated to post-apartheid social movements.

At its inception, the group was largely a talk shop, a space in which residents of disparate settlements would come together to tell one another about various problems, both of material deprivation and of political organisation. However, at this point the Housing Assembly did not function as a coordinating body for actually existing housing struggles. In tracing the origins and genesis of the Housing Assembly's politics, I want to demonstrate how its politics exceed the externally imposed limits of the pressure group model. The Housing Assembly's target, I argue, is not the state, but the market. The pressure group model is not capable of taking decommodification struggles seriously, as by its imposed criteria, these groups fail where they do not act as pressure groups or embed themselves as policy-making entities. When Housing Assembly members participate in land occupations, for example, they do not do so in order to pressure the state or attempt to dictate land policy; they do so in order to gain direct access to land.

The Housing Assembly was largely the creation of two employees of a Cape Town NGO that emerged from COSATU struggles in the late 1980s, the International Labour Research and Information Group (ILRIG). As well intentioned as they were, these NGO workers reproduced a dynamic all too common in NGO–social movement interactions. Often those who would come to Housing Assembly meetings were self-identified activists, who would use their involvement in ILRIG-sanctioned activities to legitimise their own leadership roles in their respective neighborhoods and settlements. After it later became an active group of housing activists, relatively autonomous from its unofficial institutional affiliation, its earlier reputation remained.

Even after gaining nominal independence from ILRIG, the Housing Assembly continued to hold coordinating and steering committee meetings at the NGO's offices. Largely this was a function of not having a large enough alternative space available for multi-hour meetings of this size. By the same token, one ILRIG employee was involved from the beginning, consistently giving presentations on the South African housing crisis, social policy, and the history of social movements in the 1980s and after apartheid. He was exceptional in two ways. First and foremost, he was himself a housing activist, both in his own township – Mitchell's Plain – and more generally. He was an active member of the Anti-Eviction Campaign from its inception, and before that, he was a founding member of the Cape Areas Housing Action Committee (CAHAC), a body that organised the first successful generalised rent strike in the Cape Flats and was a predecessor of the civics movement. CAHAC was always the implicit model he had in mind as he attempted to develop the Housing Assembly's organisational form.

Second, his method was intentionally one of facilitating autonomy and self-organisation. For example, he organised a six-part training session he called 'train the trainer' in which Housing Assembly members were taught how to give a presentation on the failure of post-apartheid housing delivery and the persistence of substandard housing. They would subsequently revise this presentation, and organise workshops around the housing crisis themselves. The first of these that

94   *Zachary Levenson*

I witnessed was organised for about 70 attendees from across the Cape Flats in mid-August 2013. Rather than lecturing attendees or other potential members, the goal was to begin by soliciting testimony from the crowd. One man from Khayelitsha described the parastatal electricity company's refusal to deliver electricity to his settlement, even though electricity lines ran directly above his shack. He continued, telling everyone that the municipal government refuses to extend plumbing to the neighborhood, citing an adjacent dam as the reason. There is also quite a bit of disease, most notably tuberculosis, he continued, and there has been no progress for decades.

Others gave briefer accounts. One woman told us she had five kids but only one large room separated by thin partitions. This lack of privacy and her perpetually leaking roof rendered her home miserable. Another woman described having to stay at others' houses, having to bring them gifts in order to stay in their good graces, but she complained that she did not have any disposable income to do so. A third woman living in Lost City talked about her rent increasing every month even though her landlord refused to pay the water bill. As a result, her water was regularly cut off; sometimes she was not even able to flush the toilet, she insisted. That and overcrowding make the place nearly unlivable even though it is technically a formal flat. Other participants described leaking, overcrowding, crime, and gangsterism in their living situations.

After this initial exercise, they moved on to describe the impact of these conditions on their family life. These included poor public health, no place for children to do homework, domestic violence, mental health issues, crime (resulting from lack of electricity and therefore darkness), washing with cold water, smelling like fire all the time, and having limited access to water. Women and children were scared to go outside, and people described a general loss of confidence. Of course, there were also endemic substance abuse problems, as well as high HIV/AIDS rates in their areas. One woman concluded, 'We're just waiting to die. We've given up hope. We're dead here [*pointing to her head*].'

I noted how residents in quite disparate forms of housing – rented flats, backyard shacks, informal settlements, temporary relocation areas (TRAs), crumbling RDP houses – were able to articulate problems that affected people in all of these substandard forms of housing. Residents were surprised to encounter others with similar problems in forms of housing that they otherwise viewed as viable alternatives. When shack and TRA residents were able to discuss their housing dilemmas with recipients of state-provisioned formal housing, they increasingly came to the realisation that the problem was not insufficient will or even capacity on the part of the state's delivery apparatus. Even those who had received housing were facing substantial problems, whether of the quality of structures or of being required to move to unsustainable locations far from affordable transportation or viable employment.

This is not to suggest that the shift from state to market as the target of social movement activity easily or even necessarily follows from these discussions among residents occupying various rungs in the ladder of housing distribution. There is an observable reluctance on the part of precarious residents to enter into any kind of alliance with others in a similar situation. At the ILRIG-sponsored Globalization School in September 2013, for example, housing activists from around the country gathered for a strategic dialogue about potentially building a larger organisation, though ultimately to no avail. A Housing Assembly member from an informal settlement in Athlone insisted that everyone in the room's living situations were connected, related to the same crisis of housing and service delivery, and through analysis the housing activists could begin to think about strategy. His interventions were immediately resisted. Some of this was a sense of proprietorship over one's own experience; for many participants, equation amounted to reduction. As soon as multiple experiences were rendered comparable, the thinking went, variation was erased altogether. Thus one participant from the Eastern Cape decried the Housing Assembly chairperson's invocation of 'the working class', a concept, he argued, that negated his own experiences as a Xhosa man, as perpetually unemployed, and as a shack resident.

In one representative 'train the trainer' workshop, the difficulty of reaching a common perspective was abundantly apparent. Attendees insisted upon detailing their own living conditions. When pushed to connect their own situation to that of others in the room, they refused, often with a flourish of mild annoyance. Each attempted to outdo the next, presenting her own poverty as a novelty, despite the countless narratives that were already described. Much of this emphasis on the particularities of each housing situation seems to be related to a desire for adequate representation in a context of perceived political abandonment, a stubborn refusal to fully dispense with the notion that a faulty system of housing delivery was to blame for their respective predicaments. Indeed, there appears to be a commonplace understanding in many settlements that through forcefully narrating their respective plights, they might attract the attention of the municipal state.

The irony is that the refusal to be represented at the level of the neighborhood occurs at the same time as residents state that they want representation at the level of the municipality. The bulk of skepticism remains directed at local representatives – in most cases, people's neighbors – rather than the city or the province. It is to the Housing Assembly's great merit that it has been able to begin to transcend some of the barriers of localism, shifting focus from competition over limited state resources to a critique of capitalist housing markets and their inhibiting effects on distribution itself. In the following section, I provide an account of the Housing Assembly's organisational model, focusing in particular on how multiple organisational scales are articulated into a coherent strategy that both incorporates localised discontent and posits a generalised theory of the post-apartheid housing crisis. But this organisational model alone is insufficient to unite various housing identities under the rubric of a unitary social movement. It was only through a process of actual, material struggle – through participating in and defending land occupations – that the Housing Assembly was able to form a coherent bloc. The penultimate section details this process of struggle, taking the Housing Assembly's involvement in three land occupations in Mitchell's Plain as the crucial moment in uniting its disparate membership into a fighting body.

96 *Zachary Levenson*

Devolution to the districts

Cape Town–based housing struggles have a long history of federated structures rooted in neighborhood-level branches, from the United Democratic Front of the 1980s[21] to the Anti-Eviction Campaign of the early 2000s[22] – both of which, incidentally, were launched in Mitchell's Plain. The Housing Assembly is no different. However, as discussed extensively at Coordinating Committee meetings, previous Cape Town–based post-apartheid social movements faced two major barriers to effectively utilising their federated structures. First and foremost, branches became mired in a parochial localism, unable to transcend neighborhood-level concerns and make use of the organisation as a whole. The Housing Assembly consciously attempted to overcome this limit by holding regular (ranging from weekly to monthly) report-backs to a central Coordinating Committee that included both district-level conveners and organisation-wide elected officials. The sole purpose of these meetings was to ensure that local strategies accorded with the Housing Assembly's overarching strategy as determined by its membership. This makes the Housing Assembly unique in a period characterised by two notable features: nearly all of the post-2000 urban social movements in South African cities have collapsed, and those militant struggles that have emerged more recently (around service delivery, housing, jobs, and education) have rarely been connected to a coordinating movement organisation.

A second major limit to previous iterations of district-level organising is that despite maintaining the organisational form of a federated structure, previous organisations were frequently dominated by a handful of charismatic personalities. In such cases, directives typically ran from these individuals to local branches instead of vice versa. In some instances, these individuals were able to stand in for branches themselves, creating the appearance of district-level power, but in practice resulting in one or two figures substituting their individual wills for those of the local committee. This critique was the one most frequently voiced in the Housing Assembly's discussions of previous social movements.

To reinforce branch autonomy, the Housing Assembly divided the Cape Flats into five districts (see Figure 6.1), and each of these into a number of neighborhood committees. The Mitchell's Plain district, for example, convened meetings in Tafelsig and Beacon Valley, two large, well-established neighborhoods; and in Siqalo, an informal settlement with an estimated 30,000 residents. At the neighborhood committee level, organisers would decide upon the frequency of meetings. I attended a handful of such meetings in four of the five districts, and I attended every district meeting in Mitchell's Plain's Beacon Valley and Tafelsig neighborhoods over a four-month period. At their peak, these occurred weekly. This was the strongest district at the time, and so it would be inaccurate to extrapolate from this experience, but by the time I left, Athlone and Khayelitsha were reportedly holding meetings of comparable strength.

A major function of these meetings was to coordinate *huisbesoek*, Afrikaans for door-to-door campaigning. Every Sunday at 2 pm, Beacon Valley residents would meet at the convener's front gate, and for two hours they would systemically work through the neighborhood. They would bring petitions with them, which were

Social movements beyond incorporation 97

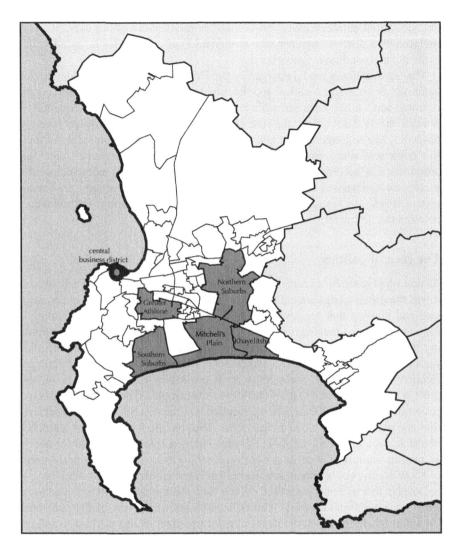

Figure 6.1 Housing assembly districts in relation to the Cape Town city centre

actually less petitions and more condensed versions of the Housing Assembly's draft program, describing the organisation's politics in some detail. Signing the document was a means of expressing interest in the organisation, and every week *huisbesoek* would draw in one or two additional members. Given the centrality of this collective activity to the Housing Assembly's local strategy, there were very few opportunities for opportunistic activists to act on behalf of the group. In the rare instances where this occurred, the offending activists were formally rebuked by the Steering Committee, to whom they would have to report back periodically in order to monitor their progress. In the case of one particularly intransigent

98 *Zachary Levenson*

district convener who continued to speak on behalf of her neighborhood without substantial outreach work, the Committee relieved her of her duty. She was replaced by a district convener who reinitiated *huisbesoek* in his informal settlement and surrounding neighborhoods.

The organisational model adopted by the Housing Assembly then safeguarded against both excessive localism and the threat of demagoguery. However, organisational form alone does not sufficiently account for the Housing Assembly's politics, directed not toward the state but the market. As Andrew Walder recently observed, 'we no longer have explanations to offer about variation in the substantive content of a movement – the type of politics that it represents'.[23] Instead, prominence is accorded to organisational form and effective mobilisation; the means are emphasised at the expense of the ends. Moving beyond the formal means, it is to the Housing Assembly's development of a politics beyond incorporation that I now turn.

The ends of politics

As described to me by an early Housing Assembly member from Mitchell's Plain, it was the group's engagement with a concrete series of struggles over access to land and housing that solidified the organisation's political identity, elevating it from an occasional meeting space to a citywide coordinating committee for housing struggles. He told me how backyarders led two occupations in 2011 in Tafelsig, the poorest neighborhood in Mitchell's Plain, just before the 2011 municipal elections: one at the field across from the Kapteinsklip Metrorail station, and the other at the field adjacent to the Swartklip sports complex. The Kapteinsklip occupation initially had 5,000 people, he recalled. On the first Sunday of the occupation, the police showed up and cleared the field, but the following day a number of shacks would go back up. Small groups retained hold of each field for nearly 18 months until most occupants were successfully evicted. A small encampment of a few dozen people remains on the field at Kapteinsklip.

Despite the ultimate clearance of the land occupation, activists' sustained experience of frontal conflicts with police and representatives of the municipal Department of Human Settlements transformed their politics. These conflicts, in combination with the necessity of constantly reconfiguring strategy simply to retain access to the land, increasingly led Housing Assembly–affiliated participants to view the local state as an adversary. Whereas many housing-related social movements make demands on the state's delivery apparatus, participants in and supporters of the Tafelsig occupations were largely backyarders who had slipped through the cracks of the post-apartheid housing delivery scheme. Their perception of the local state was not as a potential source of housing and services, but as a coercive entity that sought to evict them. The fact that this squatted land was municipally owned – not even private property – was doubly alarming to these activists, not least because the City of Cape Town had no immediate plans to develop the land adjacent to the Kapteinsklip station. Thus clashes with the City – its Anti-Land Invasion Unit and the Department of Human Settlements – and the

Social movements beyond incorporation 99

South African Police Service remained participants' primary interaction with the state.

Often, however, conflicts between residents and the state took a more subtle form. In drawing out the implications of occupation-level factionalism for thinking about the role of the municipal state, Housing Assembly affiliates made sense of otherwise quite complicated dynamics. In the Kapteinslip occupation, a sizable faction aligned itself with opportunists, forming blocs aligned with various outside entities. Its members were interested in dialoguing with philanthropists or small political parties that would appear at the land occupation in search of a constituency. One Housing Assembly member described the scene to me in impassioned detail, clearly growing agitated as she explained the source of conflict. She recounted battle lines quite literally drawn, with one opposing faction proposing to work with the police. The idea was that if they could eject immigrants from the land occupation, perhaps they could legitimate their own position and gain at least a temporary reprieve from the City. The Housing Assembly member was not having this. She told me that just a few days before this squabble, she met the man from ILRIG and through him, she built a relationship with a number of Housing Assembly affiliates. She was immediately drawn to the group's politics and began attending their occasional meetings and workshops closer to the city centre when she could; he would reimburse her taxi fare. Through these encounters, she told me, she gained a sense of programmatic politics for the first time. From this day forth, she laughed, she could only think of politics – it was all she would discuss with her husband. Housing Assembly members who would visit the occupation stood in solidarity with her, and a number of other occupiers were drawn into the organisation.

Through discussions of their experiences at the two Tafelsig occupations (as well as a third Mitchell's Plain–based land occupation a few months later), Housing Assembly members began to rethink their relationship to the City. Rather than a benevolent delivery state, residents encountered municipal agencies that either criminalised them, or else attempted to relocate them to semi-permanent encampments on the far periphery of the municipality. This was not only a conflict with the City, but also a campaign against the commodification of land. Of course, this was not their language, but the concept remains the same: The Housing Assembly's politics emerged from its experience of reappropriating land that the City deemed too valuable, or else unfit for use.

At the centre of the organisation's Draft Statement – its most important document and essentially its founding program – is an explicit defense of land occupation as a legitimate tactic:

> We believe that occupations are a legitimate means for both people fleeing poverty and unemployment elsewhere in the country, as well as for evicted people, backyarders and those in overcrowded housing, to take their struggle for decent housing forward.[24]

This set of politics is reiterated in the group's central document adopted at the formal launch of the organisation in March 2014, coupled with a cautionary note

100 *Zachary Levenson*

on engaging the state: Their aim is 'to promote an understanding among affected communities that the cheap policies such as site-and-services, the upgrading of informal settlements and backyard dwellings, "re-blocking" initiatives, self-help schemes, among others, are hopelessly inadequate changes and unacceptable as alternatives to decent housing for all.'[25] Their argument then is that revising existing policy is not only too little too late, but not even particularly effective. If the new national housing policy Breaking New Ground was supposed to spur a shift from relocations to peripheral greenfields to in situ upgrading, it did nothing of the sort.[26] Above all, according to these two Housing Assembly documents, this failure of housing policy is attributable to the dominance of private interests in its implementation, from the nepotistic contracts granted to Black Economic Empowerment (BEE) companies to the use of for-profit subcontracting more generally.[27] The primacy placed on the value of real estate over the right of residents to live in decent housing is at the centre of the Housing Assembly's critique, and above all, acting as a pressure group on policymakers will do little to reverse this tendency in their estimation.

The few cases in which Housing Assembly members did see squatters gain access to more durable forms of housing were invariably disappointing. In one case, a half dozen participants in the Swartklip occupation accepted state-provisioned alternative accommodation. These turned out to be peripherally located corrugated zinc shacks in a temporary relocation area (TRA). This TRA was notorious among residents for its high concentration of gang violence and petty robberies, and these relocated residents were extremely dissatisfied. Within a couple of months, they had returned to the Housing Assembly. In another case, squatters from an occupation in another township (Grassy Park) received formal housing in a nearby development. The walls and floors of these structures were crumbling before they even moved in.[28] Despite being home recipients, they too remained active in the Housing Assembly. From these experiences, the Housing Assembly drew two major lessons. First, state-provisioned housing is nearly always distributed on an individualised basis, forcing households to compete with one another over a limited supply of housing stock. Second, even in cases where formal housing is distributed, it is rarely what recipients envisioned it to be beforehand. In both cases, the municipal state is encountered as an adversary rather than a potential partner. Instead of engaging this state then, Housing Assembly members were skeptical of the strategic efficacy of doing so. They certainly kept an eye on housing policy, convening study groups on Breaking New Ground and Connie September's housing Green Paper, to name but a couple, and organising workshops on the history of housing interventions since the demise of apartheid. But the Housing Assembly's social movement strategy was aimed not toward the state, but the market, rejecting the mediation of the Department of Human Settlements in favor of advocating direct land seizure.

Beyond incorporation

Rather than an abstentionist critique of engagement, the Housing Assembly has developed a programmatic alternative to what it views as the futile efforts of the

Social movements beyond incorporation   101

pressure group model in a period marked by the failure of housing and service delivery. Its direct participation in and defense of land occupations as a viable strategy for gaining access to housing is at the root of its ability to bypass the morass of localism. In a period dominated by scattered service delivery protests, however increasingly frequent, and following the demise of most post-2000 social movements, the recent emergence of a citywide housing organisation would appear anomalous. As I argue in this chapter, this ability to transcend localism is grounded in two major strategic developments that distinguish it from many previous housing-oriented organisations: the active construction of a novel agent of struggle – the subject of a generalised housing crisis, as opposed to distinct and fragmented housing identities; and involvement in decommodification struggles instead of acting as a pressure group on the municipal state.

This market-orientated approach stands in stark contrast to strategies easily explained by the various proponents of the pressure group model, as discussed previously. Above all, this approach signals a break with Chatterjee's valorisation of political society, which he notoriously describes as 'popular politics in most of the world'.[29] If for Chatterjee, politics in informal settlements concerns the formation of settlement-level organisations competing with one another for recognition from a delivery state, the case of the Housing Assembly demonstrates quite clearly that poor people's politics need not be inherently competitive. Indeed, it is precisely the limits of this competitive mode of politics that drove the organisation to develop its citywide approach in the first place. Rejecting the prevailing social movement approach of identifying in terms of one's immediate conditions – as shack residents, as backyarders, as RDP house recipients, and so on – the Housing Assembly seeks to unite all of these residents as subjects of a capitalist housing crisis under the political identity of being 'working class'.[30] It is division into these sectional interests that reduces the effectiveness of housing-related mobilisation in the first place, they argue, and so Chatterjee's reinscription of neoliberal governmentality as a form of popular politics from below misses the mark. Rather than a potentially effective challenge to a municipal state that continues to exacerbate the housing crisis, the political society approach to social movement politics simply engages the state on its own terrain.

Given the vast literature on social movement organisations involved in land occupations, electricity reconnections, and other active forms of decommodification, it is the task of social movement theorists to think these movements beyond direct engagement with the state. A growing literature on Northern social movements that target the market rather than the state[31] indicates a shift in the way we talk about contemporary social movements more broadly. Yet this tendency remains to be fully considered by social movement theorists in general[32] and, as I hope I have demonstrated in this chapter, analysts of South African social movements in particular. Certainly the post-Marikana strike wave in the platinum belt and the Western Cape wildcats of 2012–13 were described in such terms, but when it comes to social movements struggling not at the point of production but at the point of *re*production, no such allowance is made.

The case of the Housing Assembly clearly demonstrates the need to situate organised struggles for decommodification within a more wide-reaching

102   *Zachary Levenson*

theoretical scaffolding that takes movements' own goals seriously. The challenge will be to consider both market- *and* state-orientated struggles, developing specific accounts of each without abandoning the concept of 'social movement' altogether. Political variation should not pose a problem to theorists of these movements, but instead serve as their point of departure. The Housing Assembly and other decommodification movements[33] should not be represented as deviations from a set of goals presumed in advance to accurately represent social movement strategy. Certainly the majority of social struggles and movements in contemporary South Africa do target the state, and the Housing Assembly is atypical in this regard. But its attempt to veer from a course that has yet to yield substantial gains does not render it misguided or aberrant. Social movement theorists must reject teleological approaches rooted in organizational theory and begin to take movements' own politics seriously.

Notes

1   This chapter benefited greatly from critical feedback from Marcel Paret, Trevor Ngwane, Noor Nieftegodien, and Carin Runciman, as well as from the participants in a one-day conference on Contentious Politics, Capitalism, and Social Movement Theory organised by the Social Change Research Unit at the University of Johannesburg.
2   Peter Alexander, 'Rebellion of the Poor: South Africa's Service Delivery Protests – A Preliminary Analysis,' *Review of African Political Economy* 123 (2010): 25–40; Peter Alexander, Carin Runciman, and Trevor Ngwane, 'Media Briefing: Community Protests' (paper presented at Social Change Research Unit, University of Johannesburg, February 12, 2014).
3   Carin Runciman, 'The Decline of the Anti-Privatisation Forum in the Midst of South Africa's "Rebellion of the Poor",' *Current Sociology* 7 (2015): 961–79.
4   During the lead-up to the formal launch, I attended every citywide Housing Assembly meeting, ranging in frequency from monthly to three times per week. I also sat in on every Mitchell's Plain district meeting, and I lived with the Mitchell's Plain district convener during this entire period, regularly interacting with new recruits in the area. I occasionally attended meetings in other districts (described in subsequent notes), as well as recruitment meetings and workshops in areas beyond the five core districts.
5   Richard Ballard, Adam Habib, and Imraan Valodia, eds., *Voices of Protest: Social Movements in Post-Apartheid South Africa* (Scottsville: University of KwaZulu-Natal Press, 2006); William Beinart and Marcelle C. Dawson, eds., *Popular Politics and Resistance Movements in South Africa* (Johannesburg: Wits University Press, 2010); Marcelle C. Dawson and Luke Sinwell, eds., *Contesting Transformation: Popular Resistance in Twenty-First-Century South Africa* (London: Pluto, 2012); Peter Dwyer and Leo Zeilig, *African Struggles Today: Social Movements since Independence* (Chicago: Haymarket, 2012); Nigel C. Gibson, ed., *Challenging Hegemony: Social Movements and the Quest for a New Humanism in Post-Apartheid South Africa* (Trenton: Africa World Press, 2006).
6   Adam Habib, *South Africa's Suspended Revolution: Hopes and Prospects* (Johannesburg: Wits University Press, 2013); Steven L. Robins, *From Revolution to Rights in South Africa: Social Movements, NGOs & Popular Politics after Apartheid* (Woodbridge: Currey, 2008); Elke Zuern, *The Politics of Necessity: Community Organizing and Democracy in South Africa* (Madison: University of Wisconsin Press, 2011).
7   Robins, *From Revolution to Rights in South Africa.*
8   Zuern, *Politics of Necessity.*

Social movements beyond incorporation 103

9 Robins, *From Revolution to Rights in South Africa*, 171.

10 Zuern, *Politics of Necessity*, 18.

11 Ibid., 184.

12 Ibid., 42–3, 50, 67.

13 Partha Chatterjee, *The Politics of the Governed: Reflections on Popular Politics in Most of the World* (New York: Columbia University Press, 2004); Partha Chatterjee, *Lineages of Political Society: Studies in Postcolonial Democracy* (New York: Columbia University Press, 2011). Chatterjee's work has been increasingly cited by South Africanists in recent years, including in Marcel Paret's contribution to this volume (Chapter 4), as well as in Claire Bénit-Gbaffou and Sophie Oldfield, 'Accessing the State: Everyday Practices and Politics in Cities of the South,' *Journal of Asian and African Studies* 46 (2011): 445–52; Gillian Hart, 'Political Society and Its Discontents,' *Economic and Political Weekly* 50 (2015): 43–51; Prishani Naidoo, 'Struggles around the Commodification of Daily Life in South Africa,' *Review of African Political Economy* 111 (2007): 57–66; and Thiven Reddy, *South Africa: Settler Colonialism and the Failures of Liberal Democracy* (London: Zed, 2015).

14 Chatterjee, *Politics of the Governed*, 38–9.

15 Chatterjee, *Lineages of Political Society*, 150.

16 David Harvey, *Rebel Cities: From the Right to the City to the Urban Revolution* (New York: Verso, 2012); Neil Brenner, Peter Marcuse, and Margit Mayer, eds., *Cities for People, Not for Profit: Critical Urban Theory and the Right to the City* (London: Routledge, 2011); Helga Leitner, Jamie Peck, and Eric Sheppard, eds., *Contesting Neoliberalism: Urban Frontiers* (New York: The Guilford Press, 2006); Don Mitchell, *The Right to the City: Social Justice and the Fight for Public Space* (New York: The Guilford Press, 2003).

17 Patrick Bond and Peter McInnes, 'Decommodifying Electricity in Postapartheid Johannesburg,' in *Contesting Neoliberalism: Urban Frontiers*, ed. Helga Leitner, Jamie Peck, Eric S. Shepard (New York: The Guilford Press, 2007), pp. 157–178.

18 David A. McDonald and Greg Ruiters, eds., *The Age of Commodity: Water Privatization in Southern Africa* (London: Routledge, 2004); David A. McDonald and John Pape, *Cost Recovery and the Crisis of Service Delivery in South Africa* (London: Zed, 2003).

19 Alf Gunvald Nilsen, *Dispossession and Resistance in India: The River and the Rage* (London: Routledge, 2010), 200.

20 Karl Polanyi, *The Great Transformation: The Political and Economic Origins of Our Time* (Boston: Beacon Press, 2001), 79–80.

21 Ineke van Kessel, *'Beyond Our Wildest Dreams': The United Democratic Front and the Transformation of South Africa* (Charlottesville: University of Virginia Press, 2000); Jeremy Seekings, *The UDF: A History of the United Democratic Front in South Africa 1983–1991* (Athens: Ohio University Press, 2000).

22 Sophie Oldfield and Kristian Stokke, 'Building Unity in Diversity: Social Movement Activism in the Western Cape Anti-Eviction Campaign,' in *Voices of Protest: Social Movements in Post-Apartheid South Africa*, ed. Richard Ballard, Adam Habib, and Imraan Valodia (Scottsville: University of KwaZulu-Natal Press, 2006), 111–32; Faranak Miraftab and Shana Wills, 'Insurgency and Spaces of Active Citizenship: The Story of the Western Cape Anti-Eviction Campaign in South Africa,' *Journal of Planning Education and Research* 2 (2005): 200–17.

23 Andrew G. Walder, 'Political Sociology and Social Movements,' *Annual Review of Sociology* 1 (2009): 398.

24 Housing Assembly, 'Draft Statement of the Housing Assembly' (n.d.), 3.

25 Housing Assembly, 'What the Housing Assembly Stands For' (2014), 1.

26 Marie Huchzermeyer, *Cities with 'Slums': From Informal Settlement Eradication to a Right to the City in Africa* (Cape Town: University of Cape Town Press, 2011).

104 *Zachary Levenson*

27 Housing Assembly, 'Draft Statement of the Housing Assembly.'
28 Zachary Levenson, ' "We Are Humans and Not Dogs": The Crisis of Housing Delivery in Post-Apartheid Cape Town,' *Berkeley Journal of Sociology* 58 (2014): 15–22.
29 Chatterjee, *Politics of the Governed.*
30 Housing Assembly, 'Draft Statement of the Housing Assembly'; Housing Assembly, 'Final Draft Statement on the Elections and the United Front Call' (2014).
31 Harvey, *Rebel Cities*; Brenner et al., *Cities for People, Not for Profit*; Leitner et al., *Contesting Neoliberalism*; Mitchell, *Right to the City.*
32 Gabriel Hetland and Jeff Goodwin, 'The Strange Disappearance of Capitalism from Social Movement Studies,' in *Marxism and Social Movements*, ed. Colin Barker, Laurence Cox, John Krinsky, and Alf Gunvald Nilsen (Leiden: Brill, 2013).
33 Carin Runciman, *Mobilisation and Insurgent Citizenship of the Anti-Privatisation Forum, South Africa: An Ethnographic Study* (PhD Dissertation, University of Glasgow, 2012); Marcelle C. Dawson, ' "Phansi Privatisation! Phantsi!": The Anti-Privatisation Forum and Ideology in Social Movements,' in *Popular Politics and Resistance Movements in South Africa*, William Beinart and Marcelle C. Dawson, eds., *Popular Politics and Resistance Movements in South Africa* (Johannesburg: Wits University Press, 2010), 266–85; Ahmed Veriava and Prishani Naidoo, 'From Local to Global (and Back Again?): Anti-Commodification Struggles of the Soweto Electricity Crisis Committee,' in *Electric Capitalism: Recolonising Africa on the Power Grid*, ed. David A. McDonald (Cape Town: Human Sciences Research Council, 2009), 321–37; Patrick Bond and Peter McInnes, 'Decommodifying Electricity in Postapartheid Johannesburg'; Oldfield and Stokke, 'Building Unity in Diversity'; Anthony Egan and Alex Wafer, 'Dynamics of a "Mini-Mass Movement": Origins, Identity and Ideological Pluralism in the Soweto Electricity Crisis Committee,' in *Voices of Protest*, Richard Ballard, Adam Habib, and Imraan Valodia, eds., *Voices of Protest: Social Movements in Post-Apartheid South Africa* (Scottsville: University of KwaZulu-Natal Press, 2006), 45–66.

Part III
Local state formations

7 Party politics and community mobilisation in Buffalo City, East London

Tatenda G. Mukwedeya and Hlengiwe Ndlovu

Grassroots community struggles across many of South Africa's townships and informal settlements have been escalating from 2004 onwards. They have tended to be relatively autonomous and localised, with little or no links to other community-based organisations beyond their localities. Most of the concerns raised during these protests revolve around issues of service delivery such as access to housing, water and electricity among others, hence their characterisation as 'service delivery protests' regardless of their causes and nature. This upsurge in community-based mobilisation captured the imagination of the academic left and activists who viewed them as representing a radical transformation but, as Sinwell points out, 'they do not necessarily reflect a new kind of politics'.[1] Nonetheless, a burgeoning literature emerged dedicated to recording and analysing these struggles and their relationship with the state.[2] However, there is scant research on the relationship between these forms of community-based mobilisation and the ANC as the dominant political party. As Sinwell suggests, the interface between popular mobilisation and political parties has not been explored in a thorough manner as parties are often considered demobilising and/or corrupt.[3] Despite this, some of the protests in post-apartheid South Africa have been attributed to internal divisions and power struggles in local ANC structures by individuals who want to benefit from state resources.[4] This chapter contributes to our understanding of the interface between popular mobilisation and political parties.

The regularity and increasing incidence of violent protests has drawn analogies of a rebellion or an insurgency.[5] However, after 12 years of sustained service delivery protests in South Africa, they seem to remain largely localised and have not resulted in a radically new kind of politics as postulated by Sinwell.[6] Key to understanding why this is the case is the role of party politics in mediating the relationship between the state and community-based organisations. Particularly, this chapter examines how factional politics in the ANC depolitices community concerns by reducing them to individual factional struggles. We observe that the significance and role that political parties play is one major difference between the global wave of protest spurred by the Arab Spring and South Africa's service delivery protests. Whilst the global wave of protests is a revolt against mainstream politics, in South Africa, in many instances movements do not seek an alternative politics, particularly where the ruling ANC is dominant. Focusing on protests and the 2006 local government elections, Booysen in her analogy of 'the ballot and

108 *Tatenda G. Mukwedeya and Hlengiwe Ndlovu*

the brick' points out how protest and voting comfortably coexist. Particularly, she notes that, despite grassroots protest over poor service delivery, what is even more interesting is the electoral support for the ANC that is still relatively unwavering.[7] Whilst there was a decline in ANC support to just under 62% in the May 2011 local government elections from 66% in 2006, the ANC still commands substantial support.

The chapter draws on separate ethnographic research projects on local politics in Buffalo City by both authors over a cumulative period of two years between 2011 and 2014. The research drew on interviews, observation and various secondary sources. Broadly the research involved participating in the everyday life of the residents, including community meetings and protests primarily in Duncan Village, a township four kilometres outside the city centre. One of the co-authors of this chapter was born in East London and has spent most of her life in the city. This was valuable because her familiarity and social proximity allowed her to gain full access to the community to observe the inner workings of a protest. Similarly, Auyero and Swistam in their research on a poor community in Argentina highlight that familiarity and social proximity were extremely useful in reducing as much as possible the symbolic violence exerted through the interview relationship.[8] This chapter draws on just one protest in Duncan Village for a richer description that offers a window into the intricate dynamics that underlie service delivery protests in South Africa. Whilst this case cannot be generalised to the rest of the country, it is indicative of what transpires in similar protests across South African townships. It details the community concerns that inform a protest, the organising and planning of the protest, its execution and how party politics may become intertwined in community-based organisations that engage in protest action.

In contrast to Dawson's analysis (Chapter 8), which takes the ANC's political patronage as a starting point, this chapter begins with a genuine community concern and demonstrates how, later on in the process, the party becomes involved. We argue that community protests and party politics become entangled through a double process of imposition and invitation. Whilst party leaders may meddle in protests for political gain (imposition), community members sometimes seek out party officials to intervene and assist them (invitation). Not only does the party impose itself on mobilised communities, but community activists may also strategically employ the dominant party to negotiate for concessions from the state, in exchange for political support.

We argue that the involvement of ANC intra-party politics depoliticises the protests, stifling their potential to be part of a larger socio-political phenomenon with global connections. This depoliticisation entails reducing broader and long-standing concerns, around socio-economic redistribution and rampant corruption, to narrow factional party politics driven by local elites. The involvement of party politics in community mobilisation serves to increase the community's dependence on the party. Our case study thus confirms Booysen's argument that the ANC tends to reproduce its power following popular protests, which 'are the relatively benevolent partner to electoral behaviour and a valve to vent frustration whilst continuously supporting and voting for the ANC'.[9]

Parties and mobilisation in Buffalo City 109

The chapter is structured into three parts, with the first one setting the scene by situating South African protests in relation to the new global protests that flared with the Arab Spring uprisings in December 2010. The chapter then shifts to a detailed exposition of a relatively isolated protest that was organised in Buffalo City in November 2014 and then reflects on this experience in relation to social movement literature in order to enrich literature on popular mobilisation with an analysis that accounts for the role of dominant political parties.

Situating South African protests in the global protests

The self-immolation by Mohamed Bouazizi on 17 December 2010 in the Tunisian town of Sidi Bouzid became the rallying call that sparked the contemporary wave of global protests. The resultant removal of the Tunisian leadership and other long-time rulers in the Arab world is now well known. The Arab Spring, as the protests are popularly referred to, also inspired similar movements in the developed world such as Spain, Italy, Greece and Portugal. Most notably is the Occupy movement in America and the United Kingdom which in turn inspired similar repertoires of protest around the world. By the end of 2011, the spread of the Occupy protests was in about 900 cities in 82 countries.

Where was South Africa in all of this? As the Arab Spring took off, South Africa was recording its highest occurrence of service delivery protests since 2004. According to Municipal IQ, a specialised local government data and intelligence service, the country witnessed 111 protests in 2010. In November 2010 just before Bouzizi would immolate himself, residents of East London's township of Duncan Village engaged in one of many service delivery protests. *The Times* reported that 'about 80 angry residents blocked a road and attacked policemen'. Captain Stephen Marais stated, 'They blocked the Ziphunzane bypass with branches, trees, burning tyres, cement blocks . . . and then they started throwing stones and things at us [the police]. We responded by firing rubber bullets.'[10] Thus, as the global protest movement gained momentum in 2011, service delivery protests in South Africa continued, with little connection to what was happening around the world and even in other parts of the country.

As a spinoff to the Occupy movement that was successful in the United States, Europe and cities across the world, there were calls to hold countrywide occupations in various cities in South Africa in October 2011. The call was answered in Johannesburg, Cape Town, Grahamstown, Durban and East London, but the movement never managed to gain momentum as it did in other cities across the world. Occupy Johannesburg and Cape Town managed to attract 200 occupiers whilst Grahamstown and Durban had about 80.[11] In East London a mere six protestors participated for an hour and a half. Whilst the other Occupy protests across the world lasted longer, the South African Occupy movement was not sustained and it quickly fizzled out. Service delivery protests nevertheless continued to intensify, but they remained relatively localised. An important difference between South African forms of community mobilisation and the recent global movements is their relationship with political parties and the state. One of the features of

110   *Tatenda G. Mukwedeya and Hlengiwe Ndlovu*

the Tunisian-inspired 'new global culture of protest' was a suspicion of political parties in favour of networks and experiential structures.[12] However, the significant difference in South Africa is that the dominant ANC still garners widespread support tied to its liberation credentials despite signs of declining hegemony. Therefore, there is a paradoxical occurrence of protests against ANC-controlled councils that is simultaneously coupled with popular support for the party. This combination of governance failure and yet enduring party popularity is what Lawrence Piper has termed 'popular incompetence'.[13]

South Africa therefore seems to have a peculiar trajectory of community mobilisation linked to the dominant party. Despite more than 12 years of sustained mobilisation including protests, why is it that these popular movements have remained largely localised and some kind of radical change has remained elusive? A detailed account into the life of a protest sheds light on this question. The following section describes the cycle of a protest from its planning to its execution, its eventual ending and aftermath in order to illuminate the role of ANC intra-party politics in service delivery protests.

Inside a service delivery protest[14]

Within the Buffalo City Metropolitan Municipality precinct, East London and particularly the township of Duncan Village is a hotspot for service delivery protests resulting from the prevailing socio-economic conditions. It is estimated that 80,000 people live permanently in Duncan Village, crammed onto just 2% of the municipalities' land area. Houses are overshadowed by the growing number of shacks, with 3,500 formal dwellings and 14,000 shacks, while densities exceed 2,500 people per hectare in some areas.[15]According to a 2013/14 Buffalo City Public Order Policing services report, the township experiences at least one protest every two weeks. Therefore the processes and concerns underpinning the protests are likely to vary but the following case is indicative of what generally transpires.

The protest took place on the 23rd and 24th of November 2014. It was one of the many on-going protests by residents of the Florence Street informal settlement located in Duncan Village on the edge of the M2 freeway. Despite being initiated by Florence Street residents, it must be noted that their protests are tied to the broader concerns of the Duncan Village community who live under similar conditions. Community members from nearby neighbourhoods therefore participate in one another's protests.

The contentious issue that drove the protest started in 2009 when 87 residents of Florence Street informal settlement were approved for low-cost houses in Reeston, which is about 13 kilometres north east of Duncan Village. They received letters from the municipality to be relocated, and their shacks were demolished in accordance with the relocation procedure. However, when they arrived in Reeston their houses were already occupied by other residents of another informal settlement in Reeston. They returned to their informal settlement on Florence Street

Parties and mobilisation in Buffalo City 111

to re-build their shacks after the municipality failed to evict the people who had already occupied their houses in Reeston.

The group became popularly known as the 'Reeston 87' by officials and the media in their struggles to secure their houses. They have been mobilising the whole informal settlement and the neighbouring wards in their efforts to secure their homes and also around access to other basic services critical for dwellers of informal settlements. Nonetheless, Buffalo City municipality was unable to resolve the matter or to offer alternative housing to the Reeston 87. The group exhausted all legal procedures to have their houses allocated to them without success and their court case has been pending for years. Therefore, like many other organisations across the country, they have been protesting as a way to force the municipality to address their demands for decent housing.

Preceding the protest on the 23rd and 24th of November 2014, residents of the informal settlement organised a march on 12 November 2014 in which they handed a memorandum of their disputes to the mayor. They gave the mayor seven days to respond. After ten days without any response, residents of Florence Street informal settlement began organising a service delivery protest on Sunday, 23 November. As one respondent named Ayanda pointed out, 'We are going to burn on the freeway because we had a peaceful march, gave the Mayor seven days to respond to our memorandum but she has not responded yet so she will after this.'[16] The protest was therefore meant to remind the mayor that members of the Reeston 87 were still waiting for answers about their 87 houses that were occupied illegally in Reeston. This is similar to the analogy Karl Von Holdt and colleagues make of a 'smoke that calls'. It describes how collective violence (in service delivery protests) is understood as a language, a message, a way of calling out to higher authorities about the state of things in their town but its associated violence makes it a warning at the same time. One of their respondents in Voortrekker recalled how their premier undermined them and how he would see by the smoke that they were calling him. The burning of property and the 'thick, black smoke which billowed over the township' was 'the smoke that calls' and in this sense, the violence had generated a response from distant and uncaring officials.[17] Similarly, Susan Booysen observes that South Africans have crafted protest to supplement the vote, not to substitute for voting. Protest has been frequently used to pressurise the elected ANC government to do more, to deliver on election promises and to replace local leaders.[18]

Whilst most residents in Florence Street are members of the ANC, their local branch strongly discouraged them from protesting, arguing that they 'have to be responsible citizens'.[19] The ANC local officials viewed protests as undermining the legitimacy of the party which dominates the local council with 71 of the 100 seats. Therefore the protest was organised outside party structures. A small number of the residents were members of the Democratic Alliance, and they claimed that they only came together for their common struggle for houses regardless of any political affiliations. The protest was organised by a five-member committee, four of whom were women, that was elected by members of the Reeston 87 to

112   *Tatenda G. Mukwedeya and Hlengiwe Ndlovu*

represent them in the struggle for their houses.[20] All the committee members were members of the ANC though.

Important aspects of the planning for the protest were coordinated from the shack of one of the committee members. During this stage the shack was a hive of activity as people regularly came to check on the progress of the plan or to make monetary contributions towards the purchase of protest materials. The plan was to get everyone from the informal settlement to gather protest material which included tyres, wood, stones and anything that could help to start the fire. Some collected cardboards to prepare placards for grievances. Monetary donations ranged from R1 to R20 for purchasing diesel and 'airtime'. The diesel was to be used to fuel the fire, and airtime was necessary for calling the media and other community members to coordinate and execute the protest. Informing the media was central to the residents as a form of public performance to garner support and sympathy from the broader South African community and to pressure the local state.

By ten o'clock in the evening, some raw materials and members of the community were missing so the committee decided to use some coercion to ensure full participation. Residents accused of free-riding by not participating received threats to burn down their shacks or to have their electricity cut off. The electricity to the informal settlement is illegally connected; thus the community controls its distribution. Popularly referred to as *izinyoka*, electricity from power lines connected to their shacks is illegally redirected by digging up the roads and installing ordinary cables. This coercion was important to ensure the success of the protest, but it also revealed the undemocratic aspects of the protest. Around midnight, when the gathering process began, the organisers sent a group of young boys to people's shacks to inform them of the assembly whilst others were called or sent *WhatsApp* messages. Around one o'clock in the early morning, protest participants carried the cardboard, tyres and the rest of the materials to the M2 freeway. Tyres were spread over a considerable space on the road to ensure that traffic flow would be disturbed. Pieces of wood and cardboards were thrown over the tyres and finally the diesel. Following a tip-off, the police came to disrupt the protest with their infamous armoured vehicles, *nyalas*. However, after a few hours of contrived action involving constant pursuit, near captures and repeated escapes, and despite the presence of police with armoured vehicles who were dispersing the crowds, the protesting residents managed to burn their blockades around four in the morning.

At dawn, the rest of the city woke up to the disruption on the M2 freeway. As the police were trying to clear the road, the media were present recording the events and interviewing people. It was at this time that the councillor made an appearance, and he reiterated what he had told the media. He pointed out that the problems of the Reeston 87 group were political in the sense that a group in the ANC leadership was sabotaging his efforts to resolve the matter because he was associated with an opposing faction. Earlier, when the protest plan was at an advanced stage, a former councillor had visited the shack where the organising committee met and outlined to them the steps he would have taken to ameliorate the Reeston 87's challenges. According to one of the organising committee members, he was

Parties and mobilisation in Buffalo City 113

insinuating that the current councillor was incompetent and thereby campaigning for himself to return as the councillor in the upcoming elections. Thus the onset of the 2016 local government elections could have also contributed to the increased interest in the plight of the Florence Street residents.

Whether the current councillor or the former councillor is correct or not in their assertions is debateable. What was clearer is that their statements divided the residents; some began calling for the sacking of the current councillor whilst others had decided to continue with their protest as a way of engaging the municipality directly to force it to address their demands. This was not the first time ANC officials had tried to meddle in the activities of the community. Akhona, one of the leaders of the Reeston 87, pointed out in an interview how local ANC officials in previous protests offered information and resources to facilitate their housing allocation but none had ever materialised. Instead, they succeeded in delaying the community as residents waited for the officials to deliver on their word. Akhona added how the false promises had encouraged residents to disentangle their struggles with party officials.[21]

Despite this, residents of Florence Street informal settlement were paradoxically looking to senior regional members of the ANC since the party was viewed as having power to address their conundrum. The mayor to whom they had given a petition a couple of days earlier was the target of their appeal, and they believed that efforts that ignored involving ANC officials were futile altogether. Bénit-Gbaffou rationalises this tendency by observing that 'the party is more efficient in some instances to address residents' issues, through networked channels of access to powerful politicians, as opposed to the red tape and fragmentation of the current local government system.'[22] There is therefore an implicit ceding of power by the community to the party and its officials. The following section examines the consequences for popular community mobilisation of imposed or invited party politics in protests.

Party politics in community-based mobilisation

It is clear from the foregoing that the protest in the township of Duncan Village in East London was mobilised around a genuine community concern. The committee and structure around the organisation of the protest entails Cornwall's 'invented spaces' which are organic and created 'from below' by those outside the state.[23] These include spaces created from popular mobilisation, as well as spaces in which 'like-minded people join together in common pursuits'.[24] However, as the protest by Florence Street residents demonstrates, the involvement of party politics undermines these bottom-up community initiatives by bringing a top-down party machine characteristic of a dominant party. As highlighted previously, the involvement of the ANC occurs in two ways which may be inter-related. Either local politicians impose themselves to offer information and resources for political support or protestors seek out the party to use party officials strategically to garner concessions and access the state. The experiences of Florence Street residents demonstrate these two scenarios.

114 *Tatenda G. Mukwedeya and Hlengiwe Ndlovu*

Local politicians, driven by factional interests and seeking political mileage over competitors, meddle into invented spaces for community mobilisation such as protests in attempts to gain political mileage over their competitors. This was demonstrated by the former councillor who visited the organising committee and tried to channel the protesters' frustrations towards a political rival. With the involvement of factional politics, the important subject of housing is relegated to the margins and a factionalised narrative that targets the capabilities of an individual takes precedence. Some of the residents lose interest in community mobilisation and focus on the politics around municipal positions, limiting the escalation of their mobilisation.

However, local party officials are sometimes bypassed in favour of regional or national officials who may be perceived as more influential. This can be a strategic decision because calling out a senior party official in a dramatic manner such as through a disruptive protest coupled with media attention can force officials to attend to community concerns. Von Holdt and colleagues have also explored the role that violence in protests plays in attempts by communities to get governments attention. One of their respondents is quoted saying, 'Violence is the only language that our government understands. Look we have been submitting memos, but nothing was done. We became violent and our problems were immediately resolved.'[25]

Whether party officials are invited or impose themselves in various forms of community-based mobilisation, it is important to note that the sheer presence of party politics in community protests serves to entrench the power of the party. The involvement of party politics maintains the presence of the ANC in poor communities such as Duncan Village. This is similar to Argentinean local politics as pointed out by Auyero, who adds that:

> By supplying information and goods that appeal to their close followers' self-interest, local politicians ensure voluntary compliance is secured at low cost. Power is, in this sense, economical. In the act of getting help, problem holders become increasingly ensnared within the Peronist web.[26]

In the Florence Street protest already discussed, a former ANC councillor who offered information to ameliorate the community's concerns ensnared a portion of residents who supported his claim in ANC politics as shown by their call to remove the current councillor. Even the deliberate appeal to the ANC mayor by Florence Street protestors entangled their struggles within the ANC's web of influence. Their issue regarding access to housing cut across party political lines whilst confronting the challenge of systemic corruption but was nonetheless reduced to the weaknesses of an individual. The involvement of party politics, particularly factionalised politics, diluted a deeply political issue regarding access to housing which is being undermined by corruption. One consequence of this can be that acts of community mobilisation get limited to local politics around contestation between local elites, yet demands by communities usually have broader political ramifications such as curbing corruption, which is a national concern. This is exacerbated in contexts with dominant parties such as the ANC where there is a realisation that it controls access to state resources. This is illustrated by a common phrase by ANC officials that, 'it is cold outside the ANC' which implies that resistance to the party is a futile exercise. In most cases this involves losing a well-paying job or a lucrative tender vital to one's livelihood. Therefore, people consent to the party or to the local politicians' worldview and in so doing regenerate the ANC's power and that of its local officials who monopolise information and goods at the local level.

Conclusion

Service delivery protests have by and large become South Africa's dominant form of community mobilisation for the past 12 years ever since new social movements began to wane. They have become widespread across the country as the poor in townships and informal settlements struggle to secure basic services such as water, electricity, housing and even employment opportunities. Through a detailed focus of a protest in the township of Duncan Village in East London, the chapter examined the role of party politics in service delivery protests. It observes that ANC party officials become involved in community mobilisation by imposition and by invitation. That is, either local politicians impose themselves to offer information and resources for political support or protestors seek out the party to use party officials strategically to garner concessions and access the state. The imposition of party politics, on one hand, is related to patronage politics and factional competition for positions which Hannah Dawson's research in Zandspruit informal settlement on the outskirts of Johannesburg has illustrated.[27] The invitation of party politics, on the other hand, stems from the realisation that the party is more efficient in some instances to address residents' issues, through networked channels of access to powerful politicians as pointed out by Bénit-Gbaffou.[28] We argue that the involvement of party politics in community protests either by imposition or invitation serves to entrench and reproduce the power of the party at the expense of community concerns. However, the party offers some concessions through its control of the state by offering targeted access to state resources that ensure the community's consent to the dominant party's hegemony. Importantly, the consequences of the involvement of party politics in protest mean that the party is deeply embedded in urban local societies. The assimilation of the party politics into community mobilisation, taking from Auyero, means that they are co-opted by the institutionalised practices of political clientelism and thus partake in the reproduction of the hierarchic relations prevailing in the local political arena and thus in their own subordination.[29] A deep link to urban local societies for Bénit-Gbaffou also means a form of social control restricting the ability of civil society to revolt and challenge urban policies more radically.[30] This begins to contribute to an explanation of why service delivery protests in South Africa have remained largely localised instead of developing into larger movements similar to the global wave of protest.

Notes

1 Luke Sinwell, 'Is "Another World" Really Possible? Re-examining Counter-Hegemonic Forces in Post-Apartheid South Africa,' *Review of African Political Economy* 38, no. 127 (2011), 61–76.

2 Sakhela Buhlungu, *The Anti-Privatisation Forum: A Profile of a Post-Apartheid Social Movement* (Durban: Centre for Civil Society, 2004); Prishani Naidoo and Ahmed Veriava, *Re-membering Movements: Trade Unions and New Social Movements in Neoliberal South Africa* (Durban: Centre for Civil Society, 2005); R. Ballard, A. Habib, I. Valodia, and E. Zuern, 'Globalization, Marginalization and Contemporary Social Movements in South Africa,' *African Affairs* 104, no. 417 (2005): 615–34; Peter Alexander, 'Rebellion of the Poor: South Africa's Service Delivery Protests – A Preliminary Analysis,' *Review of African Political Economy* 37, no. 123 (2010): 25–40; Susan Booysen, 'With the Ballot and the Brick: The Politics of Attaining Service Delivery,' *Progress in Development Studies*, 7, no. 1 (2007): 21–32.

3 Luke Sinwell, 'Transformative Left-Wing Parties and Grassroots Organizations: Unpacking the Politics of "Top-down" and "Bottom-up" Development,' *Geoforum* 43 (2012): 190–8.

4 Malose Langa and Karl von Holdt, 'Insurgent Citizenship, Class Formation and the Dual Nature of a Community Protest: A Case Study of Kungcatsha,' in *Contesting Transformation: Popular Resistance in Twenty-First Century South Africa*, ed. Marcelle C. Dawson and Luke Sinwell (London: Pluto Press, 2012), 80–100; Karl Von Holdt, Malose Langa, Sepetla Molapo, Nomfundo Mogapi, Kindiza Ngubeni, Jacob Dlamini, and Adele Kirsten, *The Smoke that Calls: Insurgent Citizenship, Collective Violence and the Struggle for a Place in the New South Africa: Seven Case Studies of Community Protests and Xenophobic Violence.* Research Report (Johannesburg: CSVR and SWOP, 2011); Harber, Anton, *Diepsloot* (Johannesburg: Jonathan Ball, 2011).

5 Ibid.

6 Sinwell, 'Is "Another World" Really Possible?'

7 Booysen, 'With the Ballot and the Brick,' 31.

8 Javier Auyero and Debora Swistun, 'Tiresias in Flammable Shantytown: Toward a Tempography of Domination,' *Sociological Forum* 24, no. 1 (2009): 4.

9 Susan Booysen, *The African National Congress and the Regeneration of Political Power* (Johannesburg: Witwatersrand University Press, 2011), 126.

10 Service Delivery Protest Hits East London." *Times Live*, November 11, 2010, accessed March 3, 2015.

11 Jared Sacks, 'Two Reports from Occupy South Africa,' October 29, 2011, accessed December 20, 2014, http://libcom.org/news/two-reports-occupy-south-africa-29102011; Nicholas Owsley, *The Occupy Movement: A Polanyian Analysis of Contemporary Dissent.* Centre for Social Science Research Working Paper No. 317, December 2012.

12 Mohammed A. Bamyeh, 'The Global Culture of Protests,' in *In Understanding Occupy*, ed. Ruth Milkman, Benjamin Barber, Mohammed A. Bamyeh, William Julius Wilson, Dana Williams, and Deborah B. Gould, *Contexts* 11, no. 2 (2012): 12–21, accessed December 20, 2014, http://contexts.org/articles/understanding-occupy/#bamyeh.

13 The common explanation for popular incompetence is voter loyalty. That is, citizens do not use the vote to hold politicians accountable but rather, like sports fans remain loyal to their teams, they stick to their party regardless of its performance. Explanations of voter loyalty have tended to locate arguments on a continuum from ethnic or racial identity-based reasons on the one end to more contingent, interest-based reasons at the other, with various positions in between. Laurence Piper and Fiona Anciano. 'Party Over Outsiders, Centre Over Branch: How ANC Dominance Works at the Community Level in South Africa,' *Transformation: Critical Perspectives on Southern Africa* 87 (2015): 76.

14 Some parts of this case study have been presented in a Masters Research Report by one of the authors (see Ndhlovu 2015).
15 UNESCO, accessed March 3, 2015, http://www.unesco.org/most/africa12.htm.
16 Interview with Ayanda, Gompo Hall, Duncan Village, November 25, 2014. Note that this is not the respondent's real name. Pseudonyms are also used for all the other respondents in this chapter.
17 Von Holdt et al., *The Smoke that Calls*, 27, 44.
18 Booysen, *The African National Congress*, 126.
19 Interview with Thando, Protest organising committee member, Duncan Village, November 23, 2015.
20 It is interesting to note that research on mineworker strikes has documented the role of independent workers committees, sometimes popularly referred to as *five madodas* which are also composed of five members. Chinguno notes that they set up outside the unions to represent the interests of workers. Thus there are connections in the repertoires of protest between workers and community organisations concerned with service delivery. Crispen Chinguno, 'Marikana and the Post-apartheid Workplace Order,' *Society, Work and Development Institute (SWOP)*, Working Paper No. 1 (2013), 20.
21 Interview with Akhona, Duncan Village, November 25, 2015.
22 Claire Bénit-Gbaffou, 'Party Politics, Civil Society and Local Democracy – Reflections from Johannesburg,' *Geoforum* 43, no. 2 (2012): 187.
23 Andrea Cornwall, *IDS Working Paper No. 170* (Brighton: Institute of Development Studies (IDS), 2002), 17.
24 Laurence Piper and Lubna Nadvi, 'Popular Mobilisation, Party Dominance and Participatory Governance in South Africa,' in *Citizenship and Social Movements: Perspectives from the Global South*, ed. Lisa Thompson and Chris Tapscott (London: Zed Books, 2010), 213.
25 Von Holdt et al., *The Smoke that Calls*, 49.
26 Javier Auyero, *Poor People's Politics: Peronist Survival Networks and the Legacy of Evita* (Durham: Duke University Press, 2001), 116.
27 Hannah Dawson, 'Patronage from Below: Political Unrest in an Informal Settlement in South Africa,' *African Affairs* 113, no. 453(2014): 518–39.
28 Bénit-Gbaffou, 'Party Politics, Civil Society and Local Democracy,' 187.
29 Auyero, *Poor People's Politics*, 175.
30 Bénit-Gbaffou, 'Party Politics, Civil Society and Local Democracy.'

8 Protests, party politics and patronage

A view from Zandspruit informal settlement, Johannesburg

Hannah Dawson[1]

On three separate occasions in 2011, the residents of Zandspruit informal settlement on the outskirts of Johannesburg took to the streets to show their discontent with their local councillor, Maureen Schneeman, and what they regarded as a lack of service delivery and evidence of corruption. The trigger for the protests was an intra-African National Congress (ANC) rivalry over the candidate for ward councillor in the build-up to the local elections. Protests surged in support of the ANC candidate with widespread local support, Stephen Nhlapo, who was not elected in the ward as a whole. The unrest combined an internal power struggle in the local ANC with a mass movement of aggrieved residents protesting against corruption and inadequate and uneven provision of public goods and services.[2] Whereas Mukwedeya and Ndlovu (Chapter 7) document how the ANC became involved in community politics after protest action initiated by a community-based organisation, this chapter demonstrates how the local ANC itself, as a result of intra-party rivalry, initiated unrest.

The demonstrations in Zandspruit are characteristic of a surge of militant local protests in informal settlements and townships across South Africa from the mid-2000s.[3] The extensive repertoire of unrest evident in these protests has been considered elsewhere.[4] The escalation of this kind of unrest is a distinguishing feature of Jacob Zuma's presidency. Using a populist-inspired campaign to oust his predecessor, Thabo Mbeki, Zuma cultivated a reputation for being an 'accessible man of the people'[5] who brought hope of a 'new' ANC with increased urgency and opportunities for participation.[6] The election of Zuma resulted in increased expectations which when unfulfilled heightened the level of protest, with people believing Zuma to be more likely to address their demands.[7] Zuma's presidency has also been characterised by increased factionalism within the ANC, which in turn has led to protests by dissident ANC members.[8]

Recent work has drawn attention to patronage politics in South Africa.[9] Tom Lodge argues that neo-patrimonial characteristics within the ANC have become more prominent under the leadership of Zuma.[10] Lodge describes the ANC as relying increasingly on patron-client relations in which public services and resources are offered in exchange for political support.[11] There is also a substantial literature on social movements and local service delivery protests.[12] To date, however, these two literatures have existed in separation, and little attention has been paid to how patronage politics operates at the local level and interacts with and stimulates local protests.[13] This chapter seeks to fill this gap and provides an analysis 'from below' which considers the agency of the recipients of patronage.

This chapter is primarily based on three months of ethnographic research between July and September 2011 in Zandspruit but also draws upon more recent research during 2013–2014 and an analysis of the 2014 national election results. For analysis, I distinguish among three clusters of actors – leaders, brokers and protestors – who had different and shifting agendas and motivations for participation in the demonstrations. The first cluster are self-appointed community leaders who govern the four private plots of land where the majority of the protestors reside. I interviewed four members of this group – including the aspirant candidate – who instigated the first two protests. The second were six young unemployed men, or brokers, who aligned themselves with the aspirant councillor and took up the 'mandate'[14] to orchestrate the protests. Lastly, I interviewed 22 protestors – young men and women, predominantly between the ages of 18 and 30, who participated in at least one but often all three of the protests.

The chapter begins by outlining a theoretical framework to understand the relationship between patronage and protests in South Africa. This is followed by a discussion on the shared grievances of residents and how the local elections in 2011 created the terrain for intra-ANC rivalry. The chapter then fleshes out how and why the protests in Zandspruit can be understood as a battle for patronage 'from below'. This includes an analysis of how intra-ANC rivalry linked to rival candidates and followers created the mobilising structures, through informal networks and brokers, for collective action. Finally, this chapter unpacks the 'dual nature' of protests, as described by Karl Von Holdt, where protests function as a means of collective claim making for public goods and services, and as a political strategy by a local ANC faction and elite to gain access and control over state resources and service delivery.

Political patronage and protest

There is broad consensus that political patronage occurs when state resources are traded in return for political support – expressing itself within patron-client relationships. The focus of much Africanist literature has been on personalised intra-elite patronage, which binds elites to a political party through individual benefits. It has overlooked more diffused or collective forms of patronage at a societal level, which distribute collective material benefits through political parties and general government expenditure, as well as through local brokers and patrons.[15] Herbert Kitschelt and Steven Wilkinson define political clientelism as a direct exchange between a politician and a voter, of employment and public goods and services for political support.[16] Claire Bénit-Gbaffou outlines why this definition is particular in a number of respects.[17] First, it indicates that patronage does not necessarily require a personalised relationship and can develop between a politician and a group, what is referred to as 'collective clientelism'. Second, political clientelism is about the distribution of public goods such as public housing,

120   Hannah Dawson

employment contracts and access to social services. Third, political clientelism is not merely about electoral support. Political support takes many forms such as participating in party rallies and being the party watchdog in meetings.

Political patronage can manifest itself in different forms, depending on the degree of personalisation and competition between different patronage networks and structures.[18] Nic Cheeseman also highlights the agency of non-elite or subaltern groups, the recipients of patronage, to determine the terms of their incorporation into the political system and ultimately how responsive patrons are likely to be to their local needs and demands.[19] The degree of competition, and role of local elite and subaltern groups, is particularly important for understanding the protests in Zandspruit because they evolved out of the action of a rival faction within the local ANC and their corresponding candidates and followers. Contemporary Africanist literature has located agency almost exclusively with the 'big man' and discounted the agency of poor communities to inform, navigate and influence the formation and beneficiation of patron-client relations.[20] This chapter argues that the increasing factionalism within the ANC has created a context for intra-party or competitive patronage, with both local elites and subaltern groups actively engaged in demanding public goods 'from below'.

Perceptions and understandings of patronage are often value-laden, with patronage viewed as a pathology and the antithesis of democracy and accountability. Kitschelt and Wilkinson's work on clientelism debunks some of these assumptions by portraying a continuum – between programmatic policies with benefits defined as abstract 'rights' versus clientelistic policies with benefits in the form of more personal or local favours – on the basis that they both rely on a relationship between politicians and voters marked by an 'exchange of votes for benefits'.[21] From the perspective of such a continuum, patronage might be better understood as a permanent feature of the party-political system that takes on various forms.

The arena of local government, as this chapter demonstrates, is central to the study of political patronage as this is where citizens interact with the state most closely. A common denominator in the surge of protest action is indignation at local government officials and councillors who are accused of indifference, incompetence and corruption.[22] Local councillors and ward committees have therefore emerged as a political arena where the ANC has selected candidates for councils on criteria other than merit or potential. This has resulted in local government becoming the site of political battles, factionalism and patronage.

An assumption of patron-client relations, given their asymmetric and vertical relations, is that they hinder collective action and claims making, which require horizontal ties.[23] Research on poor people's movements in Latin America has shown that patronage and collective mobilisation are not inevitably conflicting political phenomena and are often mutually imbricated.[24] Auyero et al. describe four instances in which patronage and collective action intersect and interact, two of which are illustrative in the Zandspruit context.[25] The first is 'network breakdown', whereby protests emerge as a response to a disruption and malfunction of patron-client arrangements, for example, differential access to public goods. The

Protests, party politics and patronage 121

second instance Auyero et al. describe is 'relational support', whereby competitive patronage networks provide the mobilising structures for collective action.

Applied to the Zandspruit demonstrations, this framework depicts how the grievances giving rise to the protests can be understood as a breakdown in collective clientelistic arrangements between the ANC and its supporters. As a result, the development of an intra-ANC rivalry for the position of councillor created competitive patronage networks which provided the mobilising structures for protest action.

Shared grievances and competitive patronage networks

Three protests occurred in Zandspruit informal settlement between March and July 2011. These uprisings represent a wide-ranging discontent with the local councillor, Maureen Schneeman, who was accused of corruption and deficient service delivery. The protests were underpinned by a complex, wide-ranging and locally specific set of grievances that included the contested nature of land occupation and ownership, uneven service delivery, and, of central importance, the intra-ANC rivalry and leadership battle in the build-up to the local elections. The leadership battle that triggered the protests was linked to uneven access to basic services in Zandspruit and the widespread perception that the councillor and her friends had privileged access to government houses, jobs and tenders. The discontent with the councillor and accusations of corruption came largely from residents in a particular section of Zandspruit, known as the Private Properties, which is particularly over-crowded and lacking basic amenities.

Popular and scholarly portrayals of informal settlements such as Zandspruit as homogenous communities fail to capture the uneven provision of basic services and living conditions and other markers of social differentiation. For example, residents in Zandspruit include those who lived on the surrounding plots from the 1980s; the original group of residents who were moved to Transit Camp in 1994; and then multiple other groupings of people who are defined by when they arrived, what section they live in, and crucially their access to basic services such as electricity, water and sanitation, formal housing, and tenure security (through access to title deeds).

The four main sections in Zandspruit are Transit camp, Extension 9 and 10, Zenzele and what are referred to as the Private Properties. Transit Camp, the oldest part of the settlement, has tarred roads, water and sanitation within each stand but no electricity, RDP houses or secure tenure.[26] The four Private Properties refers to land that was illegally invaded in the early 2000s, and where tens of thousands of people now live in squalor. This section was described by a resident as staying 'like a pilchard, like a small fish, a pilchard, there is no space here'.[27] It is so densely populated that refuse-removal vehicles, ambulances and emergency vehicles have no access, and inadequate water drainage, dirty toilets and overcrowding has resulted in terrible living conditions.

The uneven provision of services in Zandspruit, in particular the difference between Transit Camp and the four Private Properties, was perceived by the

122   *Hannah Dawson*

leaders of the protests and protestors (most of whom lived in the Private Properties section) to be the result of the councillor privileging the older part of the settlement for development. This reinforced social differentiation and engendered resentment, rivalry and conflict within the settlement.

The grievances of residents in the Private Property section need to be understood within a historical framework whereby citizens have placed significant expectations on the ANC to provide a 'better life for all'. These expectations were strengthened under Zuma's more populist leadership, which raised hopes that support for the party would be rewarded.[28] Differential access and the complete absence of basic services in the Private Properties section contributed to the overriding grievance of unfulfilled promises along with allegations of corruption, indifference and the unresponsiveness of the councillor. This dissatisfaction was expressed by residents as one of betrayal, with the ANC accused of having 'stolen our votes'.[29]

The everyday nature of many of these grievances bred an impatience and anger which the protest leadership mobilised and channelled towards de-legitimising the current councillor and demanding her removal. The local elections created competitive patronage networks and provided the political opportunity to shift positions of power, generating a 'war for leadership'.[30]

In the run-up to the 2011 local elections the ANC undertook community consultations in an attempt to find the best or most appropriate candidate for the ward councillor.[31] Seeking to fulfil a resolution from the ANC's 2007 Polokwane conference, these consultations aimed to ensure that the broader community was involved in candidate selection processes.[32] For the first time, the ANC decided to allow communities to nominate election candidates.[33] A general branch meeting was held in Zandspruit to nominate four candidates. This was followed by community consultations to select two candidates. What transpired in Zandspruit was a bitter leadership battle within the local ANC between the existing local councillor, Maureen Schneemann, and a long-standing ANC branch member, Stephen Nhlapo.

Maureen Schneeman was elected the councillor of Zandspruit in 2006 after the ANC won the ward in the local elections that same year. Zandspruit had previously been part of a larger ward controlled by the main opposition party – the Democratic Alliance (DA). Before this position, Schneeman had been on the ward committee and served as secretary of the local ANC branch for many years. Her involvement in Zandspruit extends back to the early 1990s and included work with the AIDS support programme. Maureen Schneeman's son was on the Randburg council from 1994 and until recently was an ANC member of parliament. He was instrumental in the decision to purchase the land that is now Transit Camp and a prominent factor in Schneeman taking up the position of ward councillor. Schneeman is white and in her early seventies; she lives in a nearby suburb within the ward. This aggravates accusations of her being absent and not understanding the issues facing residents.

Stephen Nhlapo had lived in the Private Properties section for more than 12 years and was well known for his active role in the local ANC branch and local leadership structures. As a result he had extensive support from the residents of

Protests, party politics and patronage 123

this section, and he created an alliance with other ANC dissidents and powerful leaders in the Private Property areas. Nhlapo was portrayed as representing the community interests and having a greater sense of urgency to bring development because he, informants emphasised, 'also needs electricity and other services'.[34] Stephen Nhlapo channelled the grievances and anger related to the slow and inadequate delivery, poor housing, toilets which did not flush, and a clinic with insufficient services to further his claim as the aspirant councillor. Nhlapo and other local leaders thus represented what Catherine Cross describes as a 'communal governance system based on face-to-face relationships and individual patronage', providing leverage to residents who felt excluded.[35]

Whilst not directly involved in service delivery, councillors play an essential role as the interface between residents and the municipal administration. Councillors, however, are often perceived by the community as the local face of the government. They are therefore bestowed with substantial local power over access to, and allocation of, resources and responsibility over existing projects and ensuring delivery. As explained by Samuel, a broker:

> A councillor is the power. More than us. Cause we tell the councillor we want a house. She [Schneeman] has to make it move, go to the department of housing and say guys, for the budget of next year . . . but she didn't. How can she be here for 5 years without building a house.[36]

Residents in Zandspruit understood the councillor to be all powerful and were often unaware of how time-consuming and difficult it can be to mobilise development funding and get all components of the delivery machinery into movement.[37] The effect of inadequate financial management, lack of planning and project management, and inefficient and ineffective use of resources at the local government level has been amply documented.[38] Slow and inadequate service delivery and wide-ranging perceptions of corruption put immense pressure on Schneeman. This provided the leaders of the protests with a scapegoat and motivation to instigate protests. Schneeman repeatedly claimed that only some of the community felt that no services had been brought to Zandspruit, and argued that the protests were instigated by a 'few trouble-makers who have their own agendas'.[39] Schneeman believed that the instigators of the protestors used lies and accusations of corruption to mobilise crowds (from predominately the Private Property section) in an attempt to attain positions of power. This was not because of a lack of delivery, she argued, but precisely because they were aware that there was significant development in the pipe line.[40] The views of protestors towards councillor Schneeman varied. A protester named Tsoanelo acknowledged the terrible living conditions of many residents as an explanation for the protests. Yet he argued that the real reason was the leadership battle, with the leaders 'hiding behind the masses' by 'organising groups who are revolting against the councillor'.[41] In his words:

> They are calling them service strikes but for me, I don't think it is service delivery. Because so far our councillor has done a lot to show her commitment

124 *Hannah Dawson*

to the community. She has done her bit to develop the community. From my understanding, it has less to do with service delivery . . . it is more of a power struggle.[42]

On the other hand, Ben, like many other of my informants, described Schneeman as not fulfilling her promises and of being absent and indifferent to the needs of residents:

> I can tell you one thing. Not that I'm racist. But I'll tell you the truth. You know Maureen. She knows nothing about what is happening here. She comes and she goes. Even if we had a councillor that lived here it would be better. Maybe he or she could actually see our things. I mean if someone doesn't actually live here. Then how can you be a councillor. You don't know how we live. You go to a meeting and then you bounce. She doesn't know the conditions we people are living in.[43]

Schneeman and her committee were accused of 'eating money' which indicated the pervasive sense that the councillor's committee, popularly known as 'Maureen's dogs', had preferential access to jobs and houses. Some residents acknowledged that the limited provision of services was a result of substantial backlogs and the impossibility of bringing facilities to densely packed areas. These voices, however, were drowned out in the densely crowded Private Property section. These perceptions and accusations helped to mobilise support behind Stephen Nhlapo, who the residents – predominantly in the Private Property section – associated with improved accountability, urgency and representation.

Protests in Zandspruit

The first protest occurred in the run-up to the 2011 local election when the regional ANC office re-nominated Maureen Schneeman as the ANC candidate. It has been suggested that racial and gender quotas for candidates were influential in the final selection but Schneeman evidently had the support of the provincial ANC.[44] The elimination of Stephen Nhlapo from the candidacy angered the residents, especially those in the Private Property section. The majority of people interviewed were misinformed that the community consultations undertaken by the ANC did not determine the final candidate choice but were limited to nominations. The endorsement of Schneeman as the ANC candidate led to a flurry of accusations of manipulation directed at the ANC. Protest action including the blockading of the main road, burning of tyres and street battles with the police erupted alongside a threat of an election boycott if Schneeman was not replaced by Nhlapo.

After the first protest, meetings were held in the settlement and Nhlapo pleaded with the community to vote for the ANC to prevent losing the ward to an opposition party. Nhlapo made reference to Zuma's announcement that 'irregularly nominated' councillors would be removed by a task team headed by Nkosazana Dlamini-Zuma after the elections, assuring the community that he could still

Protests, party politics and patronage   125

be councillor if the ANC won. The second protest, held one month before the local elections, was orchestrated by community leaders and brokers in support of Nhlapo. A memorandum dated the same day as the second protest accused the ANC of 'tak[ing] all the decisions without our concern' and threatening again to boycott the elections. Similar tactics were used and an estimated 40 protestors were arrested. In the municipal elections the ANC won 56 percent of the vote, with a 53 percent voter turnout.[45] This compared with a 55 percent average turn-out for Johannesburg and 56 percent for Gauteng province.[46] A closer look at the two main voting stations within Zandspruit reveals that the ANC won more than 90 percent of the votes. On the basis of these figures, there was no evidence of any significant boycott of the elections in Zandspruit, indicating that the battle for patronage – in 2011 at any rate – resided within the ANC instead of against it.

The third protest occurred approximately six weeks after the local election. It was prompted by the failure of the first two protests to yield any results, including an investigation by the task team. 'We didn't vote for Maureen. We voted for the ANC', said a protestor. 'In Zandspruit, we are hungry for the task team', he continued, 'They mustn't go to Maureen's committee . . . [it] must be a task team for the people'.[47] The task team was expected to replace Schneeman with Nhlapo, who would bring greater accountability and urgency to the Private Properties section as well as investigate uneven delivery of services and cases of corruption. This disappointment, combined with allegations and rumours that probed the motivations and personal agendas of Nhlapo and the other leaders, created tensions between Nhlapo and the brokers. This created a trigger for the third protest which, unlike the first and second, erupted without the leaders' knowledge. The protest was reported as being larger and more violent, with the main road barricaded and an attack on state property. Many of the protestors, who had previously supported Nhlapo, accused the aspirant councillor of fighting for power and tenders[48] for himself and misleading the community. Mzwandile, a broker, said that he had not fully appreciated that the leaders were 'fighting because they want money' and then come 'looking for people to protest'. In Mzwandile's words, 'we [brokers and protestors] are protesting for their [the leaders of protests] own pockets'.

The three protests, although differing slightly in their specific triggers, agendas, participants and points of emphasis, stemmed from similar grievances and emerged as a result of intra-ANC rivalries in the run-up and aftermath of the local elections. The emergence and development of a rival faction within the local ANC with networks of followers – predominantly in the Private Properties section – provided, as argued in the following section, the mobilising structures for protest action in a battle for patronage 'from below'.

Protests as collective claim making

The ANC is not just a modern political party but retains its status as a liberation movement, and sees itself as the custodian and legitimate representative of the aspirations of the people.[49] This overlap has strengthened patrimonial predispositions within the ANC; blurred the distinction between the party and the state,[50]

126 *Hannah Dawson*

particularly at the local level; and nurtured the continued electoral dominance of the ANC. On the one hand, the Zandspruit protests illustrated the agency of low-income residents, who asserted demands for the provision of public goods and services. On the other hand, the protests represented a form of political opportunism with a local elite, led by the aspirant councillor, endeavouring to reconfigure local government positions to gain access and control over state resources and service delivery. This involved political brokers aligning themselves and backing the aspirant councillor – a strategy they hoped would be rewarded through localised favours. The protests therefore had various and often contradictory aims – what Von Holdt describes as the 'dual nature' of unrest – but nevertheless indicated the agency of brokers in particular to determine the terms of their incorporation within patron-client relations.

The ANC was referred to as a 'mother' by a number of informants. Lwazi referred to the ANC as 'the organisation we trusted' and then asked me, 'If you have a mother, and she disappoints you, how do you feel?'[51] The use of the word 'mother' reflects a familial and personal relationship with the ANC. Susan Booysen's description of the ANC as the custodian and legitimate representative of the aspirations of the people of South Africa hints at this, but does not fully capture the personal nature of the relationship based on norms of reciprocity and obligation. Samuel, a broker, accused the councillor who he described as the 'mother of the house' of not 'feeding [her] babies equally'.[52] The widespread discontent with local representation and accusations of corruption and differential access to state resources fuelled the candidate revolt in which residents felt betrayed by the ANC. The protests, therefore, merged a demand for a local councillor (i.e. a patron) who would distribute resources to the Private Property areas and a demand for the provision of public goods and services.

Protests, as argued by Booysen, were understood by many protestors as a principal means of bargaining with the state to attain higher levels of service delivery or government responsiveness.[53] Some informants believed a public display of violence was required to attract the attention of the government and in particular high-profile ANC cadres:

> If you want your crisis to be attended you must do something important. Maybe you can burn buses or whatever. By not doing that you cannot be attended to. They can't hear you.[54]

The lack of communication and feedback between the councillor and the residents, combined with widespread perceptions of corruption, eroded the trust residents had in the ANC to fulfil its promises. The protests signified on the one hand, the breakdown in clientelistic arrangements between the ANC and its supporters, with collective violence understood as essential to be heard. On the other hand, the protests may be interpreted as a political strategy that was employed in response to the bureaucratic indifference and exclusion that residents were experiencing.[55] What is clear is that demonstrations were the instrument through which residents felt their grievances were heard, and were essential in the process of making demands and claims on the state for the provision of public goods and services. The highly personalised and opportunistic nature of politics in Zandspruit, however, undermined the collective nature of these protests, highlighting both the possibilities and dangers of patronage politics.

Protests as political navigation

The first two protests were orchestrated in an attempt to shift the ANC's decision regarding the candidate for local councillor, with the aim of reconfiguring positions of power and the accompanying patronage networks to access state resources. Protests therefore operated as a tactic of political navigation. Both the leaders and brokers had anticipated that if Stephen Nhlapo was elected local councillor, he would not only prioritise the Private Properties area but also be responsible for the rewarding of tenders for development projects, the allocation of houses and importantly, the distribution of jobs. The competition for control over state resources in places such as Zandspruit has heightened what Tom Lodge describes as a 'new generation of politicians-turned-businessmen' who have produced new kinds of factional rivalry.[56] In Zandspruit it facilitated the emergence of political brokers who had a shrewd understanding of the political process and importantly, the necessity of political connections to the local councillor to access a house and a government job.

Many of the brokers, bearing in mind the personal relationship they had with the aspirant councillor, expressed an expectation to organise the protest. Samuel, a broker, described how Nhlapo came to his house and called him to attend meetings leading up to the protests. Others made their support of the aspirant councillor known and availed themselves in the leadership battle. These relationships consisted of complex chains of dependence and reciprocity, and the symbiotic relationship between the leaders who initiate protests and the brokers and protestors who carry them out has been highlighted in other unrest.[57] The leaders in Zandspruit could only achieve political aims through unrest that required residents (and in particular youth) to avail themselves for direct action. The brokers, who worked very closely with the leaders and mobilised the residents for protests, had expectations – what Barry Gilder describes as 'cultural instincts'[58] – that in return the leaders would ensure work opportunities for them. For example, one informant stated that, 'If they bring development here we can make sure we get jobs, even if it is housing or anything, that people get a job.'[59]

The protests largely failed the brokers as a tactic of navigation, because of their failure to oust Schneeman from the position of councillor. After the third protest the perception that the leaders had deceived brokers and protestors was widespread. A few weeks after the third protest, the aspirant councillor Stephen Nhlapo and another local leader received a tender to build a pavement and cycle lane along the edge of the settlement. This infuriated residents for three reasons. First, many people assumed that the councillor had given the tender to Nhlapo and other faction leaders in an attempt to buy them off and therefore prevent further protests. The leaders were accused of surrendering to the system of corruption and

128   *Hannah Dawson*

malpractice and forsaking the fight for an end to corruption and incompetence. Second, youth were angered because, from their perspective, paving had been prioritised over more immediate claims for houses, sanitation and electricity, and the youth and residents as a whole were not consulted. Lastly, although Nhlapo had employed people from within the settlement, the majority of my informants had not been offered a job. As a result the brokers felt cheated:

> Those guys [the leaders] I was fighting with are not committed. I've been protesting with those guys but today they won't say Samuel, there is a job. They get people from outside a job. What about me? They don't care about me. Even now when they meet me they looking down. They just use me.[60]

The foregoing quote indicates the layers of meaning protests held for brokers and the contradictory nature of their involvement. Brokers supported Nhlapo because they genuinely thought he would bring greater accountability and urgency to the claims of residents, especially in the Private Property sections. At the same time, they had personal expectations to gain access to jobs and resources which did not transpire. Participation in unrest, therefore, appears to be contradictory, condemning corruption and nepotism on the one hand while simultaneously pursuing a battle for patronage on the other.

For the residents and brokers in the underserviced Private Properties section of Zandspruit, the competitive patronage network Nhlapo represented held the possibility of distributing resources to the neglected Private Properties. Stephen Nhlapo and his network provided a humanising or personalistic manner of assistance which was sought after by the most deprived and neglected sections of a community. Some were also optimistic that these networks would provide what Auyero describes as alternative ways of 'getting things done' while avoiding bureaucratic indifference.[61] At the same time, the personalised and opportunistic nature of these relationships and the misgivings about the leaders' motivations undermined the collective demands of the protests. This was evidently the case when Nhlapo received a tender soon after the local elections to prevent further discontent. In effect, this fuelled further discontent and accusations of betrayal and corruption. The informal and contingent nature of the relationship among leaders, brokers and protestors weakens the ability of these networks to build and sustain action over time. These dynamics have also shown to generate a culture of mistrust and cynicism around the effectiveness of such political action.

Conclusions

Most scholarship on protests has not paid close attention to the struggles within the ANC, nor explored the local dynamics of patronage politics and the way this shapes the formation of collective action.

Residents' grievances are a result of a complex interplay of factors generating frustration, anger and accusations of abandonment and betrayal towards the

Protests, party politics and patronage 129

ANC. These grievances, most notably differential access to public goods, represent a breakdown in collective clientelistic arrangements between local ANC representative and residents. In addition, the development of competitive patronage networks in Zandspruit, as a result of an intra-ANC rivalry, has been shown to provide the mobilising structures for collective action. As such, this analysis supports Auyero's proposition that patron-client relations (based on vertical and asymmetric relationships) and collective action (requiring horizontal ties) are not inevitably conflicting political phenomena.[62] That said, the fragility and fluidity of loyalties between leaders and brokers, given the highly personalised and opportunistic nature of their relationships, can weaken the collective demands and power of demonstrations.

While not seeking to obscure the dangers and dysfunctions of patronage politics, this chapter shows how patron-client relations serve various functions, many of which remain unexamined in the local context in South Africa. The analysis supports Tom Lodge's argument that neo-patrimonialism is increasingly prominent within the ANC. But by providing a view 'from below', it also challenges his assertion that ANC supporters are 'passive clients' rather than 'assertive citizens'.[63] The protests in Zandspruit demonstrate that low-income residents, and brokers in particular, are actively engaged in strategies to determine and assert the terms of their incorporation and rewards within patron-client relations. A view 'from below' also highlights that it is not necessarily the patron who establishes the relationship with possible clientele or supporters, but instead clientele or residents who seek out patrons to secure leverage or access to resources. This case study has also shown how these strategies can fail leaders, brokers and protestors. Nonetheless, understanding how different actors and allegiances operate on the ground provides important insights into the triggers for protests and the social networks through which people are mobilised and organised in complex, seemingly provisional patron-client relations.

Zandspruit has been the site of on-going protests since 2011. In February 2014 – two months before the national elections – growing frustration with the ANC's failure to fulfil their promises of a housing project and basic service delivery was made apparent by a further string of protests, which erupted in response to the removal of shacks by the police. During this same period both the official opposition party, the Democratic Alliance (DA), and the newly formed Economic Freedom Fighters (EFF), were actively campaigning in Zandspruit, capitalising on disillusioned ANC members and positioning themselves as an alternative to the ANC.

A few key figures in the ANC faction who supported Stephen Nhlapo in the 2011 elections, and initiated the protests discussed here, were actively campaigning for the DA in the run up to the national elections. One of these leaders, a close ally of Stephen Nhlapo in 2011, told me on the day of the national elections in 2014 that 'people were not scared anymore [unlike 2011] to be DA'. The EFF in Zandspruit only established itself a few months before the national elections but gained significant traction, positioning itself as the party that would bring economic change and jobs. After explaining that South Africans are still not 'economically free', an EFF supporter said he was voting for the EFF to 'wake up the ANC'.

130   Hannah Dawson

The 2014 elections saw the ANC's support erode by more than 11 percent within the ward as a whole, and by 15 percent in the two main voting sites within Zandspruit. These results suggest that unresolved grievances and protest action over a sustained period ruptured the ANC's hegemony, providing inroads for opposition parties and the EFF in particular. The effect of diminishing ANC support and growing party competition on forms of patronage and protest is yet to be seen. It will be an important area for future research.

Notes

1 This chapter is a shortened and updated version of a paper entitled, 'Patronage from Below: Political Unrest in an Informal Settlement in South Africa' previously published in *African Affairs* 113, no. 453 (2014): 518–39. The chapter's argument benefitted from presentations at the 'Contentious Politics, Capitalism, and Social Movement Theory: South Africa in Global Perspective' colloquium hosted by the South African Research Chair in Social Change, University of Johannesburg and at the Wits Institute for Social and Economic Research (WISER). Special acknowledgements must go to Claire Bénit-Gbaffou, Karl Von Holdt and the anonymous reviewers and editors of *African Affairs* for their invaluable comments.

2 This is what Karl Von Holdt has described as the 'dual nature' of protests; see Karl Von Holdt, et al., *The Smoke that Calls: Insurgent Citizenship, Collective Violence and the Struggle for a Place in the New South Africa*. Research Report (Johannesburg: CSVR and SWOP, 2011). Susan Booysen has also argued that candidate revolts in the 2011 local elections seamlessly blended into, and triggered service delivery protests. See Susan Booysen, 'The Ballot and the Brick – Enduring under Duress,' in *Local Elections in South Africa: Parties, People, Politics*, ed. Susan Booysen (Bloemfontein: Sun Press, 2012).

3 South Africa's police recorded an average of 2.9 unrest incidents per day over the period from 2009 to 2012. This is an increase of 40 percent over the average of 2.1 unrest incidents per day recorded for 2004 to 2009. See Peter Alexander, 'Rebellion of the Poor: South Africa's Service Delivery Protests – A Preliminary Analysis,' *Review of African Political Economy* 37, no. 123 (2010): 25–40.

4 Alexander, 'Rebellion of the Poor'; Lucius Botes et al., 'The New Struggle: Service Delivery-Related Unrest in South Africa' (unpublished paper, Centre for Development Support, Bloemfontein, 2007); Susan Booysen, *The African National Congress and the Regeneration of Power* (Johannesburg: Wits University Press, 2011); Von Holdt, et al., *The Smoke that Calls*.

5 Tom Lodge, 'Neo-Patrimonial Politics in the ANC,' *African Affairs* 113, no. 450 (2014): 1–23.

6 Booysen, *The African National Congress and the Regeneration of Power*, 90, 119.

7 Alexander, 'The Rebellion of the Poor.'

8 Ibid.; Claire Bénit-Gbaffou, 'Against Ourselves – Local Activists and the Management of Contradicting Political Loyalties: The Case of Phiri Water,' *Geoforum* 43 (2012): 207–18; Anton Harber, *Diepsloot* (Jeppestown: Jonathan Ball Publishers, 2011).

9 The Mapungubwe Institute for Strategic Reflection (MISTRA) published a book on patronage politics in South Africa in 2013; see Mcebisi Ndletyana, 'Pholoana Oupa Makhelemele and Ralph Mathekga,' *Patronage Politics Divides Us: A Study of Poverty, Patronage and Inequality in South Africa* (Johannesburg: Real African Publishers, 2013).

10 Lodge, 'Neo-Patrimonial Politics,' 3.

11 Ibid., 2–3.

12 Doreen Atkinson, 'The State of Local Government: Third Generation Issues,' in *State of the Nation: South Africa 2003/2004*, ed. John Daniel, Adam Habib and Roger

Southall. (Pretoria: Human Sciences Research Council, 2003), 118–40; Doreen Atkinson, 'Taking to the Streets: Has Developmental Local Governance Failed in South Africa?' in *State of the Nation: South Africa 2007*, ed. Sakhela Buhlungu, John Daniel, Roger Southall and Jessica Lutchman. (Pretoria: Human Sciences Research Council, 2007), 53–77; Alexander, 'The Rebellion of the Poor"; Susan Booysen, 'With the Ballot and the Brick: The Politics of Attaining Service Delivery,' *Progress in Development Studies* 7, no. 1 (2007): 21–32; Hein Marais, *South Africa Pushed to the Limit: The Political Economy of Change* (London: Zed Books, 2011).

13 For an analysis of protests in the context of local patronage politics, see Malose Langa and Karl Von Holdt, 'Insurgent Citizenship, Class Formation and the Dual Nature of a Community Protest: A Case Study of "Kungcatsha",' in *Contesting Transformation: Popular Resistance in Twenty-First Century South Africa*, ed. Marcelle Dawson and Luke Sinwell (London: Pluto Press, 2012); and Claire Bénit-Gbaffou, 'Party Politics, Civil Society and Local Democracy – Reflections from Johannesburg,' *Geoforum* 43 (2012): 178–89.

14 Karl Von Holdt, 'Overview: Insurgent Citizenship and Collective Violence: Analysis of Case Studies,' in *The Smoke that Calls: Insurgent Citizenship, Collective Violence and the Struggle for a Place in the New South Africa: Seven Case Studies of Community Protests and Xenophobic Violence*, ed. Karl Von Holdt, Malose Langa, Sepetla Molapo, Nomfundo Mogapi, Kindiza Ngubeni, Jacob Dlamini, and Adele Kirsten, Research Report (Johannesburg: CSVR and SWOP, 2011).

15 Abdul Raufu Mustapha and Lindsay Whitfield, 'Conclusion: The Politics of African States in the Era of Democratisation,' in *Turning Points in African Democracy*, ed. Abdul Raufu Mustapha and Lindsay Whitfield (Suffolk, United Kingdom: James Currey, 2009), 202–28, 220.

16 Herbert Kitschelt and Steven Wilkinson, eds., *Patrons, Clients and Policies: Patterns of Democratic Accountability and Political Competition* (Cambridge: Cambridge University Press, 2007), 2.

17 Claire Bénit-Gbaffou, 'Up Close and Personal – How Does Local Democracy Help the Poor Access the State? Stories of Accountability and Clientelism in Johannesburg,' *Journal of Asian and African Studies* 46 (2011): 453–64.

18 Nic Cheeseman, 'The Rise and Fall of Civil Authoritarianism in Africa: Patronage, Participation and Parties in Kenya and Zambia' (PhD dissertation, University of Oxford, 2006).

19 Ibid.

20 Mustapha and Whitfield, 'Conclusion: The Politics of African States,' 221.

21 Kitschelt and Wilkinson, *Patrons, Clients and Policies*.

22 Alexander, 'The Rebellion of the Poor'; Booysen, 'With the Ballot and the Brick'; Marais, *South Africa Pushed to the Limit*.

23 Javier Auyero, 'From the Client's Point of View: How Poor People Perceive and Evaluate Political Clientelism,' *Theory and Society* 28 (1999): 297–334; Robert Gay, 'Rethinking Clientelism: Demands, Discourses and Practices in Contemporary Brazil,' *European Review of Latin American and Caribbean Studies* 65 (1998): 7–24.

24 Gerrit Burgwal, *Struggle of the Poor: Neighborhood Organization and Clientelist Practice in a Quito Squatter Settlement* (Amsterdam: CEDLA, 1995); Robert Gay, 'Community Organization and Clientelist Politics in Contemporary Brazil: A Case Study from Suburban Rio de Jeneiro,' *International Journal of Urban and Regional Research* 14 (1990): 648–66.

25 These include network breakdown, patron's certification, clandestine support and reaction to threat. See Javier Auyero, Pablo Lepegna and Fernanda Page Poma, 'Patronage Politics and Contentious Collective Action: A Recursive Relationship,' *Latin American Politics and Society* 51, no. 3 (2009): 1–31.

26 RDP houses are state-subsidised dwellings which were originally promised in the ANC's 1994 RDP manifesto called the Reconstruction and Development Programme (RDP).

132 *Hannah Dawson*

27 Author interview, Samuel (broker), Zandspruit, September 14, 2011.
28 Lodge, 'Neo-Patrimonial Politics.'
29 Interview, Ashley (protestor), Zandspruit, August 15, 2011.
30 Interview, Tsoanelo (protester), Zandspruit, September 16, 2011.
31 Booysen, *The African National Congress and the Regeneration of Power.*
32 The 52nd ANC national conference held in 2007 in Polokwane is associated with the battle for party leadership between the sitting President Thabo Mbeki and Jacob Zuma.
33 Phindile Ntliziywana and Jaap de Visser, 'Assessing the Risks of Zuma's Call for "Fresh Elections" after 18 May' (unpublished Report, University of the Western Cape, 2011), accessed June 6, 2015, http://www.ldphs.org.za/publications/publications-by-theme/local-government-in-south-africa/local-government-elections/municipal-elections-2011/Assessing_the_risks.pdf.
34 Author interview, Samuel (broker), Zandspruit, September 14, 2011.
35 Catherine Cross, 'Local Governance and Social Conflict: Implications for Piloting South Africa's New Housing Plan in Cape Town's Informal Settlements,' in *Informal Settlements: A Perpetual Challenge?* ed. Marie Huchzermeyer and Aly Karam (South Africa: Juta Academics, 2006), 261.
36 Interview, Samuel (broker), September 14, 2011.
37 Cross, 'Local Governance and Social Conflict,' 260.
38 Atkinson, 'The State of Local Government'; Atkinson, 'Taking to the Streets'; David Hemson, Jonathan Carter, and Geci Karuri-Sebina, 'Service Delivery as a Measure of Change: State Capacity and Development,' in *State of the Nation: South Africa 2008*, ed. Peter Kagwanja and Kwandiwe Kondlo (Pretoria: Human Sciences Research Council, 2008), 151–77.
39 Interview, Maureen Schneeman (local ward councillor), Zandspruit, August 3, 2011.
40 At the time of the research, the ANC had recently finalised the purchase of nine plots of land (including the four Private Properties) which would allow for housing development. By early 2016, no further development has transpired.
41 Interview, Tsoanelo (protestor), Zandspruit, September 16, 2011.
42 Ibid.
43 Interview, Ben (protestor), Zandspruit, August 15, 2011.
44 Booysen, *The African National Congress and the Regeneration of Power.*
45 In the longer version of this chapter published in *African Affairs* 113, no. 453 (2014), I incorrectly state that the ANC won 77 percent of the vote (Ward 100). A few months before the 2011 elections Zandspruit moved to Ward 114 which includes neighbouring suburbs that would have voted differently. This is evident in the discrepancy between the ANC getting 56 percent in the ward overall and more than 90 percent at the specific voting stations within Zandspruit.
46 Booysen, *The African National Congress and the Regeneration of Power*, 155.
47 Interview, Caswell (protestor), Zandspruit, July 25, 2011.
48 A tender is a written offer to contract goods or services at a specific cost or rate. The term 'tenderpreneurship' has, in South Africa, come to denote the activities of a government official or politician who uses his or her power and influence to secure government tenders and contracts.
49 Booysen, *The African National Congress and the Regeneration of Power*, 86.
50 Lodge, 'Neo-Patrimonial Politics,' 17–18, 87.
51 Interview, Lwazi (broker), Zandspruit, August 23, 2011.
52 Interview, Samuel (broker), Zandspruit, September 14, 2011.
53 Booysen, 'With the Ballot and the Brick'; Booysen, *The African National Congress and the Regeneration of Power*.
54 Interview, Tsepho (protestor), Zandspruit, August 22, 2011.
55 Robert Gay has argued similarly that clientelism should be seen as a strategy that is selectively employed and the product of a sophisticated and reasoned grasp of the

political process as a whole. See Gay, 'Rethinking Clientelism,' 16. See Auyero, 'From the Client's Point of View,' 4.
56 Lodge, 'Neo-Patrimonial Politics,' 20.
57 Von Holdt, 'Overview: Insurgent Citizenship.'
58 Barry Gilder has argued that there exist 'cultural instincts' to come to the aid of a comrade, friend, family and community. See Barry Gilder, *Songs and Secrets: South Africa from Liberation to Governance* (Auckland Park: Jacana, 2012), 399.
59 Interview, Martin (broker), Zandspruit, August 10, 2011.
60 Interview, Samuel (broker), Zandspruit, September 14, 2011.
61 Auyero, 'From the Client's Point of View.'
62 Auyero et al., 'Patronage Politics and Contentious Collective Action.'
63 Lodge, 'Neo-Patrimonial Politics,' 21.

Part IV
Labour formations

9 Changing forms of power and municipal worker resistance in Johannesburg

Carmen Ludwig and Edward Webster[1]

The city of Johannesburg has a long history of struggle over municipal services since its establishment as a gold mining town in the late nineteenth century.[2] By early 1918 there were signs of great discontent among both white and black workers on the Rand, especially in Johannesburg. Indeed, syndicalists in March 1918 appealed to white workers of Johannesburg to implement their own version of the Russian revolution by occupying the power station.[3] In May, the Johannesburg Council's refusal to improve black workers' working conditions led to the 'bucket boys' strike, which City authorities suppressed by arresting sanitary workers. Although black workers were not able at this stage to translate their struggle into organisational power, they began to see their power through collective resistance.[4] However, black workers remained vulnerable to deportation to the rural areas, as they were only allowed to enter what was seen as the 'white man's city' temporarily, and were tightly controlled by the pass system.

In this chapter we examine how black workers in the Johannesburg municipality struggled to build union power during the apartheid and post-apartheid periods. Drawing on the power resources approach, we identify four dimensions of trade union power: structural, associational, symbolic and institutional. The extent to which unions may utilise any or all of these resources depends on whether they are available or can be developed. The question raised by our analysis is whether these struggles in the Johannesburg municipality are discrete and disconnected instances of resistance, or whether they can be linked to other movements from below. Do these struggles represent examples of Marxian-type struggles against exploitation or Polanyi-type struggles against commodification? Or are they sometimes a combination of both; workplace struggles over wages (exploitation) and protests against privatisation (commodification)?

This chapter is based on research conducted by Carmen Ludwig between 2012 and 2014 as part of two projects: a PhD project on trade union strategies in organising precarious and informal workers in the municipal sector in South Africa; and a study of externalised workers for the South African Municipal Workers' Union (SAMWU), conducted jointly with Lawrence Ntuli. The research was based on a prolonged period of participant observation at national and local union and workers' meetings, including the Johannesburg region. Besides field notes and document analysis, the data were further gathered through 20 in-depth interviews and

138 *Carmen Ludwig and Edward Webster*

group discussions with union officials and shop stewards at the regional (Johannesburg), provincial (Gauteng) and national level, as well as with municipal and outsourced workers in Johannesburg.

We divide the chapter into two parts. In the first part we develop an analytical framework based on different forms of worker power. In the second part of the chapter we use this analytical framework to show how the goals and forms of power changed in the different cycles of resistance. We identify three cycles of municipal workers struggles against privatisation and contract work, framed around the repertoires of inclusion and exclusion. We demonstrate that trade unions are able to draw on new forms of power, logistical and symbolic power, which extend traditional forms of workers power. The struggles of municipal workers are furthermore best seen as a Marx-Polanyi dialectic in which Marx's focus on struggles around exploitation in production are intensified by labour market flexibility through the process of commodifcation introduced by privatisation.[5] While the Marx/Polanyi distinction refers to the goal or object of struggle (anti-exploitation vs anti-commodification), the different forms of power capture the leverage that actors use to achieve the goal. Our cases suggest that these are two relatively independent variables, which may, at times, influence each other.

Part one: developing an analytical framework of changing forms of workers' power

Karl Polanyi, some 70 years ago, wrote in *The Great Transformation* that 'the idea of a self – adjusting market implied a stark utopia. Such an institution could not exist for any length of time without annihilating the human and natural substance of society.'[6] This became known as the 'Polanyi problem': creating a fully self-regulated market economy requires that human beings, nature and money be turned into pure commodities. But, he argued, land, labour and money are fictitious commodities, because they are not originally produced to be sold on a market. Polanyi went on to show how society took measures to protect itself against the disruptive impact of unregulated commodification. He conceptualised this as a 'double movement' whereby ever – wider extensions of free market principles generated counter-movements to protect society. A central problem with Polanyi's theory is that the concept of power is largely missing.

By way of contrast, 77 years earlier, Karl Marx had focused on production, rather than the market, showing how the expansion of capitalism initiated a process of proletarianisation based on the separation of workers from the means of production.[7] This, Marx argued, led to the exploitation of this new working class as capital, in its relentless drive for profit, appropriated the surplus generated by the producers. For Marx, and the Marxists that followed, exploitation rather than commodification is the central experience of capitalism. While there are powerful resonances between Marx and Polanyi, especially in the early writing of Marx on money and alienation from which Polanyi draws, Michael Burawoy argues that there are fundamental divergences between their commentaries.[8] Polanyi sees, in

Power and municipal worker resistance 139

contrast to Marx, commodification rather than exploitation as the central experience of capitalism, with the consequence that the focus shifts from production to markets, and from classes to society.

Drawing on Marx and Polanyi, Silver distinguishes between two forms of workers' struggles: whereas in Marxian struggles workers fight for control over the work process, in Polanyian struggles workers fight for the protection of society against the ravages of the self-regulating market system.[9] Both types of struggles depend on workers' ability to influence the structural imbalance of power relations between capital and labour through the mobilisation of power resources. While Marx has a theory of both workers' structural and associational power, Polanyi's double movement or countermovement, on the other hand, is primarily concerned with associational power, though he is vague about who it is that builds associational power – the working classes, landed classes and others.

We propose that collective struggles differ in respect to the forms of power that workers deploy. To overcome the lack of an emphasis on power, Silver introduced Erik Olin Wright's distinction between associational and structural power.[10] While *associational power* derives from the formation of collective workers' organisations such as trade unions or political parties, *structural power* develops from the status of specific groups in the economic system or in the labour market.[11] Structural power can take two forms: Marketplace bargaining power describes a form of structural power that evolves from tight labour markets, scarce skills in demand by employers, low levels of unemployment, or the ability of employees to exit the labour market. In contrast, workplace bargaining power results from a specific strategic position of a group of workers within production.[12] It is in particular the dynamics of production and in the broader sense, of capitalism, which shape this particular form of workers' power. For instance, the location of workers in key industrial sectors and in highly integrated production lines or value chains enhances their ability to effectively interrupt production through collective action. In a more general sense, the link between the economic structure and mobilisation has also been highlighted in social movement studies from a Marxist perspective.[13]

Associational power cannot fully replace structural power but compensates it to a certain degree. Basically, associational power refers to the collective strength of workers which is grounded in organisation. Associational power refers to trade unions' infrastructural resources which encompass material and personal resources of trade unions, including the role and organisational experience of full-time officials, shop stewards and union activists.[14] We see similarities between associational power and resource mobilisation in social movement theory. Both share the basic outlook that organisation is not an obstacle to mobilisation but a prerogative. The resource mobilisation approach argues that mobilisation depends on movements' access and ability to accumulate and utilise resources in collective action. Besides its focus on material resources and money, resource mobilisation has also pointed to the relevance of conceptual tools, knowledge, infrastructure, social networks, and the experience, skills and strategic orientation of leadership in movement organisations.[15]

140 *Carmen Ludwig and Edward Webster*

As a third form of power, *institutional power* refers to social compromises which are fixed in laws or institutions and pre-structure future processes of negotiations and trade union strategies.[16] Institutional power takes the form of a secondary source of power as it derives from previous workers' struggles and therefore rests on associational and structural power. Collective bargaining agreements or labour laws are an expression of trade union's institutional power. Furthermore, where unions have established access to government through institutionalised tripartite or legislative processes, one would expect them to embark on a strategy to enhance their institutional power and to use more formal strategies such as social dialogue, lobbying and meetings with ministers and decision makers.[17] Institutional power is similar to the notion of political opportunity structures in that both underscore the centrality of political structures or institutions such as laws and state agencies.[18]

Silver argues that weaknesses in structural power might encourage experiments with new forms and ways to strengthen workers' associational power.[19] Webster, Lambert and Bezuidenhout take this analysis further by arguing that trade unions can also be able to draw on new forms of power, which compensate for a lack of traditional sources of workers' power. They argue that logistical power has become particularly relevant in the light of rising labour protests in the global South. Logistical power can be regarded as a form of structural power which primarily rests on workers' ability to disrupt flows of capital and people in public spaces.[20] It is therefore based on the ability of workers to extend disputes from the workplace into the public domain. Taking the strike of farm workers' in De Doorns in 2012 as an example, workers compensated their lack of structural power by blocking roads and highways.[21]

Furthermore, by appealing to notions of social justice, workers can also draw on what Chun calls symbolic power.[22] Symbolic power can be expressed in two ways, by building coalitions with other social groups such as social movements and by influencing the public discourse. Although we regard symbolic power as closely related to associational power, for the purpose of conceptual clarity we treat it as a separate form of power. While associational power is founded in workers' organisation, symbolic power derives from alliances of trade unions with other social groups in society. In essence, symbolic power transcends the conflict between capital and labour into wider societal struggles that expand from the workplace into the public.

Chun demonstrates that precarious workers in Korea and the United States compensated for their lack of structural power by building coalitions with student movements and social movements and by winning public recognition and legitimacy for workers' struggles.[23] As Lévesque and Murray convincingly argue, power resources are a necessary but insufficient condition to respond to the changing conditions affecting unions' grievances.[24] It needs actors assigning meaning to these conditions in order to transform grievances into mobilisation.[25] The union's ability to generalise their grievances and demands in framing processes is therefore decisive for building symbolic power.

Power and municipal worker resistance   141

On the one hand, the two new forms of power – logistical and symbolic – have in common that both seek to address 'the public' by extending disputes from the workplace into the public domain. On the other hand, tensions also exist between logistical and symbolic power: Whereas symbolic power essentially depends on gaining public support, logistical power may turn citizens against the protests and de-legitimise its demands in the eyes of the wider public. This distinction points to the fact that the relationship between union's different power resources is not to be understood as simply additive or complementary, but also potentially conflictual.

Part two: cycles of contestation

First cycle: contesting the labour regime

The first cycle of municipal workers' resistance, 1980 to 1995, was framed against racial discrimination by demanding an inclusive, democratic citizenship. This was a period of municipal workers' militancy and of building associational power as illustrated by a mass strike of municipal employees in Johannesburg in July 1980. The strike started in the Orlando Power Station over the demand for a minimum wage, and quickly spread to other departments. After two days, approximately 10,000 black workers had joined the strike. Mobilisation was fuelled by long-standing grievances in depots and compounds, uniting skilled and unskilled workers, and contract and non-contract workers. The strike that 'shook Johannesburg' lasted one week and was finally crushed through massive police intervention. More than 1,000 workers were deported to the rural Bantustans.[26]

The disruptive collective action of municipal workers centred on demands for higher wages and trade union recognition, but the strike was also an attack on the exploitative social relations of the migrant labour system. Contract labour was a central pillar of the apartheid system and was used as a means of 'influx control' and of forcing workers into the lowest paid sectors. For recruitment, the Johannesburg City Council (JCC) relied primarily on the most remote districts of rural Transkei, where poverty was high and workers were forced to take the most unpleasant jobs, particularly as sanitation workers.

The JCC employed more than 12,000 'migrant' workers out of a total workforce of about 14,000 black workers in 1980.[27] The 'migrant' workers from the Bantustans usually received one-year contracts and call-in cards for contract renewal. The majority were classified as unskilled workers and trapped in that position. Two thirds of the municipal workforce lived in tightly controlled and overcrowded compounds located close to their workplaces.[28]

Although the state had started to widen the area of legality by providing for trade union recognition of black workers, as a result of the 1979 Wiehahn Commission, institutional power remained weak for municipal employees who faced employer resistance to unionisation. Workers primarily relied on their structural power even though they remained vulnerable to dismissal and deportation. Associational power was also only in the process of being built. The

142   *Carmen Ludwig and Edward Webster*

Black Municipal Workers' Union (BMWU), created to counteract management efforts to establish a sweetheart union, was only one month in existence when the strike erupted. Despite being premature in its organisational capacity, the BMWU played an important role in support of the strike: First, the leadership of the BMWU consisted of workers who had challenged management before and gained experience in trade union organising. Second, the union had already organised sections and this proved to be crucial for fostering solidarity between contract and non-contract workers. Third, the controlled compounds were turned into the central site of trade union recruitment of contract workers and laid the basis for workers' militant actions.[29]

Municipal workers' struggles in the first cycle were directed against exploitation, depending predominantly on workers' structural power. Associational power was difficult to sustain because of massive state repression, particularly in the public sector, as well as to trade union fragmentation.

Second cycle: contesting the commodification of public goods

The second cycle covers the shift to privatisation, 1996 to 2000, when intense ideological contention focused on the opposition to privatisation, with workers demanding public goods. With the end of apartheid, trade unions were able to significantly increase their associational power and SAMWU became one of the fastest-growing unions in federation, the Congress of South African Trade Unions (COSATU).[30] The end of apartheid also led to a brief 'honeymoon' period of institutionalisation, which saw an increase of trade unions' institutional power. Because they had played a significant role in the fight against apartheid, trade unions gained 'policy dividends' and 'institutional dividends'.[31] The former came in the form of progressive labour laws, in particular the Labour Relations Act (LRA), which eliminated discrimination in the labour market. The latter refers to the establishment of corporatist institutions, in particular the National Economic Development and Labour Council, NEDLAC, which gave unions a say in policymaking. For the first time, black municipal workers also negotiated wages and social benefits in a sector-wide Bargaining Council. However, the African National Congress' (ANC) macro-economic policy shifted in 1996 from a commitment towards state intervention and redistribution, as formulated in the Reconstruction and Development Program (RDP), to the highly contested program Growth, Employment and Redistribution (GEAR), which entailed a market-orientated strategy, including trade liberalisation, privatisation, tax reduction and fiscal-deficit reduction, amongst others.[32] In line with this policy shift, the Johannesburg City Council adopted a plan in 1999, iGoli 2002, to transform and restructure the municipality. This led to a far-reaching model of 'contracting out' as municipal departments were turned into utilities, agencies or corporatized entities.[33]

The iGoli 2002 was embedded in a wider neoliberal agenda, thereby facilitating what Rosa Luxemburg called capitalist *Landnahme*, processes of commodification and the expansion of capital into areas that were previously excluded from profit maximisation.[34]

Power and municipal worker resistance   143

GEAR resulted in severe cuts in inter-governmental grants from national to lower levels, thereby reducing the transfers for the Greater Johannesburg Metropolitan Municipality (GJMC) from 500 million rand in 1993 to 24 million in 1999.[35] At the same time, incentives by the World Bank and the Department of Finance were set in order to support the realisation of the iGoli 2002. This put the municipality under a great deal of pressure.

Advocates of the iGoli 2002 process, including the ANC-led Johannesburg Council and business, framed the implementation as an optimization of services through cost recovery, and by creating 'commercial imperatives for improved performance and efficiency' with an underlying assumption of market efficiency in contrast to state bureaucracy.[36] Therefore, the challenge, as described in the iGoli 2002 plan, was 'to transform the current bureaucracy into a business approach because the city is a "big business." '[37] Correspondingly, citizens were regarded as customers of the outsourced services.

In contrast, SAMWU's post-apartheid strategy was to pursue a double track of opposing the privatisation of municipal services, and of engagement in the reorganisation of municipal services on the basis of the social rights entrenched in South Africa's democratic constitution.[38] In the protracted conflict around iGoli 2002, SAMWU highlighted that privatisation would lead to rate increases, job losses and little access of the unemployed to basic services such as water and electricity. SAMWU emphasised labour-community links and social citizenship, realised through a democratically controlled public service. Accordingly, the union also criticised the lack of participation of labour and the community in the process as, similar to the adoption of GEAR, iGoli 2002 was the result of an internal government process with private consultants' involvement. SAMWU commented:

> In South Africa the workers' movement has never confined struggles to narrow interests of organised workers only. The SA Municipal Workers Union (SAMWU) is committed to an affordable and efficient public sector delivery that is accountable to the communities we serve; and that includes democratic community and worker participation.[39]

The anti-privatisation campaign demonstrated the relevance of symbolic power. SAMWU followed a strategy of inclusive solidarity, which went beyond the narrowly defined economic interests of its members by highlighting the relevance of a public service for all. First, in the 'propaganda war' around iGoli 2002, SAMWU managed to gain a high media presence. Second, SAMWU was also able to mobilise symbolic power through coalition building with social movements.

A senior city official even regarded the union as the major player with the capacity to 'make or break Johannesburg's ability to move on privatisation'.[40] However, the momentum that was built in the campaign was difficult to sustain because it also brought to the fore the tensions and the disunity that existed within the labour movement in defining its relationship to the ruling party, the ANC. Although SAMWU revived its strategy of social movement unionism to fight against privatisation, as Lier und Stokke argue, this strategy was limited

144 *Carmen Ludwig and Edward Webster*

by COSATU's alliance with the ANC, which made it difficult for SAMWU to fundamentally oppose privatisation in Johannesburg.[41] SAMWU's campaign was therefore constrained by an 'underlying tension between loyalty to the ANC and loyalty to the labour movement'.[42]

Although SAMWU was involved in the foundation of the Anti-Privatisation Forum (APF) in 2000 as a coalition of anti-privatisation movements and organisations, including sections of COSATU, the union increasingly withdrew its support from the APF because of 'strategic differences'[43] between social movements and the COSATU affiliates, centred on their relationship with the ruling party. As Ngwane concludes, the campaign lost drive as the government offered some concessions and the unions compromised.[44] Overall, SAMWU's campaign focus shifted from a strategy of inclusive solidarity, fundamentally opposed to privatisation, to a more exclusive approach focusing on its immediate membership interests and job protection. As a former SAMWU officer concluded, the 'fight was not lost outside, it was lost within. The members, staff – we were not as one. Although we had one resolution, the implementation of it became a problem.'[45]

As reflected in internal discussion documents, it became increasingly difficult for SAMWU to combine the two faces of unionism, being a 'sword of justice' on the one hand, and a 'defender of vested interests' on the other:[46]

> If we simply engage at the level of negotiations and discussions we disarm ourselves of the possibility of engaging in a wider social struggle for our positions. Worse still we allow our members and communities to simply watch the 'negotiators' without strengthening them both politically and organisationally – a fatal mistake given our predictions of the real consequences for workers and communities should iGoli be implemented.[47]

This also affected the set of repertoires used by the union. SAMWU's campaign strategy was based on 'a combination of mass action and strategic engagement',[48] including the struggle for public opinion, workers mobilisation, negotiations with the GJMC and political negotiations with the ANC.[49] On the one hand, the union made use of disruptive forms of contention, including mass mobilisation, strike action, sit-ins and the disruption of road traffic.[50] On the other hand, by focussing on negotiations, SAMWU increasingly gave preference to containing forms of protest, agreeing even to temporarily abstain from protest action.[51] In contrast, crisis committees and citizens' forums preferred direct action to institutionalised processes.[52]

In the second cycle, municipal workers' struggles were directed against the commodification of public services. Despite its limitations, SAMWU was able to exert symbolic power and to influence the 'contest over meaning'[53] through its anti-privatisation campaign. As McKinley reflects, SAMWU's campaign 'involved sustained efforts to forge alliances with community organizations.'[54] The union's ability to exert symbolic power was limited through the labour movement's alliance with the ruling party, which suggests that symbolic power depends on unions' ability to maintain their autonomy in the face of party loyalties.

Third cycle: mobilising contract workers, rebuilding union power

In the third cycle, 2001 to 2011, the union confronted the consequences of flexibilisation and the return of contract labour. As a result of the lost fight against iGoli 2002, the City of Johannesburg's waste removal company Pikitup was created as a utility in 2001. Pikitup is owned by the City of Johannesburg, but is run like a private company. Permanent and temporary municipal employees were absorbed into the new entity. Despite promises made to workers when Pikitup was created, as Samson describes, conditions rapidly deteriorated. Pikitup started reducing its workforce through 'natural attrition' by not replacing workers who left, were dismissed or died. On the one hand, Pikitup increased the workload and pressure on the remaining workforce to get the same amount of work done as before.[55] On the other hand, Pikitup also made increasing use of subcontractors and labour brokers over time in non-revenue areas, especially in the labour-intensive task of street cleaning.

Labour brokering and subcontracting involves a triangular employment relationship among client, third-party contractor and employee.[56] Pikitup as the client is on top of the triangular power relationship and in control of all terms of contracts with labour brokers or subcontractors, without having to bear the risks associated with being the employer. Contracts between Pikitup and subcontractors did not entail regulations about workers' rights, and Pikitup also did not ensure that companies abided by labour laws. Consequently, many third-party contractors would deny basic workers' rights.[57] Workers from third-party contractors and labour brokers were performing the same work as general workers in Pikitup, but earning about half of what Pikitup workers were earning. In addition, third-party contractors were paying, at best, contributions to the Unemployment Insurance Fund (UIF), but denying their workers all other benefits, such as medical aid or the pension fund.

Ten years after its creation, permanent employees in Pikitup found themselves to be in the minority in the workplace. By 2011 externalisation had increased to such an extent that about 60 percent of the workforce was externalised, with the majority of workers provided by labour brokers. The increase of contract work in Pikitup diminished SAMWU's structural power as well as its associational power.

In 2011 SAMWU embarked on a campaign to turn this situation around and to make all casual workers permanently employed by Pikitup. SAMWU intensified organising efforts among outsourced workers, thereby strengthening its associational power. Solidarity of permanent and contract workers was key to ensuring that any strike in Pikitup had an effect on the employer, and therefore that the union would be able to exercise its structural power.

Therefore, shop stewards at Pikitup started recruiting externalised workers for the union, making use of the joint workplace at depots and in the streets. SAMWUs strategy aimed at building a relationship between the union and externalised workers on the one hand, and between workers from Pikitup and third-party contractors on the other. These relationships were created through general meetings at the workplace that included all employees working directly or indirectly for Pikitup. In addition, SAMWU also tried to sustain the relationship that it had built

146   *Carmen Ludwig and Edward Webster*

with organised workers of third-party contractors by maintaining their employment. When a contract between Pikitup and a service provider expired, and a new company received the tender, SAMWU applied pressure to ensure that the new contractor provided trucks and tools, and absorbed the employees that were employed by the previous contractor. SAMWU managed to reach a recognition agreement with some third-party contractors, where it established shop steward structures that worked closely together with shop stewards in Pikitup.

When negotiations between SAMWU and Pikitup deadlocked in the Local Labour Forum, workers embarked on a one-week go-slow on 1 April, and a two-week protected strike on 7 April 2011. Pikitup management tried to interdict the strike through the Labour Court, but was not successful. SAMWU's key demand was for Pikitup to take over all externalised workers on a permanent basis and to end corruption at Pikitup.[58] A broad majority of the workforce of Pikitup, which consisted in 2011 of about 2,800 employees, participated in the strike as did employees of third-party contractors.[59] An innovative feature of the Pikitup strike was that temporary and permanent workers went out on strike together.

The result of the strike was that no refuse collection took place in the City of Johannesburg, which put its management as well as the City of Johannesburg under significant pressure. Strikers closed down depots and halted waste collection with the effect that:

> Johannesburg was stinking in such a way that it was difficult even for us who are staying in town to walk around. That also puts pressure on the City Council to say 'Resolve this labour dispute because we want to walk in a clean city as we used to do.'[60]

During the strike, Pikitup workers increased the impact of the strike by trashing the streets. 'Trashing' served a number of different purposes. For workers in solid waste it was seen as a means to 'undo the work we do', and therefore make the work they usually perform visible. It was therefore also a means to turn the street, as the workplace, into a public site of contestation, thereby exercising logistical power. It also demonstrated workers' determination and militancy in the conflict with the employer. At the same time, trashing significantly increased the impact of the strike and therefore, enhanced workers' structural power. Images of trashed streets demonstrate that waste on the streets blocks or hampers the flow of traffic and the movement of pedestrians:

> Because if we were just marching after that the next person that comes can't see anything, he won't recognize that there was something which was taking place. [. . .] If it's clean there is no need for them [the employer] to say that this strike should come to an end but if it's not clean they will see the need of those people, that these people are important. Let us listen to them so then they must go and do their job.[61]

However, it was SAMWU's ability to exert symbolic power by gaining public recognition which shifted the balance of power in favour of workers. Through its strong anti-corruption frame, the union was also able to harmonise symbolic and logistical power. Although the media picked up on the issue of street trashing, in contrast to previous SAMWU strikes it did not receive significant attention. Instead, the media focused on the issue of corruption. As a result, SAMWU's preferred framing and definition of the situation prevailed in the media coverage. Shop stewards also shared the impression that communities were sympathetic and in support of the workers strike because the union was 'blowing the whistle' on how the process of issuing tenders had fostered corruption at Pikitup. In entities such as Pikitup, where the public is intensely affected by a strike, influencing public opinion plays an important role. Although the Pikitup board initially denied that there was a problem with tenders and corruption, the managing director and all but one member of the board resigned.[62] The exposure of corruption added to the existing pressure on Pikitup and gave public legitimacy to the SAMWU strike. In addition, the approaching local government election a few weeks after the strike, in May 2011, provided a political opportunity for applying pressure and gaining concessions from the City Council. That way, the union also held the City Council as the sole shareholder responsible for its entity Pikitup.

SAMWU also received active support from COSATU who saw the struggle at Pikitup as a chance to enhance its campaign on the ban of labour broking.

The outcome of the strike was a victory for SAMWU as the parties agreed to absorb contract workers involved in the core cleaning service.[63] Pikitup also agreed not to enter into new outsourced core cleaning services without embarking on a meaningful joint consensus-seeking process with SAMWU, and to a forensic investigation into the allegations of corruption. The company hired auditors to investigate 11 of its contracts, worth nearly R366 million. The auditors' draft report found irregularities in all but one of them.[64] As a result of the strike, Pikitup's workforce was increased to about 4,600 employees.[65] Although Pikitup started implementing the bargaining agreement and absorbing externalised workers in 2011, the process stalled in 2012 and about 500 former contract workers are still fighting to be absorbed by Pikitup.[66]

Conclusion

Reflecting on the changing face of municipal work it is clear that it has moved in a circle: from the fight against contract work, which led to a new participatory labour relations regime, and then back to the rise of contract work through privatisation. In the 1980s trade unions increasingly challenged the pass system, gradually eroding its base and culminating in its abolition in 1986. In the 1990s a new workplace regime was institutionalised, which introduced labour laws in favour of unions and the promise of a new participatory labour relations regime.[67] However, this did not last long because of a shift of power in favour of employers as South Africa moved from a three-tier cheap labour market regulated through a *racial state* to a multi-tier labour market regulated through the *market*. In essence, race was declining in significance and class was becoming more salient. Municipal workers in the core gained through the new labour dispensation, but the policy shift in government towards neo-liberalism undermined these institutional gains.

148   *Carmen Ludwig and Edward Webster*

Munck, analysing the making and re-making of the working class on a global scale, argues that neither the Marxian nor the Polanyian approach on its own is sufficient but that it is their close interplay and interweaving that goes a long way to unravelling the contemporary processes affecting labour.[68] The changing power dynamics in the three cycles shows that exploitation and commodification become increasingly interrelated. In the first phase the strike in Johannesburg in 1980 can be understood as a Marxian struggle, directed against exploitation in production with the precarious nature of the migrant worker status deepening workers' exploitation. Structural power was the most relevant power resource to contest the exploitation inherent in the apartheid workplace regime.

In the second cycle, municipal workers' resistance against privatisation and iGoli 2002 was framed as a struggle for social rights and SAMWU mobilised symbolic power in order to challenge the shift to privatisation. Although struggles in production remained relevant, commodification became the most salient experience that, at least temporarily, created a link between workers and social movements. A comparison of the first two cycles indicates that Marxian struggles revolve around structural power, whereas in Polanyian struggles the mobilisation of symbolic power becomes particularly relevant. Commodification, as the case study indicates, can hardly be fought at the workplace alone but depends on its extension into the broader society.

In the third cycle, exploitation is deepened by the precarious nature of contract work. At the same time, municipal workers began to connect the sphere of exploitation (the workplace) with the sphere of commodification (privatisation). SAMWU found itself in a significantly weakened position as its structural and associational power came under pressure as a result of privatisation. In the Pikitup strike of 2011 SAMWU followed a strategy of inclusive solidarity in the workplace by organising and uniting a fragmented workforce. The union was able to re-build its associational power by drawing in and uniting a heterogeneous workforce. During the strike, workers increased their leverage through the use of logistical power. Besides the struggle against exploitation at the workplace level, SAMWU gained public support through framing its strike as a struggle against corruption. iGoli had been framed by the Council as an increase in public efficiency. In the Pikitup strike SAMWU mobilised symbolic power by exposing privatisation and 'tenderisation' as a source of corruption, self-enrichment and exploitation, thereby highlighting the importance of public control. Although in the third cycle, the experience of exploitation was initially the most salient for workers, SAMWU was able to transcend this experience into a broader discourse on the necessity of accountability and public control.

The case study of Johannesburg's municipal workers demonstrates that unions can develop innovative strategies and mobilise new sources of power, such as logistical and symbolic power, in the face of workplace restructuring and the privatisation of public services. However, unless these innovations are consolidated, they are hardly sustainable. One obstacle to sustaining associational and symbolic power has been the alliance with the ruling party, as our analysis of the iGoli 2002 process has indicated. Conflicts on how to relate to the ruling party and on how to build the organisation have significantly increased in the labour movement recently. The situation came to a head at a Special Congress in December 2013 when NUMSA, the largest affiliate in COSATU, decided not to give electoral support to the ANC in the forthcoming general election. These differences on how to relate to the ruling party led to the expulsion of NUMSA from COSATU, and attempts to form a rival trade union federation. NUMSA's initiative triggered a debate in the labour movement on how rank-and-file dynamism could be revived, and how unity could be built across the formal/informal divide and across political lines.

In SAMWU, internal differences led to the fragmentation of the union. SAMWU has been weakened by serious allegations of corruption and a decline in internal democracy. Since 2014, union officials and shop stewards, who were demanding financial accountability from the leadership, have been suspended or expelled from the union, including many from Pikitup and the Johannesburg region. Although for now, SAMWU remains the dominant union in the sector, the union is increasingly challenged by two break-away unions, the Democratic Municipal and Allied Workers Union of South Africa (DEMAWUSA) and the Municipal and Allied Trade Union of South Africa (MATUSA), which were formed in 2015 by former SAMWU leaders. The new unions aim at reviving the notion of worker control, and support NUMSA's decision of breaking with the alliance and of forming links with social and community-based movements instead. The development of SAMWU over time illustrates the dilemma that labour is facing: Does it focus on defending its narrow interests through a strategy of exclusive solidarity or does it pursue its interests in ways that include those of other constituencies and movements from below – the union as sword of justice? The recent developments demonstrate that the goals of the labour movement and the form in which union power is built is an open and contested process, whose outcome also depends on trade union's strategic choices.

Notes

1 We thank Marcel Paret and the anonymous reviewer for the very useful comments on earlier drafts.
2 Franco Barchiesi, 'Privatization and the Historical Trajectory of "Social Movement Unionism": A Case Study of Municipal Workers in Johannesburg, South Africa,' *International Labor and Working Class History* 71 (2007): 50–69.
3 Jonathan Hyslop, *The Notorious Syndicalist: J.T. Bain: A Scottish Rebel in Colonial South Africa* (Johannesburg: Jacana Media, 2004), 280, 286.
4 Luli Callinicos, *Working Life 1886–1940: Factories, Townships and Popular Culture on the Rand. Vol. 2* (Braamfontein: Ravan Press, 1987), 89.
5 Ronaldo Munck, 'The Precariat: A View from the South,' *Third World Quarterly* 34 (2013), 754–6.
6 Karl Polanyi, *The Great Transformation: The Political and Economic Origins of Our time* (Boston: Beacon Press, 2001), 3–4.
7 Karl Marx, *Capital: A Critique of Political Economy, Volume 1* (London: Penguin Books, 1976).
8 Michael Burawoy, 'From Polanyi to Pollyanna: The False Optimism of Global Labor Studies,' *Global Labour Journal* 1 (2010): 301.

150   *Carmen Ludwig and Edward Webster*

9 Beverly Silver, *Forces of Labor: Workers' Movements and Globalization since 1870* (Cambridge: Cambridge University Press, 2003), 20, 182.

10 Beverly Silver, *Forces of Labor*, 18; Edward Webster, Robert Lambert, and Andries Bezuidenhout, *Grounding Globalization: Labour in the Age of Insecurity* (Oxford, Cambridge: Blackwell, 2008), 11–13.

11 Erik O. Wright, 'Working-Class Power, Capitalist-Class Interests, and Class Compromise,' *American Journal of Sociology* 4 (2008).

12 Silver, *Forces of Labor*, 13.

13 For instance, Goodwin and Hetland as well as Barker et al. have criticised social movement studies for detaching mobilisation processes from the economic structure of a capitalist society. Colin Barker, Laurence Cox, John Krinsky, and Alf Gunvald Nilsen, 'Marxism and Social Movements: An Introduction,' in *Marxism and Social Movements*, ed. Colin Barker, Laurence Cox, John Krinsky, and Alf Gunvald Nilsen (Leiden: Brill, 2013); Gabriel Hetland and Jeff Goodwin, 'The Strange Disappearance of Capitalism from Social Movement Studies,' in *Marxism and Social Movements*, ed. Colin Barker, Laurence Cox, John Krinsky, and Alf Gunvald Nilsen (Leiden: Brill, 2013).

14 Christian Lévesque and Gregor Murray, 'Understanding Union Power: Resources and Capabilities for Renewing Union Capacity,' *Transfer: European Review of Labour and Research* 16 (2010): 340.

15 Bob Edwards and John D. McCarthy, 'Resources and Social Movement Mobilization,' in *The Blackwell Companion to Social Movements*, ed. David A. Snow, Sarah A. Soule, and Hanspeter Kriesi (Malden, MA/Oxford/Victoria: Blackwell, 2004), 125–8.

16 Klaus Dörre, Hajo Hajo, and Oliver Nachtwey, 'Organizing – A Strategic Option for Trade Union Renewal?' *International Journal of Action Research* 5 (2009).

17 Donna McGuire, *Re-Framing Trade Union Mobilisation against the General Agreement on Trade in Services (GATS)* (München: Rainer Hampp Verlag, 2013), 97.

18 Doug McAdam, 'Political Opportunities: Conceptual Origins, Current Problems, Future Directions,' in *Comparative Perspectives on Social Movements*, ed. Doug McAdam, John D. McCarthy, and Mayer N. Zald (Cambridge: Cambridge University Press, 1996), 27.

19 Silver, *Forces of Labor*, 172.

20 Webster et al., *Grounding Globalization*, 13.

21 Jesse Wilderman, *Farm Worker Uprising in the Western Cape. A Case Study of Protest, Organising, and Collective Action* (Johannesburg: Wits University, 2014).

22 Jennifer J. Chun, *Organizing at the Margins. The Symbolic Politics of Labor in South Korea and the United States* (Ithaca, NY and London: Cornell University Press, 2009). In the Jena approach it is referred to as 'societal power' which includes two subtypes, discursive and cooperative power, with the first referring to unions' ability to influence public perceptions and the second to coalition-building with social movements. Arbeitskreis Strategic Unionism, 'Jenaer Machtressourcenansatz 2.0,' in *Comeback der Gewerkschaften. Machtressourcen, innovative Praktiken, internationale Perspektiven*, ed. Stefan Schmalz and Klaus Dörre (Frankfurt/New York: Campus, 2013).

23 Chun, *Organizing at the Margins*, 18.

24 Christian Lévesque and Gregor Murray, 'Renewing Union Narrative Resources: How Union Capabilities Make a Difference,' *British Journal of Industrial Relations* 51 (2013): 779.

25 Robert D. Benford and David E. Snow, 'Framing Processes and Social Movements: An Overview and Assessment,' *Annual Review of Sociology* 26 (2000): 615–21.

26 Jeremy Keenan, 'Migrants Awake – The 1980 Johannesburg Municipality Strike,' *South African Labour Bulletin* 6 (1981): 4.

27 Ibid., 10.

28 Labour Research Committee, 'State Strategy and the Johannesburg Municipal Workers Strike,' *South African Labour Bulletin* 6 (1981): 68.

29 Keenan, 'Migrants Awake,' 7–10.

Power and municipal worker resistance 151

30 Franco Barchiesi, *Precarious Liberation: Workers, the State, and Contested Social Citizenship in Postapartheid South Africa* (Scottsville: UKZN-Press, 2011), 152.
31 Sakhela Buhlungu, *A Paradox of Victory: COSATU and the Democratic Transformation in South Africa* (Scottsville: UKZN-Press, 2010), 164.
32 Webster et al., *Grounding Globalization*, 165–7.
33 Sandra van Niekerk and Ronnie Roger, 'The SAMWU Experience,' in *New Forms of Organisation* (Cape Town: ILRIG, 2009), 31.
34 Klaus Dörre, 'Social Classes in the Process of Capitalist Landnahme: On the Relevance of Secondary Exploitation,' *Socialist Studies* 6 (2010).
35 Khetso Gordhan, *Moving towards a Restructured Jo'burg*, January 4, 2000.
36 Greater Johannesburg Metropolitan Council, *iGoli 2002: Making the City Work – It Cannot Be Business as Usual* (Johannesburg, 1999).
37 Ibid., 6.
38 Hilary Wainwright, 'Transformative Resistance: The Role of Labour and Trade Unions in Alternatives to Privatisation,' in *Alternatives to Privatisation: Public Options for Essential Services in the Global South*, ed. David A. McDonald and Greg Ruiters (Cape Town: HSRC, 2012), 78.
39 SAMWU, Pamphlet, April 6, 1999.
40 Quoted in Jo Beall, Owen Crankshaw, and Susan Parnell, *Uniting a Divided City: Governance and Social Exclusion in Johannesburg* (London: Earthscan Publications, 2002), 103.
41 David Christoffer Lier and Kristian Stokke, 'Maximum Working Class Unity? Challenges to Local Social Movement Unionism in Cape Town,' *Antipode* 38 (2006).
42 Interview, SAMWU national official, Cape Town, November 9, 2012. Furthermore, the unwillingness of COSATU to seriously challenge its alliance partner on the issue of privatisation further negatively affected SAMWU's campaign and led to political opportunities, such as the local government election in 2000, not being explored.
43 Interview, SAMWU national official, Cape Town, November 9, 2012.
44 Trevor Ngwane, 'Labour Strikes and Community Protests: Is There a Basis for Unity in Post-Apartheid South Africa?' in *Contesting Transformation: Popular Resistance in Twenty-First Century South Africa*, ed. Marcelle C. Dawson and Luke Sinwell (London: Pluto Press, 2012), 130.
45 Interview, former SAMWU national office bearer, August 8, 2012 (together with Hilary Wainwright).
46 Alan Flanders, *Management and Unions* (London: Faber, 1970), 15.
47 SAMWU, discussion document, December 9, 1999.
48 Interview, SAMWU national official, Cape Town, November 9, 2012.
49 Maria van Driel, 'Unions and Privatisation in South Africa, 1990–2001,' in *Rethinking the Labour Movement in the 'New' South Africa*, ed. Tom Bramble and Franco Barchiesi (Aldershot/Burlington: Ashgate, 2003), 75.
50 Mojalefa M. Musi, *Evaluating IMATU and SAMWU Policy Responses to iGoli 2002* (MA Thesis, University of the Witwatersrand Johannesburg, 2010), 89.
51 At the same time, the Johannesburg Council did not agree to a moratorium to put the implementation of iGoli 2002 on hold for the period of negotiations, which further put SAMWU at a disadvantage.
52 Barchiesi, *Precarious Liberation*, 158.
53 Sidney G. Tarrow, *Power in Movement: Social Movements and Contentious Politics* (Cambridge: Cambridge University Press, 2011), 12.
54 Dale T. McKinley, *Labour and Community in Transition: Alliances for Public Services in South Africa* (Ottawa: Municipal Services Project, 2014), 14.
55 Melanie Samson, *Dumping on Women: Gender and Privatisation of Waste Management, 2003*, accessed June 29, 2015, http://www.gdrc.info/docs/waste/005.pdf, 68.
56 Jan Theron, 'Intermediary or Employer? Labour Brokers and the Triangular Employment Relationship,' *Industrial Law Journal* 26 (2005): 619.

152 *Carmen Ludwig and Edward Webster*

57 Samson, *Dumping on Women*, 64–5.
58 In addition, workers demanded a look at existing wage disparities in the department, thereby combining demands that benefited all employees. SAMWU, press statement, April 6, 2011.
59 Pikitup, *Annual Report 2010/11* (Johannesburg: Pikitup, 2011), 9.
60 Interview, SAMWU regional official, Johannesburg, October 1, 2012.
61 Interview, Pikitup shop steward, Johannesburg, February 24, 2014.
62 Pikitup, *Annual Report 2010/11*.
63 To avoid that, Pikitup would have to breach its contracts with subcontractors; externalised workers were absorbed into Pikitup when their contracts expired. A concession SAMWU made was that the salary of absorbed externalised workers in June 2011 who started at R3000 per month be increased by July 2012 to the minimum wage of R4900.
64 Pikitup admitted that the forensic probe of 2011 revealed misuse and irregularities of tender issuing by several high-ranking officials. However, the full report has still not been released. In August 2013, a joint investigation by the *Sunday Times* and the organisation Corruption Watch found that Pikitup had commissioned a R6-million investigation into corruption but halted the probe in October 2012 before the auditing firm Ernst & Young could finalise the report. The Right2Know campaign highlighted the Pikitup workers' struggle against corruption in their whistleblowers calendar 2014. On the forensic probe: Pikitup, 'Pikitup Forensic Investigation,' press statement, October 26, 2012. On the investigation: (Times Live 7.8.2013). On the Right2Know whistleblowers calendar, http://www.r2k.org.za/2014/01/01/samwu/.
65 Pikitup, *Annual Report 2011/12*, 10.
66 At the time of writing, SAMWU has taken the matter to the Labour Court.
67 Edward Webster, 'The Promise and the Possibility: South Africa's Contested Industrial Relations Path,' *Transformation: Critical Perspectives on Southern Africa* (2013): 81–2.
68 Munck, 'The Precariat,' 757.

10 Organic intellectuals and leadership in South Africa's contemporary mineworkers' movement

Luke Sinwell

Born in 1979 in a village in Kwa-Zulu Natal, one of South Africa's nine provinces, Solomon was to become an indispensable leader in the contemporary mineworkers' movement in the country.[1] Considering the extent to which the events surrounding the massacre at Marikana shook the nation, and in particular the nature of left-wing forces outside of the African National Congress (ANC)'s alliance, including the Economic Freedom Fighters (EFF) and the National Union of Mineworkers of South Africa (NUMSA) (see Paret, Chapter 1 and Nieftagodien, Chapter 11), Solomon could be considered one of the most important activists involved in 'contentious politics'[2] since the advent of democracy in South Africa in 1994. Unlike the iconic 'Man in the Green Blanket', as Mgcineni 'Mambush' Noki would come to be known given his position as spokesperson of the workers before the massacre at Lonmin in Markana, Solomon survived to tell his story following the 2012 unprotected strikes.

Solomon later became a foremost shop steward of the Association of Mineworkers and Construction Union (AMCU) in 2013. He was at the forefront of the 2014 protected strike by AMCU members at three platinum mines – Amplats, Impala, and Lonmin – in what became the longest strike in South African mining history. The 2014 strike was especially significant because it carried forward the demand for a living wage of R12,500 per month, which initially emerged in the context of the 2012 strike at Lonmin platinum mine. Neither Noki, nor Joseph Mathunjwa (founder, president and spokesperson of AMCU), were present when Solomon, a seemingly ordinary worker with no leadership position within any union, was in his Reconstruction and Development Programme (RDP) rental house in Siraleng, Rustenburg, conceptualising an even more substantial demand: a monthly wage of R16,070, which was more than 100 percent of the existing salaries for most workers.

This chapter employs a social-biographical approach to understand the events under investigation. The strength of this approach, according to Brigitta Busch, 'lies in the change of perspective from the observed object to the perceiving and experiencing subject'.[3] Rather than bend a singular argument in relation to an abstract generalisation, this chapter follows the ethnographic tradition exemplified by David Graeber, as it lays bare the mineworkers' 'cultural universe' in relation to the movement that they initiated and sustained.[4]

154   *Luke Sinwell*

Like any good ethnographer, I needed, alongside Siphiwe Mbatha who undertook research with me on this project at the time, to be patient and on many days we waited hours to speak, or simply to spend time, with people. Our intention was not only to collect archives, conduct in-depth interviews and then simply report our findings to an academic audience. We also spent as much time as possible with mineworkers in their own social settings: cooking together, eating, driving, having informal conversations, listening to speeches at mass meetings and, in the most trying of times, visiting leading mineworkers while they were in jail (on trumped-up charges of public violence). During a relatively short period in 2013, we lived with one of the key activists in the area in his spare room in Siraleng, a mining community just outside of Khuseleka, Amplats. This activist was a close political ally of Solomon.

Solomon epitomised the most radical and democratic practices of the independent workers' committees at any of the three mines. In this chapter I uncover the hidden forms of leadership and patterns of organisation of the committee. The chapter argues that individual organic intellectuals, through the workers' committees which they were central in forming and maintaining, fuelled the 2012 strike at Amplats and the 2014 strike which took place across the Rustenburg platinum belt. Before getting into the ethnographic detail, I present a section on hegemony, organic intellectuals, and leadership. The next section provides information for the reader to understand the context in which Solomon and other leaders at Amplats enacted their agency. Thereafter the sections provide much detail about the informal networks which were established in a relatively short period and by a small number of workers at the mine. Finally, the conclusion discusses the significance of individual leadership in the development of collective actions.

Hegemony, organic intellectuals, and leadership

Solomon played, I argue, a central role in framing the demands of the mineworkers. According to McAdam, McCarthy, and Zald, framing includes 'the conscious strategic efforts of groups of people to fashion shared understandings of the world and of themselves that legitimate and motivate collective action'.[5] While there was a general understanding amongst workers that they were being underpaid, they had not yet collectively identified a radical demand, nor had they identified coherent plans to unite in strike action. The demand of R16,070 would capture the imagination of virtually all the workers at the largest platinum mine in the world, Amplats, where Solomon would assume significant responsibility as a leader.

While the demands made were reformist (higher wages), the methods employed by the workers did – in the end – challenge the hegemony of capital and reshape the structural conditions of the employment relationship. According to Gramsci, a political group is hegemonic when it is ideologically dominant. This means that the direction of society that they envision goes largely unchallenged, and is considered to be 'legitimate' often even by those who have contradictory long-term interests. The rank and file maintains this hegemony by adopting the cultural beliefs of the hegemonic group, thereby giving their active 'consent'. The 'common sense'

Organic intellectuals and leadership   155

of labour relations, which is inscribed in the minds of rank-and-file workers, may therefore be the same as that which is envisioned by those in power – for example, management.[6]

For Gramsci, intellectuals play a critical role in both maintaining and, possibly also, contesting hegemony. He argues that 'all men are intellectuals, one could therefore say: but not all men have in society the function of intellectuals'.[7] While hegemony is maintained by traditional intellectuals, who seek to preserve the dominant social order in favour of their economic interests, counter-hegemony occurs when organic intellectuals, acting in the interests of the working class, challenge the hegemonic system of beliefs. These intellectuals provide an alternative value system on which to base the future development of society.

This chapter demonstrates that Solomon was a formidable working-class organic intellectual in the Gramscian sense, as he developed counter-hegemonic ideologies rooted within the material conditions and discourses of the working class. At the core of an organic intellectual's ability to be effective at achieving counter-hegemony, as well as unity amongst the working class, is arguably the notion of leadership. In part because of an attempt to avoid 'great man' theories of history, leadership has been a neglected area in the study of social movements.[8] Furthermore, Barker, Johnson, and Lavalette point out that:

> Few academics want to revive conservative 'agitator' theories which imply that there would be no strikes, no militant movement activity, were it not for the malign trouble-makers who cause them. We must, it is argued, pay proper attention to the real grievances motivating movements, just as we must avoid treating movement members as nothing but mindless sheep.[9]

Social movements and leadership are inextricably connected since leadership is required to conceptualise a common set of demands, unite sympathisers, and exert power. While a strike is not a social movement in itself, the workers' committees and the rank and file at Amplats and Lonmin constituted one since they engaged in 'contentious politics'[10] as part of a collective and sustained attempt to force authorities to concede to their demands.

Partially because of a failure to identify leaders, previous scholars have missed the potential for agents (on the inside or the outside) to shape social movement struggles in particular directions through leadership skills and qualities. The leader may act as 'both sculptor and marble'.[11] Johnson argues that 'democratic leadership is a *conversation*, spoken *within* the movement, sustained by leader and follower, concerning the *goals* both can agree to pursue, pragmatically, in light of their changing interpretations of circumstances and experience, and the *means* to achieve those goals against an adversary'.[12] Effective democratic leadership is significantly defined by one's ability to dialogue with those who one wishes to lead in a particular direction. Johnson correctly points out that 'a genuine leader is not a searcher of consensus, but a moulder of consensus'.[13] To a significant extent, as I suggest herein, the workers' committee leaders at Amplats reflected this in practice.

156 *Luke Sinwell*

Setting the context

In January 2012 Impala platinum mine witnessed the beginning of that year's major unprotected strike wave. Later that month, the unrest had spread beyond the confines of Rock Drill Operators (RDOs) and virtually the entire workforce had downed tools. They won an increase to R9,000 and the strike ended on 3 March. Discontent with the National Union of Mineworkers (NUM) had come to a head at Impala because the union had opposed the popular unprotected strike. By the end of the strike, management had fired 18,000 of the striking mineworkers, which would have ended their union membership. About 11,000 others had resigned as NUM members at Impala by 30 March 2012. Perceived shortcomings of the union at each of the three major platinum mining houses, especially its failure to defend workers subject to dismissal for engaging in unprotected strikes, provided the conditions on which informal workers' committees took hold, first at Impala and then at Amplats and Lonmin, respectively.

By 9 August, RDOs at Lonmin platinum mine had downed tools in demand of R12,500. After being attacked outside the offices of their own union, the NUM, workers armed themselves with dangerous traditional weapons such as spears and machetes and took refuge at the infamous mountain in Marikana, where they then waited for their employer to address them about their wage demand. On 16 August, 34 workers, including Noki, were gunned down by the police in what has become known as the Marikana massacre. The Lonmin strikers displayed their bravery by continuing their strike for a living wage after the massacre, which had the counter-intuitive effect of strengthening their resolve for a living wage.

As the Lonmin strike was coming to a close in September 2012, Amplats workers downed tools while demanding R16,070 in an unprotected strike that lasted longer than its predecessors (at Impala and Lonmin). While each of these respective strikes was driven by independent workers' committees, workers nevertheless had simultaneously begun the process of joining the upstart union – AMCU. Its spokesperson and president Joseph Mathunjwa had gained legitimacy, particularly at Lonmin in Marikana, because he went sympathetically to the workers on the mountain (where workers were waiting for their employer), whereas NUM representatives unequivocally opposed their action. While 2012 witnessed unprotected strike action on each of the three major platinum mines, 2013 saw a struggle over union recognition, with AMCU eventually becoming hegemonic in the region. By early 2014, AMCU workers at all three platinum mines were united in strike action, carrying forth the legacy of the 2012 strike wave but this time with one voice.

This story is relatively well known. Ethnographic research, however, reveals a more hidden story of the process through which Amplats workers began mobilising following the 2012 strike at Impala. Key to the process was the formation of independent workers' committees. When Solomon began approaching merely one worker at a time in April and May 2012, he could not have fully comprehended the way in which the vast majority of workers, regardless of union affiliation, would soon readily act in unison in a bid to end their suffering and counter their oppression. The failure of the National Union of Mineworkers (NUM) to represent the genuine interests of the workers, created the conditions in which workers' committees took hold. The NUM, once an engine for the liberation of the black oppressed, had now become, as many mineworkers indicated in a play on words, 'The National Union of Management'. Alternatively, the worker committees were underpinned by notions of direct democracy in their engagements with the rank and file.

The following section details the formation of the persuasive and democratic workers' committee at Khuseleka shaft at Amplats, which can be traced back to Solomon and an elder stalwart of the mines named Anele. What began at Khuseleka soon spread to every other operation at Amplats in the Rustenburg region. A larger committee was then elected to represent the entire mine before the strike. This committee decided to go on strike in September 2012, independent of any union, as a group of people who would make collective decisions through consensus and be directly accountable to all the workers. As the strike rolled into its fourth week, the company claimed that it would fire all the workers who were on the unprotected strike, and this prompted members of the workers' committee, instead of going back to work, to unite with other regions of Amplats mine (Northam).

As the strike ended, minor concessions were given to the workers and it was agreed with the employer that wage negotiations around the R16,070 would continue the following year. The workers decided that they should continue their struggle for a living wage under the auspices of a union. They chose AMCU and in 2013 Solomon and other workers' committee leaders then became key figures of this union, which continued to take the lead from the insurgent workers. The next section discusses the establishment of informal networks, specifically workers' committees, at Amplats mine. This is followed by a discussion of the transition to AMCU and the great strike of 2014 whereby the three largest platinum mines in the world united for a living wage of R12,500.

The formation of the workers' committee at Amplats mine

Anele, who would become a key figure in the formation of the workers' committee at Amplats, was an elder who had his teeth smashed out trying to bring the NUM to the mines in the mid-1980s. Anele had shifted around from mine to mine, and during the 2012 strike wave he was working at Amplats in Khuseleka shaft. But he was living in Freedom Park, a stronghold neighbourhood of Impala employees, and he was acutely aware of the new developments at that mine which witnessed the first set of unprotected strikes in the platinum belt. As he stated, 'I was so close with the comrades at Impala'.[14] The discussions taking place across the mines played a significant role in fuelling the resistance. When he went to work at Khuseleka, he told his fellow workers about what was happening at Impala.

One of those workers was Solomon. He and Anele would become an exceptional pair of organisers whose careful articulation and framing of worker grievances would go down in history. Whereas the workers' committee which initiated

158   *Luke Sinwell*

the Lonmin strike at Marikana was led by Rock Drill Operators (RDOs – they actually drill the rock underground), the main committee at Amplats, including Solomon and Anele, were Winch Drivers (those who haul the drilled rock out from underground). As indicated previously, Solomon was born in 1979 in a mountainous town called Ingwavuma in Kwa-Zulu Natal, which is 400 kilometres from Durban and just outside the border of Swaziland. His mother died in 1981 when he was two years old, and he went to a school called Qoshama where he finished his matric in 1999. At the time of writing, he has a wife, six children (four boys and two girls), and two brothers and a sister, most of whom he assists financially. His first job, from 2003 to 2009, was as a truck driver at Goldfields gold mine in Carletonville. However, the work resulted in debilitation. Solomon noted, 'My body wasn't allowing me to drive the trucks. At that time we were doing double clutch, you can even see my leg it has been hurt. I had pulled my muscle so I am wearing a knee cap.'[15]

Solomon arrived at Amplats in January 2010. He was never a member of a union until he and his fellow workers decided to join AMCU in 2012. When asked about how people began to identify him as a leader, he said they could see his strength at mass meetings. The fact that he did not drink or smoke also contributed to his positive reputation as a respected leader.[16]

At 56, Anele was 22 years older than Solomon, who listened carefully to what the wise elder was telling him about the events unfolding at Impala. Solomon then engaged with Anele around a more concrete programme of action because of his vast experience: 'He was the one that would have better information on Anglo and why we get small salaries. And why there are different salaries meanwhile we do the same jobs. Because you can get 7,000 and I get 5,000. So I approached an old man to get clarity on these divisions in terms of salaries.'[17] Reflecting on the relationship that they had, Solomon stated that 'he can't be my friend . . . about the issues that were happening in the mine, I took him as my father.'[18]

Solomon recalled that, 'the time we met, there was already an issue at Impala, a strike. So, we started realising that the reason why Impala has gone on strike, is because of these same kind of issues. That's how we started to engage each other.' They discussed issues: 'Like it seems as if the company is robbing us here and there. The [risk] allowance we won't get it when we are working at night shift, but it is the same as if you are working during the day . . . the area that you are working at, it's risky'.[19]

Workers were clearly disgruntled, and they were having conversations about the fact that strike action would soon come to Amplats. Anele and Solomon began to provide the impetus for mobilisation. They each began to hold meetings with other workers in their respective zones:

> What we have done is that each and every day when we go underground we had meetings. So in our workplace we started explaining to our crews, we were working with different crews me and [Anele]. I was working the other section, so I had a meeting with people I'm working with, trying to address this issue from Impala about how things should go [here at Amplats]. And

Organic intellectuals and leadership   159

then before we go underground now [for meetings], after we realise we have more than twenty people, we had a meeting on the surface so other people can come. We addressed these issues and [then] we would go check the development until June [came].[20]

Anele and Solomon decided that to expand their organising efforts, they needed to draft a memorandum. It included a basic salary of R10,000, slightly more than that which was demanded at Impala. When they included a range of allowances including for safety, food, transport, and a basic salary of R10,000 the total came to R16,070. The two workers met together in an attempt to frame the grievances of the workers under one common demand: 'We draft this sitting in the changing room . . . when we went to the mass of plus minus fifty people to a hundred, we were on the surface now.' It was concluded that, 'it was simpler because everyone understood it . . . they adopted it and said it is good, it makes sense when we demand safety allowance, bonuses, basic, and I think it's six or seven demands to make it 16,070.' While they were having meetings outside the Jabula hostel, other more established organisations – in particular the NUM – were gathering inside. Solomon remembered being told that in those meetings workers were advised, 'don't stress about these meetings outside the hostels. It doesn't make any sense.'[21] Sipho explained that they met outside the hostel 'so that everybody who is interested can come'.[22]

At one shaft in particular, Khuseleka, the process of organising was beginning to gain traction. The ad hoc group of organisers tried to approach NUM several times, but to no avail. As one of the strike leaders later stated, 'We can look out for our own interests. Even AMCU is not part of this action because we do not need unions to represent us.'[23] 'As we go forward', according to Sipho, who was one of the earliest winch operators involved in the mobilisations:

Our group became large about 30, 40, 50. And as everyone was seeing that we are serious, uh, it was around July . . . where we decided that we are not talking unions here. We are talking salary adjustment. So each and every employee that feels that we are getting a little, let's come together. . . . So we went on the 12th of July to submit the memorandum of 16,070 rand . . . the whole of Khuseleka mine, known as Jabula, was there to support us. And that's where we were chosen by the workers [they said], 'Since you are in the front line, you might as well lead us for the meanwhile.' Because it might happen that if the management refuse then we choose to go on strike. And if we go on strike, when we come back we need to have new leaders because the current leaders [in NUM], they [are] failing us.[24]

Solomon and Anele met with management on at least three occasions between June and July. Solomon described a situation whereby, 'the company nominate[d] me and [Anele]. . . . I was [also] leading them [workers] on the other end.' He concluded that he was essentially a 'middleman' between the workers and company. The company took the contact details of the two workers and told them, 'as

160   *Luke Sinwell*

from today, if there are any grievances from the workers . . . we know you, we will negotiate with you.'[25] Solomon kept a diary of their meetings, explaining that, 'we were following all these processes in order that if the company wants to fire us, we show them [the records] that we have followed the proper procedures'.[26] The numbers attending the mass meetings outside Jabula hostel swelled and virtually all the workers at the shaft were now committed to the common memorandum which the two organisers had themselves constructed.

The few informal leaders had thought that it was time to go on strike some-time in August, but, 'the workers stop us and say don't. [They said] "let's follow the procedures"'.[27] Neither the unions nor the management would respond to the workers' grievances, so they decided to take the case to the Commission for Conciliation, Mediation and Arbitration (CCMA):

> On the 25th August it was the first submission of the case, which we want to go on strike. Around 1 September, we went to CCMA to get feedback and they told us that, 'no, we can't sit now, we will sit on the 25th September'. And then we came back as leadership and said, 'no, let's have a mass meeting and tell the people what the CCMA had said', and have a one-day agreement on when we will strike. So when we come from the CCMA it seems like a conniving company [to the workers since the company is delaying]. So we agree that from the 8th to the 11th we go on strike, all of us. During these three days we use to drive all the operations of Anglo trying to make sure that the strike starts on the same day.[28]

The delay of the CCMA led workers to conclude that they needed to undertake strike action if their demands were to be addressed.

The 2012 Amplats unprotected strike

As the Lonmin strike was coming to a close, workers at the largest platinum mine in the world began downing tools. What appeared as a major victory at Lonmin (a 22 percent wage increase) prompted other employees in various workplaces over the next two months to engage in unprotected strike action, including in the gold, diamond, and coal industries and eventually in the automobile, trucking, and public sectors. While organisation had already been under way for a good while under the leadership of Anele and Solomon, the massacre nevertheless provided significant impetus for the unfolding events at Amplats. The uprising, however, was not spontaneous. Someone needed to 'blow the whistle' and initiate a plan of action which could unite the workplace in collective action. What began at Khuseleka spread widely through existing informal networks to the other shafts at the Rustenburg mine: Siphumelele, Bathopele, Thembelani, Khomonani. Each of these respective shafts had issues regarding salaries and existing unions which were bubbling beneath the surface. Several leaders from Khuseleka, including Anele and Solomon, made it their central task to unite with the other shafts around the wage demand of R16,070. Indeed, they would not only successfully do this,

Organic intellectuals and leadership 161

but they would also later extend strike action further up the platinum belt, from Rustenburg (North West province) where they were based, to Northam (Limpopo province) where workers had not yet downed tools.

As at Lonmin, Amplats workers were strengthened not only by the inadequacy of the NUM, but also by other existing formal channels which failed to address their concerns. Unlike the Lonmin strike, which was a response to management feedback, at Amplats the dilatory response of the CCMA enabled them to successfully unite the entire workforce.[29] In addition, according to Lazarus Khoza, who was an important leader in Khuseleka, the Marikana massacre resulted in the general conclusion that, 'no, enough is enough, we have seen our brothers have been killed and the thing is they are fighting for a decent wage . . . we were inspired by the workers at Lonmin and we said like, "we would also like to join the struggle of the miners"'.[30] He further maintained that the massacre, 'made them brave yes . . . nothing made them to become angrier'. In addition he thought that because Lonmin is a comparatively small company, workers should be demanding more at Amplats.[31]

Sipho recalls that the leaders at Khuseleka told the other shafts that, 'we can't make it alone. Let's rather go to other operations at Anglo . . . to give the memorandum to them'.[32] At first it was difficult for other workers to join as they were afraid of being retrenched, but within the next few days, they were able to identify leaders in various shafts that bought into their programme. Solomon explains: '. . . we move[d] with them group by group to the shafts. . . . We make it simple that you here in other shafts [besides Khuseleka] will have to elect leaders here that will lead you. Because we cannot afford to come and hold the meeting here and go back to Jabula [the hostel near Khuseleka] on a daily basis'.[33]

A mass meeting for 'all employees' was then held at 1pm on 8 September 2012 at Jabula Playgrounds. A pamphlet was created calling workers to 'please join us in matters that affect us all concerning salary improvement.' The purpose of the meeting was to discuss 'feedback from the CCMA', and it was further noted, in a democratic fashion, that 'your views and imputs [sic] are valuable and very much appreciated.'[34] Workers held another mass meeting on 11 September, and it was decided that no one was to go underground. By 12 September the strike was in full swing.

By the end of September the strike had grown to 80 percent of the workforce. Moreover, as *The Citizen* reported, nearly 100,000 unprotected and protected employees were on strike nationwide.[35] The bosses at Amplats turned to intimidation. The CEO of Amplats issued an ultimatum, stating that if workers did not go back to work, the company would be forced to dismiss about 21,000 workers.[36] By 5 October the threat became a reality when Amplats announced that it would dismiss 12,000 workers who did not attend the hearings to which the company called them.[37] These threats ironically empowered the strikers:

> He [CEO Chris Griffiths] gave an announcement that 12,000 people are dismissed for going on an unprotected strike . . . those words gave us courage and we became very strong . . . we are going forward because we are already

162   *Luke Sinwell*

fired, so there is nothing [else] that we can do. We will stay on strike until they give us our money.[38]

Solomon corroborated, 'that made us move to Limpopo [Northam platinum mine] because we saw that we are already fired. . . . So those announcements and SMS's [sent by the company] that say that we are fired are the ones that made our strike to be solid.' He also indicated that the workers had concluded that, 'we don't want to go back to work until our demands are met'. They had witnessed the fact that, 'Impala went on strike and they came back with something,' and thus asked themselves, 'how come we can go to work empty-handed'?[39]

There was no time to lose. Solomon concluded that the strike was at a critical turning point and that solidarity from other mines was needed. He explained that, 'I moved fast to Limpopo [Northam] in Amandelbult section.'[40] He went together with Thebe, the key leader at Thembelani shaft at that time, in his car for the hour-long drive. This visit was successful, as they found the workers already having their own meeting:

we went on the ground and we talk to them. We told them that, 'at Rustenburg [section] we are engaging with the company. We are having this kind of problem, but you are not on strike, you are working. We want [you] to get the reality that if the company puts the money for us, it mustn't put money for you. Because you are not on strike.' So everyone needed money, so they understood that they must join the strike.[41]

Thebe and Solomon in effect shaped consensus when they requested that the workers at Northam select leaders of their shafts to represent them. By the beginning of the second week of October, both Amandelbult and Swartklip shafts were on strike for a living wage.[42]

By early November, hunger had set in amongst the mineworkers and their families and the strike was finally coming to an end. The strike was not as powerful as it had been previously; some workers were dropping out and others were getting tired. On 18 November the strike ended. According to Solomon, the workers' committee was also told that the negotiations for salaries would begin in January 2013, and that they then reported this to the workers, who decided to take an R400 salary adjustment.[43] The R400 increase was seen as a victory by the workers, though it was a drop in the ocean compared with the R16,070 which they were demanding. (The increase would have needed to be about R10,000 to meet R16,070!) One leader of the committee explained the logic behind the perception that this increase was a victory: 'The workers' committee came with R400 in two months and then NUM comes with R400 in twelve months.'[44] Moreover, no workers were fired. The collective mobilisation, which was initiated by two individuals, not only spread to the entire Amplats Rustenburg region and beyond, but it also soon linked up to the two other platinum giants, Impala and Lonmin, in 2014. While the strike of 2012 occurred under the auspices of non-union workers' committees, the 2014 strike took place under the union AMCU.

The 2014 AMCU protected strike

Solomon took centre stage throughout the 2014 strike in an attempt to assess the ongoing commitment amongst the rank and file. The power of the strike, from his perspective, was dependent entirely upon the reliance and dedication of the workers of AMCU. He took this a step further, as we shall see, in his attempt to further unite the working class more broadly by involving another major union. On 19 January 2014 a mass meeting of a few thousand workers from Amplats, Lonmin, and Impala was held by AMCU. The mood signalled that action was imminent, but none were entirely aware of the uncompromising spirit that would fuel the workers for the next five months.

Solomon addressed the large crowd encompassing the stadium. Other speakers had introduced themselves, but when it was Solomon's turn to speak, he told the crowd that, 'if you do not know me by now, then you are a spy.'[45] Indeed, few rank-and-file mineworkers, and even fewer AMCU shop stewards in the platinum belt (covering the area from Rustenburg to Northam), did not know this young man who had been at the forefront of the struggle since mid-2012.

For this key organiser, a concern had emerged about AMCU's relationship to the broader working class. Solomon had invited the National Union of Metalworkers of South Africa (NUMSA), which had broken its direct ties to the ANC the previous month, to speak at the rally:

> Before I invite NUMSA to the rally, I write an email to the head office [of AMCU], to the GS [General Secretary] and to the administrator there to notify them that NUMSA is coming to our meeting to support so that we can start a strike together in solidarity with us. One of these two said, 'I don't see any harm with them coming' so I continued with the invitation of NUMSA. They [then] come to the mass meeting of AMCU.[46]

Directly after the rally ended, as workers were leaving the stadium in preparation for strike action, I managed to speak to Solomon. He lamented that the president of NUMSA, Andrew Chirwa, was prevented from speaking. Whereas AMCU President Mathunjwa wanted AMCU to stand on its own, Solomon's previous organising experiences had taught him that their strength lay in their power to unite with one another. He put it simply when he told me, 'When workers come to support other workers, they must be given a chance to speak.'[47] Mathunjwa's practices reflected a belief that while mineworkers should join and be united within AMCU in order to fight the bosses, AMCU should not unite with any other political organisation or union. Linking to NUMSA at this stage could have further politicised the strike and AMCU more generally, enhancing the already tense relationship to the state and the ANC.

By early March, the strike was in full-swing. On 6 March, thousands of AMCU workers marched to the union buildings in Pretoria to highlight their demands. Two days earlier, they had conceded that the demand for R12,500 could be met over four years (instead of having immediate effect), but the platinum producers

164   *Luke Sinwell*

claimed that even this deal was unaffordable. One marcher from Lonmin seemed to capture the essence of the spirit of the mineworkers when he stated that, 'Our fellow workers died for a living wage. I cannot betray them. . . . Our journey for a living wage is strong[er] than before. . . . I am prepared to go on strike for future mineworkers to earn a decent wage.'[48]

As the strike became more and more prolonged, the ANC-led government – concerned about foreign investment and the price of the Rand – intervened swiftly. At the Congress of South African Trade Unions (COSATU) Workers' Day rally held in Polokwane, President Jacob Zuma reportedly 'urged unions [particularly AMCU] to "act in good faith" and avoid resorting to "blackmail as a negotiating tool"'.[49] President Zuma and his coterie were correct to be concerned, given their interest in maintaining the status quo and curtailing strike action. But their calls fell on deaf ears. Based on Solomon's deduction, the workers had become more committed than they had been in 2012: 'You know now the strike will last so long. I cannot even estimate how long because when you see the morale of the people they were too emotional now. Our strike is too [sic] militant than before. People attend [mass meetings] in numbers and numbers.'[50]

Each of the shafts held a mass meeting daily except on Sunday. On average, at Jabula, the meetings consisted of between 2,000 and 4,000 workers. 'I used to tell them that they know me from 2012 and I am their child', Solomon explained. He elaborated on the purpose of the meetings:

> Sometimes I must just come and greet them and tell them there is nothing and we go back, or we just sing that day and knock off [leave the area] . . . so when we are in a strike we must come and see each other and see whether or not we are still in the strike collectively. That is the purpose of coming to the meetings. It's not to bring feedback. So people must understand that when we go to the mass meeting it is not that we have something to discuss, we are just going to see each other.[51]

The workers were arguably more united than they had ever been. Though there were cracks in the leadership at Amplats amongst shop stewards, this had barely, if at all, extended to the rank and file. Certainly, workers at the three mines – Amplats, Impala, and Lonmin – who had gone on unprotected strikes at different times during 2012 were now working together as one.

Solomon had a habit of having informal conversations with workers as a strategy to gauge their ongoing commitment (or lack thereof) to the strike action; or, as he says, 'checking their morale'. One day he was visiting the community of Sondela, near Khuseleka. He recalled that he 'interviewed different people one by one and just asked him as an ordinary person about how the feeling is about the strike'. He summarised the response of these individuals who told him: 'Now it's where we are in the strike because we cannot say we are in a strike but I still have money, still have food in the house. So now it's where we feel the feeling of striking.' They further affirmed that, they 'cannot return to work empty handed'. In the end, when the five-month strike concluded, the workers agreed

Organic intellectuals and leadership   165

to an approximately R1,000 increase in monthly wages (equivalent to 20 percent increases each year for four years).

On several days during the great strike (and during a strike against retrenchments in September/October 2013), one could see Solomon's eyes beginning to roll over because of sleep deprivation. Committed with his heart and soul to the rank and file, this did not stop him from addressing masses of workers in fields and elsewhere, particularly outside of Jabula hostel where he was the emblematic spokesperson. When he arrived home he would simply eat and then sleep. In an interview he lamented that he was now like a 'slave'. Perhaps this is the fate of genuine activists who become leaders inside insurgent trade unions.

'I have been a leader in other organisations', he later explained, but 'it is too difficult to be a leader especially in mining.' Solomon suggested that if he was nominated to be a leader in a different company in the future, 'I will refuse.'[52] During 2012, however, it was more 'painful' because he was largely considered to be the chairperson of all the operations on strike including, to a certain extent, Swartklip and Amandabelt in Northam: 'Khuseleka nominated me and when I'm organising all these operations to join the strike they end up nominating me for [dealing with] all these operations. So I used to have this pain of knowing each and everything that is supposed to happen and driving the strike for all these mines and people depended on me.'[53] On occasion, though he sometimes struggled to maintain his own family's well-being, he would borrow money from his brother so that he could pay for petrol to travel to other operations. In addition:

> Other workers who are not able to get a single cent from the[ir] families, when you go to the mass meeting they will ask you whether or not you have some cash to lend them to do this and you find that you don't have it at all. You find that you don't have anything to survive with while you want the same things. And going to the mass meetings daily for a period of four months and [you are] having nothing to say. There is so much pressure because people expect you to have something to say to them that day. Other people just come and ask, 'when the strike will end'? So now it seems like it is your own strike.[54]

At the time of writing, I stumbled across Solomon in Johannesburg where he was attending a meeting to support the workers of Marikana and the families of the deceased who were killed in the massacre. After the meeting, I asked him: 'Did you really draft the demand for R16,070 in the change rooms?' He clarified: 'I drafted the demand at my house, I brought it to . . . [Anele] in the change rooms after work and we sold it to the workers.'[55]

Conclusion

The 2012 strikes did not occur magically or with the flick of a switch, but required immense leadership, dedication, and organisation. As Gramsci has noted,[56] a completely spontaneous action is impossible. For any collective action or popular

166   *Luke Sinwell*

uprising to emerge, someone must take the lead regardless of whether or not their names are recognized in historical accounts. The decision to approach employers peacefully and in small numbers, and subsequently to go on strike, involved an intellectual exercise and reflected the development of working-class consciousness.

This chapter has contended that the workers' committee at Amplats can effectively be traced back to one individual, Solomon, who approached a fellow mineworker about wages. He and Anele were among the most important organic intellectuals involved in the 2012 to 2014 platinum belt strike wave. Until the strike at Impala and the latter mobilisation at Lonmin and Amplats, workers had bowed to the 'common sense' of existing bargaining processes, which resulted in a roughly 9 percent increase every three years. This was the case until Anele and Solomon at Amplats met in the change rooms to demand increases from their employers. Soon thereafter, they began approaching other workers, convincing them to join the collective struggle.

Perhaps the core feature of the workers' committees at Amplats was the fact that they were dependent upon workers' involvement. According to Solomon, 'there are no good negotiators. It is [rather] a matter of the balance of forces, of power.' Leadership was not merely a manipulative process.[57] Rather, leaders of the committees simultaneously created the conditions for strike action and radical wage demands, while also taking the lead from the workers whose mood determined whether or not and when strike action would actually take place. Workers were not 'mindless sheep', but rather took further decisions about the way forward which was eventually communicated to management by the committees. The fact that they were democratically controlled does not mean that the committees, and later the union, did not shape the workers' views or decisions. The mere fact that they formed the committee around a set of key demands meant that they shaped the outcome of all subsequent decisions.

Focusing on key leaders, and the philosophies which underpinned their resolve to unite workers around transformative wage demands, enables one to better understand how the strike originated in a specific shaft at Amplats (Khuseleka) and then spread to others. It further enables us to consider whether the strikes would have taken a similar form, or perhaps not even occurred at all, had it not been for those few people who initiated the workers' committees. Without this consideration, the role of individuals in collective action will essentially be written out of this critical span of time, not only in the history of South Africa, but also in the history of radical working-class mobilisation more generally.

Notes

1   I have given pseudonyms to the workers discussed in this chapter. For the first comprehensive study of the contemporary mineworkers' movement in South Africa, see Luke Sinwell with Siphiwe Mbatha, *The Spirit of Marikana: The Rise of Insurgent Trade Unionism in South Africa* (London: Pluto Press, 2016). For an analysis of the transition from worker committees to AMCU, see Luke Sinwell, '"AMCU by Day, Workers' Committee by Night": Insurgent Trade Unionism at Anglo Platinum (Amplats) mine, 2012–2014,' *Review of African Political Economy* 42, no. 146 (December 2015).

Organic intellectuals and leadership 167

2 Sidney Tarrow, *Power in Movement: Social Movements and Contentious Politics* (Cambridge: Cambridge University Press, 1998).

3 Brigitta Busch, 'Introduction,' in *Interviews with Neville Alexander: The Power of Languages against the Language of Power*, ed. Brigitta Busch, Lucijan Busch, and Karen Press (Pietermaritzburg, SA: UKZN Press, 2014), 3.

4 David Graeber, *Direct Action: An Ethnography* (Oakland and Edinburg: AK Press, 2009).

5 Doug McAdam, John D. McCarthy, and Mayer N. Zald, 'Introduction,' in *Comparative Perspectives on Social Movements: Political Opportunities, Mobilizing Structures, and Cultural Framings*, ed. Doug McAdam, John D. McCarthy, and Mayer N. Zald (Cambridge: Cambridge University Press, 1996), 6.

6 Antonio Gramsci, *Selections from the Prison Notebooks of Antonio Gramsci* (London: Lawrence and Wishart, 1971).

7 Ibid., 9.

8 Colin Barker, Alan Johnson, and Michael Lavalette, 'Leadership Matters: an Introduction,' in *Leadership and Social Movements*, ed. Colin Barker, Alan Johnson, and Michael Lavalette (Manchester and New York: Manchester University Press, 2001), 1.

9 Ibid.

10 Tarrow, *Power in Movement.*

11 Alan Johnson, 'Self-Emancipation and Leadership: The Case of Martin Luther King,' in *Leadership and Social Movements*, ed. Colin Barker, Alan Johnson, and Michael Lavalette (Manchester and New York: Manchester University Press, 2001), 97.

12 Ibid., 98.

13 Ibid., 111.

14 Interview, Anele, June 8, 2013.

15 Interview, Solomon, Siraleng, August 9, 2013.

16 Interview, Solomon.

17 Interview, Solomon, Siraleng, May 4, 2014.

18 Interview, Solomon (2013).

19 Ibid.

20 Ibid.

21 Ibid.

22 Interview, Sipho.

23 Interview, Ramokga, in M. Magome, 'More Mines Shut Down as Strikers Dig in Their Heels for Pay Hike,' *The Star*, September 13, 2012, p. 2, http://www.iol.co.za/the-star/more-mines-shut-down-as-strikers-dig-in-their-heels-for-pay-hike-1381960.

24 Interview, Sipho.

25 Interview, Solomon (2014).

26 Interview, Solomon (2013).

27 Ibid.

28 Interview, Solomon (2014).

29 In an Anglo-American letter signed by CEO Chris Griffiths on September 25, 2012, to Rustenburg Mining Operations Employees entitled, 'Disciplinary action leading to potential dismissals to commence on Thursday, September 27, 2012,' the CEO acknowledged the fact that, 'some employees have been awaiting the outcome of the Khuseleka Mine CCMA matter before returning to work.'

30 Interview, Lazarus Khoza, Rustenburg, May 26, 2013.

31 Interview, Khoza.

32 Interview, Sipho, Rustenburg, August 17, 2013.

33 Interview, Solomon (2013).

34 Pamphlet entitled 'Meeting,' September 8, 2012.

35 Sapa, 'Strikers Swell to 100 000,' *The Citizen*, September 28, 2012, p. 23.

36 Statement by Chris Griffiths, 'Amplats Taking Action against Workers,' *The New Age*, September 28, 2012, p. 1.

168 *Luke Sinwell*

37 See: S. Bega and Sapa. 'Mines May Follow Amplats in Dismissing Strikers,' *Saturday Star*, October 6, 2012, p. 4.
38 Interview, Sipho.
39 Interview, Solomon (2013).
40 Ibid.
41 Ibid.
42 P. Tau, 'Violence Breaks Out at Limpopo Mine,' *The Star*, October 10, 2012, p. 6.
43 Interview, Solomon (2013). Solomon has a copy of the agreement which was signed by the various parties, including the committee itself.
44 Interview, anonymous worker.
45 Speech, Solomon, at Olympia Stadium, Rustenburg, January 19, 2014.
46 Interview, Solomon.
47 Solomon, personal communication with Luke Sinwell, Rustenburg, January 19, 2014.
48 Interview, Jukulunga Joka, in Sapa, 'AMCU Marches on Union Buildings,' *Mail and Guardian online*, March 6, 2014, accessed November 4, 2014, http://mg/co.za/article/2014–03–06-amcu-marches-on-union-buildings.
49 Speech, Jacob Zuma, in N. Marrian, A. Seccombe, and K. Gernetzky, 'Zuma Warns Over Strikes Descending into Anarchy,' *Business Day Live online*, May 2, 2014, accessed November 3, 2014, www.bdlive.co.za/national/labour/2014/05/02/zuma-warns-over-strikes-descending-into-anarchy.
50 Interview, Solomon.
51 Ibid.
52 Ibid.
53 Ibid.
54 Ibid.
55 Solomon, personal communication with Luke Sinwell, Johannesburg, October 23, 2014.
56 Gramsci, *Prison Notebooks*, 196.
57 For a useful discussion about how leadership may function in a way that does not necessarily manipulate crowds or masses, see Steve Reicher, John Drury, Nick Hopkins, and Clifford Stott, 'A Model of Crowd Prototypes and Crowd Leadership,' in *Leadership and Social Movements*, ed. Colin Barker, Alan Johnson, and Michael Lavalette (Manchester and New York: Manchester University Press, 2001), 178–195.

Part V
Left formations

11 South Africa's new left movements

Challenges and hopes

Noor Nieftagodien

South Africa's political landscape has been utterly transformed in the relatively brief period since the Marikana massacre of August 2012. For the first time since the advent of democracy, the ruling African National Congress (ANC) faces serious challenges to its hegemony. Although the party's parliamentary majority seems secure in the immediate future, its actual electoral support has been in decline for some time. A root cause of this political shift is that a growing number of people have lost hope in the party's ability to deliver on the promise of democracy, namely, a life of dignity, free from poverty, segregation, violence and humiliation. Poor South Africans had hoped the democratic state would be the primary agent for redistribution and development, and the guarantor of constitutional rights. Increasingly, however, parts of the state have become incapable of discharging these basic responsibilities. Corruption is endemic as officials and politicians plunder state resources to accumulate wealth, a practice facilitated and abetted by the private sector. State violence has also been on the increase, together with the growing influence of securocrats.[1] The Marikana massacre, the killing of Andries Tatane[2] and dozens of other protesters, the almost permanent harassment of movements such as Abahlali baseMjondolo[3] and the siege of Thembelihle in 2015 are manifestations of endemic state violence against poor communities. What has become evident is that the historic organisation of the country's oppressed people has become the defender of the status quo and protector of the interests of the economic and political elites, even as it claims to embody the aspirations of 'the nation' and of the poor in particular.

One of the primary aims of the post-1994 dispensation was to realise the dream of producing a rainbow people via the politics of reconciliation. It was premised on the idea of a purported collective project – of nation-building – which would overcome race and racism through healing and forgiveness, as exemplified by the supposedly cathartic process of the Truth and Reconciliation Commission. It was a political endeavour that required the black majority to forgive in exchange for political and economic freedom, a contract many black people were prepared to embrace even as they continued to live with the pain and anger engendered by generations of white racism. In the first period of democracy, instances of white racism were regarded as the aberrant behaviour of a die-hard but dying breed

172 *Noor Nieftagodien*

of racists. But the continuation and even increase in incidents of overt racism, as well as the ubiquity of thinly disguised everyday practices of racism, have highlighted a systemic problem, undergirded by the intersection of exploitation, poverty and race. Every indicator of underdevelopment in South Africa, including malnutrition, poor education, homelessness and violence is deeply racialised and gendered. Apartheid segregation continues to define the country's geographical landscape. Not surprisingly therefore, the critical issues of race and racism, although never absent, have re-emerged as primary sources of contention. In reality, the daily experiences of the majority of black people remain largely shaped by poverty, spatial exclusion and racism. Instead of delivering a 'better life for all', the ruling party's policies have resulted in a growth of inequality and poverty. Approximately 13 million citizens – a quarter of the population – live below the food poverty line, that is, they have an income of less than R320 per month. In stark contrast, between 2004 and 2014, the number of multimillionaires in the country grew by 120 percent, many of who are members of the new black elite. In 2008 the wealthiest 5 percent of South Africans accounted for 43 percent of total income, whereas the poorest 50 percent accounted for a mere 7.79 percent.[4] The combined wealth of two individuals, Nicky Oppenheimer and Johann Rupert (whose families accumulated enormous wealth during colonialism and apartheid), stands at an estimated R165 billion, which is equal to the combined wealth of the poorest 27 million people. South Africa remains the most unequal in the world, with a Gini coefficient that has consistently been among the highest, hovering around 6.9 percent.[5]

Political processes that had been gestating for some years have been brought into sharp relief since 2012. The current period is arguably characterized by three overlapping processes: the undoing of the ANC's hegemony, the crisis of the National Democratic Revolution (NDR) as the principal ideological framing of the new dispensation and the deepening malaise facing the economy. The ideological and organisational certainties of the last period – embodied in the ANC and the NDR – have been disrupted, while the Congress of South African Trade Unions (COSATU), historically the most important organisation of the black working class, has been severely weakened. From the late 1970s, as the mass struggle against apartheid gained momentum, youth, students and workers increasingly embraced the ANC as their liberation movement and gave the party an overwhelming mandate in 1994 to effect fundamental transformation. Now, that relationship is coming apart, perhaps irrevocably so. In this sense, there are important parallels with the global experiences of the evolution of the traditional parties of the working class and oppressed, which espoused radical programmes when at the head of mass struggles against dictatorships, colonialism and capitalism. But, as Fanon warned in relation to postcolonial societies, when in power, these parties came to represent the interests of the ruling elites, often against their traditional base (see Chapter 4). This pattern was discernible in the experiences of Congress Party (India), ZANU (Zimbabwe African National Union), PASOK (Panhellenic Socialist Movement in Greece), Labour Party (Britain) and PSOE (Spanish Socialist Workers' Party).[6] Of course, the trajectories and timeframes of

South Africa's new left movements 173

these processes differed in each country. In all of these instances, a salient question posed was whether alternative movements could replace the crumbling political behemoths as the representatives of the poor majority. This is arguably one of the pressing issues in South Africa.

Already new political possibilities are beginning to crystalise with the establishment of the United Front (UF), the Economic Freedom Fighters (EFF) and a new labour movement. Crucially, local protests and the various movements to which they have given birth, and which precede the organisations established in the aftermath of the Marikana massacre, continue to be in the forefront of producing contentious politics and practices. Collectively these movements may well constitute the key elements in the reconfiguration of political formations, but the *organisational* re-alignment currently under way will not be sufficient to create substantively different mass-based politics unless there is a fundamental reappraisal of radical politics and practice and recognition of the new forms of struggles by the working and poor in workplaces and locations. The chapter suggests there are important challenges facing the process of reconstituting a new mass left movement, in part because of the crisis of the capitalist economy and the restructuring of society and the working class. However, the pre-occupation with organisational re-alignment is creating self-imposed limitations to the potential and urgent need to transform the left. While this process of re-organisation is absolutely essential and long overdue, it is yet to produce a thorough reimagining of the left political project. For this to succeed, it is important to transcend the limitations of existing political frameworks and hackneyed formulae that obfuscate and provide succor only to those who repeat them like mantras. Different repertoires, politics and languages of insurgency are required, that must necessarily draw on the historical and international experiences of working-class struggles. It also requires critical self-reflection of the movements of the working class and poor.

The alliance and COSATU's subordination

NUMSA's expulsion by the COSATU leadership was a political decision aimed at excising from the federation mounting discontent over the politics of the tripartite alliance and their effects on trade unions and the working class. It was also the most dramatic manifestation of the malaise affecting the largest organisation in the history of the working class. How did we arrive at this point, considering the union federation's proud history? It is worth recalling that COSATU's launch in December 1985 was celebrated nationally and internationally as the birth of a giant of the working-class movement. At the time, the new federation represented the culmination of more than a decade of painstaking building of independent trade unions by black workers, and embodied the principles of workers' democracy and independence forged in the struggles against *baaskap*, that is, white managerial authority over black workers. While emphasising a commitment to building strong and militant workplace organisations, COSATU was also fully engaged in the struggle for broader political emancipation and

174   *Noor Nieftagodien*

to achieve socialism. On the one hand, COSATU and its affiliates flexed their muscles against recalcitrant employers, resulting in a sharp increase in industrial disputes: In 1987 alone, a record 1,148 strikes took place.[7] Despite heavy state repression COSATU continued to score important victories in terms of union recognition and wage increases, as well as against job losses, and generally mounted a serious challenge to employers' power. On the other hand, by the late 1980s, the federation was leading political campaigns (e.g., on education and against state repression) contributing to the reinvigoration of civic struggles which, in turn, put the wind back in the sails of the Mass Democratic Movement. In 1987 it called a two-day general strike against the whites-only elections. In so doing, as various scholars have noted, COSATU was an exemplar of Social Movement Unionism.[8]

COSATU's success was reflected in the rapid growth of its membership from 462,359 in 1985 to 1,258,853 in 1991,[9] an historic high for trade unions in South Africa, making it the most powerful and best-organized movement at the time of the unbanning of the exiled political parties. During the transition period, the federation continued to be hugely influential both in terms of mobilising struggles (e.g., against Value Added Tax and in countering state- and IFP-sponsored violence[10]) and in shaping policies for the new democratic order. In terms of the latter it was instrumental in formulating a new labour relations framework (principally the Labour Relations Act of 1995 and the Basic Conditions of Employment Act of 1997), which entrenched minimum labour rights. Importantly, its socio-economic policies shaped the Reconstruction and Development Programme (RDP), which became the ANC's platform in the first democratic elections. These early legislative advances and the formal commitment by the first democratic government to a nominally social democratic programme suggested a working-class bias in state policies, and apparently vindicated COSATU's decision to enter into an alliance with the ANC and SACP (South African Communist Party). Formalised in 1991, the Tripartite Alliance has been a crucial nexus of power that largely shaped the trajectory of post-apartheid politics. Jay Naidoo, COSATU'S first General Secretary, recently recalled that: 'Our alliance . . . was based on a clear programme of action to address the legacy of apartheid poverty, joblessness, poor-quality education and health, and the huge backlog of basic services to our people.'[11] However, the dual premise on which this hope rested – of a working class-led alliance committed to radical transformation – began to come under pressure from its inception.

In fact, the alliance provided a veneer of working-class leadership while augmenting the political power of the new elite. Arguably, one of its primary objectives was to bring the movements that had defeated apartheid (unions, civics, youth organisations and numerous local committees) under the political control of the leadership of the ANC and SACP. This process was reflected in the disbandment of the United Democratic Front (UDF), marginalisation of the South African National Civic Organisation and, most seriously, the subordination of COSATU to the agenda of alliance leaders. Thus, at the moment when the alliance was probably at its most productive, the configuration of power relations already signaled

South Africa's new left movements 175

an emerging de facto secondary position of the unions. By 1996 COSATU bitterly complained about the marginalisation of the alliance, pointing to the growing tendency by the ANC to ignore decisions taken at alliance meetings. With the ANC in power and assured of SACP loyalty, COSATU's influence inside the alliance and consequently over the formulation of government policies continued to wane. Buhlungu has persuasively argued that 'the post-1994 period has resulted in a marked decline in the role and influence of COSATU within the tripartite alliance'.[12] Endorsing this assessment, Khunou has pointed to the federation's failure 'to effectively challenge the passing and implementation of GEAR' as a pivotal moment when it lost its influence in the alliance. Yet COSATU continued to pin its hopes on institutional politics, further limiting its effectiveness. 'This inability', Khunou has argued, 'was reinforced when the federation prioritised engagement in NEDLAC to the exclusion of other approaches, such as building a powerful bloc of civil society organisations and the use of legal processes. COSATU's nostalgia for old political relationships that fail to yield results currently reduces their ability to act strategically.'[13] The marginalisation of COSATU was only one dimension of the transformation of alliance politics. What also became increasingly evident was the growing influence of national and international capital in shaping policy, which was exemplified by the ANC's adoption in 1996 of the neoliberal macro-economic framework (GEAR), which produced an increasingly contentious relationship between the federation and the government.

From the late 1990s, as the adverse of effects of the government's macro-economic policies were being felt, especially with increasing levels of unemployment and the implementation of privatisation, COSATU embarked on campaigns of mass action, including general strikes to force the government and employers to agree on ameliorative interventions. These actions sometimes produced minor shifts in policy but more often only prompted rhetorical commitments from the ANC to breathe new life into the alliance. The COSATU leadership invariably responded to these gestures from the ruling party by extolling the virtues of the alliance. However, as it became increasingly apparent that the alliance was ineffective as a vehicle for determining government policy, COSATU's efforts shifted to supporting supposedly sympathetic leaders in the ANC, in the hope of asserting some influence in the corridors of power. Unionists were also deployed to national and provincial legislators (as ANC members) to bolster what became a vain endeavour to ensure the representation of workers' interests. The consequence of this strategy was that union leaders became entangled in the factional struggles of the ruling party, which was less about overhauling the ANC's policies than about which faction would control the levers of state power to ensure preferential access to the pathways of accumulation. Buhlungu observed the development of a 'symbiotic relationship' between the ANC leadership and trade union bureaucracy, with both interested in self-preservation, securing privileges and political advancement. The consolidation of a bureaucratic layer spread across the constituent parts of the alliance and overlapping with the state bureaucracy reinforced the idea of the unity of the alliance. It led some scholars to conclude that 'a dramatic break-up of the alliance' was unlikely, while some analysts

176 *Noor Nieftagodien*

argued that COSATU's relationship with the ANC was characterised by 'flexible independence', oscillating between autonomy and subordination.[14] Like an elastic band it was at times stretched to a breaking point, but inevitably returned to its original position of tense co-existence seemingly destined to persist through the continuously extended lifespan of the first phase of the NDR.

When tensions between COSATU and the ANC reached a fever pitch under the Mbeki regime, it seemed possible that the trade union federation might break from the alliance and carve out an independent path for itself. In hindsight, the prospects for a neat split between the trade union movement and the elite of the ANC/SACP were actually unlikely. Instead, a far more complicated process has ensued, characterised by several divisions and new convergences. The alliance will, of course, continue in name, cohering around the authority of the ANC in government, but will be utterly different from what its founders envisaged in the early 1990s. Factional struggles are now endemic in the ANC, having already resulted in splits, the most important of which led to the formation of the Economic Freedom Fighters (EFF). Critically for the workers' movement and, indeed, for left politics generally, is the break-up of COSATU, which represents a setback for the struggle of the working class and poor. However, the current crisis has created the conditions for the birth of a new trade union movement, freed from the shackles of the Tripartite Alliance. The weakening of and splits in COSATU, and especially the expulsion of NUMSA, means for the first time in the democratic era the majority of trade union members may not formally be allied to the ruling party (although many may still vote for the ANC), opening the possibility of reclaiming the independence of the union movement. But unshackling unions from the alliance will not be a sufficient precondition for rebuilding and reinvigorating this movement.

COSATU in crisis

After 30 years of being the leading workers' movement, COSATU faces an existential crisis: It is riven with deep divisions and internecine factional disputes, allegations of corruption and widespread financial troubles, as well as the entrenchment of a bureaucratic leadership increasingly alienated from rank-and-file members. Long-serving and now expelled General Secretary of COSATU, Zwelinzima Vavi, pointed to some of the dimensions of this crisis in a statement made before his expulsion: 'The paralysis of COSATU has left workers defenseless on the ground, demoralised, and angry at the leadership for betraying them in this fashion. . . . The once mighty COSATU is slowly being reduced to an irrelevant toothless dog whilst the material conditions of workers continue to deteriorate.'

He proceeded to paint a gloomy picture of the dire financial situation in the federation:

> COSATU is currently living R300 000 a month beyond its income. COSATU staff could only be paid in February and March by raiding the Political Fund (designated for other purposes). This source will dry up soon. Campaign activities – the core of our work – will be curtailed, and there is the likelihood

of having to go with a begging bowl to our class enemies for money to hold a Congress later this year. This is a recipe for a complete loss of independence.[15]

Over the past few years, a number of COSATU affiliates have suffered debilitating crises. Chemical, Energy, Paper, Printing, Wood and Allied Workers' Union (CEPPWAWU), comprising two of the oldest independent unions (chemical and paper), has been paralysed by leadership struggles over control of the union's assets in its investment company. Leaders have been suspended, reinstated and re-suspended, in a merry-go-round of power games, resulting in the weakening of unions in a key sector of the economy. South African Commercial, Catering and Allied Workers' Union's (SACCAWU) financial crisis, arising from allegations of mismanagement of the union's provident fund, threatens its very existence. As one of the few unions with a significant female membership, its demise would represent a major setback for the workers' movement. Previously, claims of abuse of millions of rands were made against the South African Transport and Allied Workers' Union (SATAWU) leadership, triggering a bitter struggle in the union, which culminated in a split and the formation in 2012 of a new union, the National Transport Movement (NTM). Over the past two years South African Municipal Workers' Union (SAMWU) has been consumed by a divisive dispute centered on accusations of corruption against the union's leaders. Those who raised concerns about financial impropriety have been expelled and the union has become embroiled in a damaging court case. A report by the Save our SAMWU (SOS) campaign claims to have uncovered irregular transfer of large amounts between accounts and massive over-expenditure on the renovation of the union's new head office.[16] The centrality of finances in the crises besetting various unions is rooted in a number of intersecting factors. Foremost among these is the role of investment companies, which have become an albatross around the neck of unions. Hailed as a route to financial stability and independence for the unions, these companies have generated significant wealth and consequently have become a critical source of contention. They have been used as vehicles for the enrichment of former unionists and their entry into the upper echelons of the economic elite. Union bureaucracies have become less dependent on membership dues, contributing to a decline in accountability of officials to the rank and file. With the salaries of union officials escalating and far outstripping the wages of members, occupying positions of leadership has become lucrative. As a result, the lifestyles of union leaders are often completely disconnected from the experiences of their members. The mixing of money and politics has been ruinous for the union movement, as factions are pre-occupied with disputes over control of resources and political patronage, rather than serving the interests of workers. In the process the federation seems to have moved inexorably away from the defining characteristics of the independent unions of the 1970s and 1980s, namely of workers' independence and democracy, and militancy.

The crises besetting the progressive trade movement prompted far-reaching responses in the mining and metal sectors, suggesting the current crisis could inaugurate a revival of radical unionism. NUMSA's historic decision in 2013 not

178 *Noor Nieftagodien*

to support the ANC in the national elections of 2014 and to initiate a process to create a United Front and Movement for Socialism emanated from its assessment that the alliance no longer served the interests of the working class and poor. By challenging the SACP's ideological hold on COSATU, the metal workers' union drew a line in the sand, which eventually led to the COSATU and SACP leadership orchestrating its removal from the federation. In so doing, a path has been opened for the country's largest trade union to build a new federation, the success of which depends on its ability to attract workers and unions from other sectors of the economy, particularly from the mining sector where unionism has experienced a major change.

Until 2012 NUM was the undisputed representative of hundreds of thousands of black workers on the mines and one of the giants in COSATU. However, the strike wave on the platinum belt in 2012 exposed deep dissatisfaction with the NUM among miners, who complained of a leadership out of touch with the needs of members. Mass resignations from NUM occurred in 2012 and 2013 as workers proceeded to swell the ranks of AMCU: the latter's membership in the sector escalated to 120,000, constituting about 70 percent of the workforce, while NUM's share of the membership plummeted to 20 percent.[17] It marked an important shift in workers' politics as a traditionally loyal base of the ANC demonstrated a willingness to break with the ruling alliance and join an alternative union. AMCU's leading role in the historic five-month strike in 2014 has cemented its position among platinum workers. However, the spectacular growth of the union has come at the expense of independent workers' committees, which not only played the leading role in the struggles on the mines in 2012 and 2013, but were also instrumental in the rapid growth of AMCU in early 2013. As the union consolidated its position, the existence of these committees was increasingly regarded as a threat to the authority of the leadership. The rise of AMCU on the back of one of the most militant struggles in the history of mining challenged the status quo created by NUM and the mining companies. Yet, the attempt to demobilise autonomous workers' committees and to silence dissenting voices represents an assertion of the authority of the union bureaucracy, echoing the practices of its rival, the NUM.

COSATU's crisis has brought to the surface the deep-rooted and multi-faceted problems afflicting most unions. The splits and re-alignments under way are producing a complete transformation of the trade union movement, although the final configuration of federations still has to be decided. An alliance between NUMSA and AMCU could constitute the basis of a significant new federation, although the leadership of both unions still seems reluctant to consider this option. However, even a cursory glance at the state of the union movement suggests serious weaknesses and problems, which will not disappear through a process of organisational regrouping. An overhaul of unions is required, starting with a critical appraisal of bureaucratisation and reliance on investment companies. Equally important, unions need to organise the unorganised sections of the working population.

Organising the precariat

Perhaps the biggest problem facing the entire trade union movement is quite simply that the majority of workers are not members of unions. This may appear counter-intuitive because South African unions have managed to maintain and, in some cases, even grown their membership over the past 20 years, contrary to international trends. In COSATU, this counter-trend has been due to the relative success of unions in defending members' rights and the significant growth of public sector unions. Nonetheless, the character of the membership is revealing: Surveys of union membership demonstrate that COSATU consists mainly of permanent and full-time workers. In fact, 92 percent of its members are permanent workers and, reflecting the emerging importance of the public sector, more than 60 percent are white-collar employees.[18] Put differently, trade unions do not represent casual, outsourced, temporary and marginalised workers – the precariat. These are workers who enjoy little, if any job security, earn low wages, have few benefits (such as medical aid and provident funds) and tend to be employed by labour brokers.[19]

South Africa has followed the experiences of neoliberalism globally, which 'has entailed a restructuring of workplace relations which has led to greater labour casualization which has resulted in growing precariousness, all carried out in the name of the need for greater "flexibility"'.[20] According to the Workers' Advice Office (WAO) there was a 64 percent growth in temporary employment between 2000 and 2011. Labour broking has proliferated, with one study estimating more than '3000 firms operating in the formal economy alone, with potentially as many as 9000 operating in what it refers to as the informal economy'. In sectors such as retail, hospitality and construction, the WAO asserts, casualised or informal work has become the 'norm'.[21] Domestic workers and farmworkers are arguably the two sectors with the longest histories of precariousness. The strike wave in 2012/13 that engulfed the farm regions of the Western Cape exposed the oppressive conditions farm workers and their families have endured for generations. Yet, it estimated that less than 3 percent of farmworkers nationally are organised in unions. This weakness of formal organisation did not prevent thousands of farmworkers from embarking on a bitter struggle for decent wages, even as they faced intimidation from farm owners and violence from the state. An important victory was scored when the sectoral minimum wage was increased from R69 to R105 a day.[22] Since then, according to unions, several farmers have been on a revenge campaign and have evicted families, employed more casual workers and have dismissed those regarded as 'agitators'. The most severely affected is the independent union, the Commercial, Stevedoring, Agricultural and Allied Workers' Union (CSAAWU), which has been organising farm workers for many years and played a prominent role in the 2012/13 strike. The union faces bankruptcy because of court cases it lost in defending workers and consequent orders to pay the R600,000 cost of the employers. None of the major unions, nor COSATU itself, have offered solidarity to CSAAWU and farm workers generally. Again, an

180 *Noor Nieftagodien*

opportunity seems to have been lost to support the unionisation of one of the most marginalised sections of the working class.

There is now a similar failure to organise the rapidly growing ranks of the precariat. While recognising that organising such workers is a huge task, the WAO suggests it is necessary 'to discover new forms of organizing that better correspond with the changes in the workplace'.[23] This must surely be one of the most urgent tasks for any new union movement. In the process of reconfiguration and probable creation of a new labour movement, the current problems besetting unions require frank and transparent engagement. Bureaucratisation, the adverse effects of investment companies, the decline of workers' democracy and independence, and the almost complete absence of organisation of the precariat will ultimately lead any new reconfiguration of unions down the same cul-de-sac as COSATU now finds itself. It would also be a serious error in judgement if the production or revival of militant, social movement unionism were to exclude those unions remaining in COSATU. Whatever criticisms may be directed at the leadership of the federation and individual affiliates, who are under the sway of the SACP, the ordinary members of the unions cannot be abandoned. Unity of the working class, in particular uniting community movements and workplace struggles, should remain a principal objective.

Community rebellions

On 25 February 2015 scores of residents from Thembelihle informal settlement, situated to the south of Johannesburg, took to the streets to demand decent housing and service delivery. It was a form of action which they had engaged in repeatedly over many years and to which the state responded with little more than promises to attend to the community's grievances. When officials stonewalled again, residents decided again to march to one of the main roads to bring their concerns to the attention of a wider community. In what has become a standard form of mobilisation, the community blocked a main road, which guaranteed media attention and thus forced a response from the authorities. Inevitably, the police intervened violently to disperse the protesters, triggering clashes with the residents that lasted an entire weekend and resulted in scores of injuries. A total of 72 people were arrested, including local leaders who had attempted to mediate between the police and residents, and were subsequently charged with public violence. For a month after the original march, Thembelihle was under a siege, reminiscent of the clampdown by security forces during the states of emergency under apartheid.

Thousands of similar events have occurred across the country for the past decade and half, in what has been a sustained (albeit fragmented) movement of localised protests. Various writers have highlighted the salience of these protests in contemporary politics, and it is generally agreed South Africa has among the highest rates of protest per capita in the world.[24] Conventionally, they have generally been described as 'service delivery protests': poor residents demanding the provision of basic services such as water, electricity and housing from the state. While this characterisation is not inaccurate, it is inadequate as an analytical register with which to understand the political complexities and local nuances constituting protest movements. Communities have mobilised against corruption and administrative inefficiencies, suggesting a desire for a more effective government. Protests have been directed at local authorities, or particular officials/ politicians, to highlight incompetence or corruption in order to root out malpractices. A common thread running through these protest movements is of citizens demanding substantive local democracy: They want their proposals and plans for development, political views and representative organisations to be taken seriously by the authorities. These local movements have consistently over a protracted period struggled against the unaccountable and undemocratic practices of local politicians and power brokers.[25] Thus, while the underlying causes of these protest movements are similar, their forms and character are shaped by specific and changing political constellations. Their local character has produced fragmented and disconnected politics, which resembles the location-bound popular urban protests of the 1940s that were animated by local problems affecting the lives of black people in poor townships and squatter camps.[26] Then, as now, these location-bound contentious movements represented a significant, albeit fragmented, challenge to official policies. At various times since the late 1990s, local movements have succeeded in transforming squatter camps, informal settlements, inner-city slums, apartheid townships and post-apartheid RDP housing complexes into contentious spaces, beyond the control of states and parties.

In localities across the country, numerous local and regional movements have been created (e.g., crisis committees, concerned residents' groups, new civic organisations, people's assemblies, etc.), some of which have enjoyed only brief existences, while many others have persisted.[27] NUMSA's critique of this rebellion as 'lacking revolutionary leadership'[28] is a useful but flawed observation. In fact, these movements produced a new layer of activists who have mainly been politicised outside of the ruling alliance. These activists tend to be young and unemployed, but also include older women (who carry a disproportionate burden of tending to the numerous ailments afflicting residents of poor communities) and informalised workers. They have built organisations and mobilised campaigns under extremely difficult conditions such as state violence and a dire lack of resources.

One such local social movement is the Thembelihle Crisis Committee (TCC), which has been leading the struggle for houses and services in the informal settlement for more than a decade. The TCC generally enters public discourse when violent protests, such as referred to previously in this chapter, occur. Yet, the everyday political and social life of the movement goes unnoticed. For years members of the TCC, who are young and old, mostly unemployed and with a significant proportion of women, have been involved in a wide range of activities. They meet weekly to discuss politics, to plan campaigns and other activities, or to receive reports from sister organisations. One of the strengths of the TCC is its solidarity work: Since 2012 alone it has supported the platinum miners, farm workers and other poor communities struggling for better services, and it has marched to support climate jobs and justice for Marikana victims and to oppose xenophobia.

182   *Noor Nieftagodien*

Activists have participated in a wide range of external organisations, including the Anti-Privatisation Forum, Marikana Support Campaign, Democratic Left Front, UF and the Right To Know Campaign. They have also participated in elections and engaged the local ward committee.[29] Similar local movements exist across the country and are involved in various forms of politics, usually debated and elaborated independent of formal parties. What this reveals is a world of activism, certainly not without challenges, but which operates beyond the limited horizons of official society and mainstream media.

Many activists in these movements are critical of political parties, viewing them with healthy suspicion. Too often they have encountered politicians who promise delivery of services when on the election trail but quickly forget about the poor when occupying positions of power. It is for this reason that the slogan – 'No land, no vote' – gained popularity among poor communities who were tired of the empty promises issued from the forked tongues of politicians. Among several of these movements, efforts have been made to engender non-hierarchical politics, to create spaces where the voices of the poor could shape debates, programmes and the organisations themselves. Success in this regard has been uneven, and undermined by a range of external (constant harassment by the state, daily survival) and internal (lack of resources and factional squabbles) factors. Nonetheless, the aspiration to produce political practices substantially different from the top-down political cultures of political parties has been a hallmark of many of these movements.

An important limitation of the community-based movements and labour struggles has been their disconnection from one another. In fact, discernible enmity has existed between trade unions and several of the new social movements. Various general and specific factors explain the persistence of this division, but it was arguably mainly due to the COSATU leadership's reluctance to be associated with social movements that were sharply critical of the ANC. In the late 1990s, COSATU was instrumental in launching campaigns against neoliberalism and the privatisation of services. During this period, a strong convergence between unions and community organisations seemed to be on the horizon and promised to revive the community-workplace solidarity that characterised the anti-apartheid struggle in the 1980s. Since then, however, these forces have diverged to the point of antagonism. To its credit, COSATU supported the campaign by the TAC for access to cheap anti-retroviral medication, including criticising the Mbeki regime's AIDS denialism. But it deliberately remained aloof from the 'rebellion of the poor', with its members rarely involved in the hundreds of protests that engulfed significant parts of the country. The COSATU Workers' survey of 2008 highlighted that only a minority of COSATU members (about 44 percent) participated in community protests, despite a consistent decline from 1998 in workers' perception of the state's delivery of basic social services. COSATU members seemed to be wrapped in a contradiction of acknowledging the problems with the government but remaining loyal to the alliance, believing, as Motsoetsa has argued, 'that the government will deliver, but it needs to be given time'.[30] But it is a view that no longer holds the same currency. As new politics surge through

South Africa's new left movements   183

parts of the union movement, bridging the divide between community and workplace struggles seems like a realistic possibility. A similar situation pertained in the early 1980s when the independent unions coalesced in FOSATU. Then, youth played a crucial role in forging united struggles between these two sectors of the working class.

Student and youth politics

On 9 March 2015 Chumani Maxwele covered the statue of Cecil John Rhodes at the University of Cape Town (UCT) with feces to express his anger at the statue's anachronistic centrality at the university. Within days the demand – *Rhodes Must Fall!* – became a rallying cry for hundreds of mainly black students at the university. Although the removal of the statue was their immediate objective, students also voiced serious concerns about transformation at UCT. Their actions ignited intense debate about the extent and meaning of transformation, the place of statues of imperialists and white heroes in the post-apartheid landscape, the intensity of black pain in the face of white supremacy and the inability of many whites to understand 'what the fuss was about'. In Grahamstown, where the university still bears the name of the nineteenth century's most infamous imperial conqueror in southern Africa, black students renewed a campaign for Rhodes University to be renamed. At Wits University, students organised solidarity meetings with these struggles and constituted the Transform Wits Movement to campaign for the decolonisation of the university. Their campaign linked up with long-standing solidarity action between students and workers against outsourcing, as well as robust campaigns against exclusions. A further sign of the political winds beginning to blow through the campuses is the recent challenge to South African Students Congress (SASCO)'s predominance at some universities, with the EFF scoring victories in the Students Representative Council (SRC) elections at the Vaal University of Technology and the University of Limpopo. While SASCO and its allies in the Progressive Youth Alliance (PYA) remain politically dominant among university students, there are signs of ferment and fragmentation, reflecting processes in broader society. Campaigns in 2015 on several campuses for the decolonisation of universities were indicative of a new wave of radicalisation among students. These events proved to be the precursors to the most important student protest in the democratic era, when tens of thousands of students nationally in October 2015 participated in the 'Fees Must Fall' campaign, which forced the government and university management to agree not to increase fees in 2016. It was an historic struggle led by black students, most of whom either study at poorly resourced and badly administered institutions or are at formerly white universities where their experience of transformation is unsatisfactory.

These nascent movements are beginning to catch up with the struggles by young people in townships and informal settlements. Black youth have arguably borne the brunt of the country's stuttering development, experiencing high levels of unemployment, poor education and exposure to crime and violence. Internationally, young people face similar conditions, especially with historic high levels of unemployment (ILO 2013). In Greece and Spain, the countries of the global North worst affected by the 2008 economic meltdown, youth unemployment in 2013 stood at 62 percent and 56 percent, respectively.[31] Young people have therefore been in the forefront of struggles against austerity, especially as part of the Spanish *indignados* and in support of Syriza in Greece. In 2015, thousands of British youth marched against the austerity measures imposed by the ruling Tories. In the United States, the Occupy Movement saw tens of thousands of young people rejecting corporate greed, embodied by the financiers of Wall Street. In mid-October 2011, demonstrations occurred in nearly a thousand cities across the world. In Chile, between 2011 and 2013 hundreds of thousands of high school and university students took to the streets and occupied educational institutions to demand an increase in state funding for public education. Similar student movements have occurred in Colombia and Argentina.[32] These youth movements have been characterised by their independence from existing political parties and support for anti-austerity or new left-wing organisations.

A similar process is discernible in South Africa, where most young people eschew formal politics, refuse to participate in elections and form only a minority in the youth wings of the major political parties. In fact, there has been a disconnection between new forms of youth contentious politics and political organisations, which is perhaps most notable in relation to the African National Congress Youth League (ANCYL). Since its relaunch in 1991, the ANCYL has claimed to be the only legitimate representative of the aspirations of black youth. After displacing the Youth Congresses and independent youth formations built from the late 1970s, the ANCYL's main role has been to support the ANC's policies and to silence critics within and outside the tripartite alliance. After 1994 it became a platform for young activists to launch their political and business careers, rather than a movement of the growing army of poor youth. Leaders of the ANCYL became preoccupied with factional struggles in the ANC in order to facilitate their climb up the ladder of the ruling party and government. In the 25 years of its reappearance on the political scene, the ANCYL has failed to launch a single campaign to challenge the underlying causes of the extraordinary hardships experienced by the majority of young black people. That would require a critique of state policies and mobilisation against the ruling alliance, which the ANCYL seems incapable of doing. For this reason, the ANCYL has been left behind in the emerging struggles of young people.

The Economic Freedom Fighters has benefited most from the rising discontent and political radicalisation among young black people. From the time of their expulsion from the ANC to the elections in 2014, Julius Malema and his lieutenants appeared to have inaugurated a new wave of activism among this section of the population. In many senses, the launch of the EFF represented the most significant youth movement since the early 1990s, reflected in its capacity to attract tens of thousands to rallies and marches, with participants donning red berets and proclaiming support for the party's radical programme. The clarion call, 'Economic freedom in our lifetime', is simultaneously a powerful critique of the elite establishment and an expression of the deep frustration and anger of youth at the slow pace of change in the country. Spurred on by the political crisis affecting the alliance in the aftermath of the Marikana massacre, the EFF performed admirably in the national elections, becoming the third largest political party and by openly challenging Zuma on the Nkandlagate scandal established itself as the main left electoral party.[33]

Initially, the EFF reflected the mood of discontent among black youth especially and the concomitant desire to craft new radical politics. Its early fusion of Congress, Black Consciousness and Africanist ideas and self-definition of being Fanonian, Sankarist, Bikoist and anti-capitalist[34] wove together some existing radical political strands and seemed to create space for the formulation of novel ideas. By openly challenging the ANC and SACP leadership, the party struck a chord with many people who had grown impatient with failed promises of the ruling alliance. However, it became apparent in the preparations for the first elective conference that views contradicting those of the axis of power, centered on Malema and Shivambu, would not really be tolerated. Inevitably, the marginalisation and even expulsions of dissenters followed. What the aforementioned conference achieved was an assertion of the dominance of the former Youth Leaguers.

This development coincided with the party's transformation from being a quasi-movement – energised by youth radicalism – to becoming a formal electoral party, which captures youthful insurgency and subjects it to the organisation's hierarchical discipline, rather than allowing it to shape the politics of the party. In this sense, the EFF evinces a political praxis inherited from the ANCYL. Despite its much publicised successes, it remains to be seen whether the EFF can establish substantive connections with local movements that have been in the forefront of community protests, which is likely to be further complicated as it seeks to become a political force in municipalities. The party's self-proclamation as the 'vanguard' of the struggle exposes an appropriation of Stalinist ideas of vanguardism, namely, to impose its programme from the outside on the movements of the working class.[35] An aspect of this was evident in the way the party attempted to usurp students' struggles against the Rhodes statue by launching its own campaign against all statues. Whereas the former developed organically and was widely supported, the actions of the EFF were limited to its own cadres. The EFF has similarly attempted to use the Fees Must Fall movement to pursue its national political agenda, mostly tied to parliamentary politics, rather than contribute to building a viable national student movement. The EFF will for the foreseeable future remain an important force in any potential revival and reconfiguration of youth and student politics, and on the evidence of its growing popularity increasingly also among adults. For all its radical rhetoric and penchant for public spectacles, the party remains essentially an amalgam of populism and vanguardism, aiming to impose its predetermined programme on youth and the working class as a whole.

Hope deferred?

NUMSA's Special Congress in 2013 marked a very important and hopeful moment of reimagining the left in South Africa, including the prospect of

186 *Noor Nieftagodien*

building a United Front (UF) inspired by the experiences of the United Democratic Front of the 1980s. Initially slow to materialize the UF held a Preparatory Assembly in December 2014, attended by about 70 organisations. Thereafter dozens of local movements nationally joined, allowing the UF to establish regional chapters. United by their opposition to 'anti-poor and pro-rich policies', 'corruption and unaccountable government' and 'inequality and poverty', the delegates at the founding assembly agreed to build a new movement based on the principles of radical feminism, non-sexism, anti-racism, anti-xenophobia, non-sectarianism and accountability.[36] Crafting an anti-capitalist framework was arguably a relatively straightforward exercise, considering the preponderance of socialist activists involved in this initiative. Equally significant was the UF's explicit commitment to producing a political praxis shaped by mutual respect for different political ideas and traditions, acknowledging the value of ideological plurality and participatory learning, and eschewing reliance on trans-historical blueprints for revolution. The creation of spaces where different movements could participate in a process collectively to constitute new radical politics signaled a necessary departure from the top-down politics that has suffocated movements on the left.

However, the process of building the UF stalled, primarily due to challenges inherent to what has been called the 'NUMSA Moment'. From the outset, the UF was heavily dependent on NUMSA for political and material support and, considering the onslaught the union encountered from the leadership of COSATU and the SACP, it proved difficult to give the requisite attention to the UF. Internally, the UF faced familiar challenges, including impatience among some activists who wanted immediately to transform the UF into a workers' party that would be geared to electoral politics. Perhaps more problematically was the pre-occupation by some of the union's leaders with the idea of creating a new vanguard party – a non-Stalinist version of the SACP – that would stake a claim as the authentic inheritor of communist traditions and defender of the Freedom Charter. In fact, this exercise has thus far proven to be a diversion from building a new mass movement. Thus, the NUMSA leadership, which has taken a brave and principled stand against the ANC-SACP leadership and, in so doing, opened the door for reimagining and rebuilding a left movement, is in danger of imposing limitations on this possibility.

If it is to regain momentum the United Front needs to draw on lessons from our own recent history: the success of the United Democratic Front in the 1980s was an outcome of concerted efforts to build civic movements, student and youth organisations, and of mobilizing solidarity campaigns with workers' struggles. The proliferation of radical ideas, emphasis on popular democracy and solidarity in action were the hallmarks of the latter movement, and are now required to develop a new left movement. Launching a national initiative cannot replace the hard and consistent work of building radical and democratic organisations at local and regional levels. The 'NUMSA moment' of 2013 promised to inaugurate the rebuilding of a mass left movement cohering around the authority of the country's largest and most militant trade union. Since then it has become clear that the constitution of such a movement will face numerous challenges, as was evidenced in the efforts to mobilise a national campaign aimed at forcing Jacob Zuma to resign,

South Africa's new left movements 187

which prompted heated debates about the character and politics of alternative mass movements. As poverty, unemployment, racism, gender discrimination and state violence continue to escalate, the need for a democratic left movement is all the more urgent. For such a movement to become a serious left alternative, it must avoid the twin dangers of populism and narrow vanguardism, while uniting the numerous and currently fragmented movements of dissent in townships, informal settlements, workplaces and education institutions.

Notes

1 Jane Duncan, *The Rise of the Securocrats: The Case of South Africa* (Johannesburg: Jacana, 2014).
2 Andries Tatane was a community leader from the small town of Ficksburg (Free State Province) who was killed in 2013 by police during a service delivery protest.
3 Abahlali baseMjondolo is South Africa's foremost shack dwellers' movement, which has struggled for decent housing and basic services for more than a decade. It is principally based in Durban where its campaigns have been met with severe police brutality.
4 Giliad Isaacs, 'Mike Schussler Is Wrong about Inequality: Here's Why,' *Daily Maverick*, July 23, 2014, https://www.dailymaverick.co.za/article/2014-07-23-op-ed-mike-schussler-is-wrong-about-inequality.-heres-why./#.WFG8UqI9YnI.
5 Statistics South Africa, *Poverty Trends in South Africa: An Examination of Absolute Poverty between 2006 and 2011* (Pretoria: Statistics South Africa, 2014).
6 The European mass parties of the working class differ from the others in at least one important respect, namely, they did not constitute postcolonial governments. PSOE and the Labour Party were the traditional parties of the Spanish and British working class respective in the twentieth century. PSOE and PASOK's reputations were enhanced in the struggle against military dictatorships in Spain and Greece, respectively, which led to massive growth in their support from the 1970s.
7 Jeremy Baskin, *Striking Back: A History of COSATU* (Johannesburg: Ravan Press, 1991).
8 Eddie Webster, 'The Rise of Social Movement Unionism: The Two Faces of the Black Trade Union Movement in South Africa,' in *State Resistance and Change in South Africa*, ed. P. Frankel, N. Pines, and M. Swilling (London: Croom Helm, 1988); Rob Lambert and Eddie Webster, 'Southern Unionism and the New Labor Internationalism,' in *Place, Space and the New Labor Internationalisms*, ed. Peter Waterman and Jane Wills (Oxford: Blackwell Publishers, 2001) and for a more critical view, Karl Van Holdt, 'Social Movement Unionism: The Case of South Africa,' *Work, Employment and Society* 16, no. 2 (2002).
9 Sakhela Buhlungu, 'Union Party Alliance in the Era of Market Regulation: The Case of South Africa,' *Journal of Southern African Studies* 31, no. 4 (2005).
10 After the launch of COSATU and especially in the early 1990s, Inkatha, a Zulu nationalist movement supported by the apartheid government, launched violent attacks against independent trade unions and township residents in Natal and the Pretoria-Witwatersrand-Vereeniging region (now Gauteng Province), which resulted in the deaths of thousands of people.
11 Jay Naidoo, 'The Workers Dream of Unity, Assassinated: A Eulogy to COSATU,' *Daily Maverick*, March 2015.
12 Sakhela Buhlungu, 'Union Party Alliance in the Era of Market Regulation: The Case of South Africa.'
13 Grace Khunou, 'COSATU's Influence on Policy-Making in Post-Apartheid South Africa,' in *COSATU's Contested Legacy: South African Trade Unions in the Second*

188 *Noor Nieftagodien*

Phase of Democracy, ed. Sakhela Buhlungu and Malehoko Tshoaedi (Pretoria: HSRC Press, 2012).

14 Devan Pillay, 'The Enduring Embrace: COSATU and the Tripartite Alliance during the Zuma Era,' *Labour, Capital and Society* 44, no. 2 (2011).

15 Zwelinzima Vavi, 'COSATU: I Have Come to the End of the Road,' *Politicsweb*, March 29, 2015.

16 Save Our SAMWU Report (2015).

17 Lonmin Labour Relations Update, May 17, 2013, https://www.lonmin.com/downloads/media_centre/news/press/2013/Lonmin_labour_relations_update_170513_-_FINAL.pdf.

18 Ari Sitas, 'COSATU, the "2010 Class Project" and the Contest for "The Soul" of the ANC,' in *COSATU's Contested Legacy: South African Trade Unions in the Second Phase of Democracy*, ed. Sakhela Buhlungu and Malehoko Tshoaedi (Pretoria: HSRC Press, 2012).

19 Labour broking involves the placement of temporary/casual workers by labour subcontractors or temporary employment services. See, David Dickinson, *Fighting Their Own Battles: The Mabarete and the End of Labour Broking in the South African Post Office*. SWOP Working Paper (2015).

20 Sam Ashman and Nicolas Pons-Vignon, 'NUMSA, the Working Class and Socialist Politics in South Africa,' *Socialist Register* 51 (2014).

21 Casual Workers' Advice Office, 'The Context of the Casual Workers' Advice Office,' accessed June 2015, http://www.cwao.org.za/about-context.asp.

22 Daneel Knoetze, 'Farmworkers Union CSAAWU Should Be Saved,' *Groundup*, November 17, 2014.

23 Casual Workers' Advice Office, 'The Context of the Casual Workers' Advice Office,' accessed June 2015, http://www.cwao.org.za/about-context.asp.

24 Peter Alexander, 'Rebellion of the Poor: South Africa's Service Delivery Protests – A Preliminary Analysis,' *Review of African Political Economy* 37, no. 123 (2010).

25 Ibid.

26 Noor Nieftagodien, 'Popular Movements, Contentious Spaces and the ANC, 1943–1956,' in *One Hundred Years of the ANC: Debating Liberation Histories Today*, ed. A. Lissoni, et al. (Johannesburg: Wits University Press, 2012).

27 Patrick Bond, 'South African People Power since the Mid-1980s: Two Steps Forward, One Back,' *Third World Quarterly* 33, no. 2 (2012).

28 National Union of Metalworkers of South Africa, 'Secretariat Report' to NUMSA Special National Congress, December 2013, 17.

29 Anneke Le Roux, 'Contesting Space: A Ward Committee and a Social Movement Organisation in Thembelihle, Johannesburg,' (MA Dissertation, University of Johannesburg, 2014).

30 Sarah Mosoetsa, ' "What Would You Do If the Government Fails to Delivery?" COSATU's Memberships' Attitudes towards Service Delivery,' in *COSATU's Contested Legacy: South African Trade Unions in the Second Phase of Democracy*, ed. Sakhela Buhlungu and Malehoko Tshoaedi (Pretoria: HSRC Press, 2012).

31 *The Guardian*, August 30, 2013.

32 Alcinda Honwana, *Youth and Revolution in Tunisia* (London: Zed Books, 2013).

33 Noor Nieftagodien, 'The Economic Freedom Fighters and the Politics of Memory and Forgetting,' *The South Atlantic Quarterly* 114, no. 2 (April 2015).

34 Floyd Shivambu, *The Coming Revolution: Julius Malema and the Fight for Economic Freedom* (Johannesburg: Jacana, 2014).

35 Martin Legassick, *Towards Socialist Democracy* (Scottsville: UKZN Press, 2007).

36 Dinga Sikwebu, 'United Front Takes Baby Steps to Redefine SA Politics,' *Mail and Guardian*, December 22, 2014.

Index

African National Congress (ANC) 1, 6, 10, 25, 39, 44, 58, 153; Anti-Privatisation Forum and 68; Cato Manor protest and 79; challenges to political leadership of 80–3; EFF rival 69; electricity connections and 91–2; Growth Employment and Redistribution (GEAR) policy 39; political leadership challenged 80–3; protests as collective claim making against 125–7; tensions between COSATU and 175–6; Youth League 10, 184
Alexander, Peter 40, 72
Amplats mine: 2012 unprotected strike 160–2; workers' committee formation at 157–60; *see also* mineworkers, Marikana
Anti-Eviction Campaign 7, 46
Anti-Globalisation Movement 7
Anti-Privatisation Forum (APF) 7–8, 46, 67–9, 72, 89
apartheid 6–7, 43, 59, 171–2
Arab Uprisings 3–4, 23, 27, 109
associational power 139
Association of Mineworkers and Construction Union (AMCU) 153
Auyero, Javier 120–1, 128

Bamyeh, Mohammed 3
Barker, Colin 155
Bauman, Zygmunt 24
Bekkersdal, South Africa 63–6
Bell, Daniel 28
Bénit-Gbaffou, Claire 115, 119
Bezuidenhout, Andries 140
Black Economic Empowerment (BEE) companies 100
Black Municipal Workers' Union (BMWU) 142

Bond, Patrick 41
Bond, Peter 91–2
Booysen, Susan 44, 72, 107–8, 111, 126
Bouazizi, Mohamed 3, 23, 109
Bourdieu, Pierre 11, 33
Breman, Jan 21
Buffalo City, East London 108–9, 115; protest as spinoff of Occupy movement 109–10; service delivery protest 110–13
Bushbuckridge Residents Association 45
Buthelezi, Bheki 74

Cape Areas Housing Action Committee (CAHAC) 93
capitalism: driving global marketization 22, 32–3; electoral democracy hijacked by 43–4; post-apartheid 7; *see also* marketization
Cato Manor protest 73, 75–6, 79; challenge to political leadership 81; as counter hegemonic challenge 83–5
centrality of demands for community recognition 65
Centre for Civil Society (CCS) 73
Ceruti, Claire 9
Chatterjee, Partha 13, 21, 55, 61–2, 65–7; on concept of political society 91, 101; on populism 68
Cheeseman, Nic 120
Chemical, Energy, Paper, Printing, Wood and Allied Workers' Union (CEPPWAWU) 177
Chirwa, Andrew 163
Chun, Jennifer J. 140
Citizen and Subject 56
civic movement 45–6
Coleman, James Samuel 10
collective claim making 125–7

190 *Index*

collective clientelism 119–20
Comaroff, Jean 21
Comaroff, John 21
Commercial, Stevedoring, Agricultural
and Allied Workers' Union (CSAAWU)
179–80
Commission for Conciliation, Mediation
and Arbitration (CCMA) 160
commodification of public goods,
contestation of 142–4
commodity fetishism 26–7
Communist Manifesto, The 26
community formations 13
community rebellions 180–3
Concerned Citizens Forum 7
Congress of South African Trade Unions
(COSATU) 6, 10, 15, 39–40, 58, 164,
172; commodification of public goods
and 142–4; in crisis 176–8; launch
and power of 173–6; organising the
precariat 179–80
Connell, Raewyn 10–11
contentious democracy in South Africa 8–10
contestation, cycles of 141–7
counter-hegemonic challenges 73, 83–5
Cox, Laurence 36, 38
Cross, Catherine 123
cycles of contestation 141–7
cycles of protests 37

democracy: direct 45–6; electoral 43–5;
participatory 24
Democratic Alliance 10
Democratic Left Front (DLF) 73
digital communications 42–3
direct democracy 45–6
direct rule 59–60
dispossession 29, 31
Dlamini-Zuma, Nkosazana 124–5
dominant hegemony 72
D'sa, Desmond 76
Durban protests: challenging existing
political leadership 80–3; connections
between protesters 74–7; as counter
hegemonic challenge 73, 83–5;
rejecting procedural channels 77–80;
three case studies 73–4
Durkheim, Emile 10, 33

Economic Freedom Fighters (EFF) 1, 15,
21, 69, 153, 173, 176; youth politics and
184–5
Egyptian Revolution 5

electoral democracy 43–5
exclusionary politics 22–4; postcolonial
61–3

Facebook 42
Fanon, Frantz 13, 21, 55–8, 61, 172
fascism 30, 32
feminism 33
fictitious commodities 26–32, 39

Gauteng province, South Africa 63
Giddens, Anthony 10
Gilder, Barry 127
global formations 13
Global Justice Movement 7
Global North 10, 21–2; defining social
movements and 37; Polanyian analysis
focused on 32
global resistance: Arab Spring and 3–4,
23, 109; movements beyond movements
9; political significance 12; situating
South African protests in 109–10; South
Africa as model of 2–3; start of current
wave in Tunisia, 2010 3; taking place in
the Global South 4; workplace militancy
9–10
Global South 4, 21–2; defining social
movements and 37; destruction of nature
in 28; perspectives and critical theory
10–13
Goodwin, Jeff 38, 55
Graeber, David 153
Gramsci, A. 154–5, 165–6
Greater Westonaria Concerned Residents'
Association 66
Great Transformation, The 22, 26, 29, 138
Growth Employment and Redistribution
(GEAR) policy 39, 142–4, 175

Hart, Gillian 9
Hetland, Gabriel 38, 55
historicity 29
Housing Assembly, Cape Flats: Cape Town
housing crisis, organisation, and politics
of representation 92–5; devolution to
the districts 96–8; ends of politics and
98–100; formation of 89–90; politics
of incorporation and 90–2; success of
market-oriented approach of 100–2

iGoli 2012 142–4, 148
incorporation, politics of 90–2
indirect rule 59–60

Index 191

Inkatha Freedom Party 60
institutional power 140
International Labour Research and
Information Group (ILRIG) 89, 93–5
International Monetary Fund (IMF) 7, 8

Johnson, Alan 155

Khunou, Grace 175
Kitschelt, Herbert 119, 120
knowledge as fictitious commodity 28–9,
31–2
Krinsky, John 43

labor: commodification of 27;
recommodification of 31
labour formations 14
Lambert, Rob 140
Landless People's Movement 7
Latin America 22–4
Lavalette, Michael 155
Left formations 14–15, 171–3; alliance
and COSATU's subordination of other
organisations 173–6; community
rebellions and 180–3; new hope through
United Front 185–7; organising the
precariat 179–80; youth politics 183–5
Lévesque, Christian 140
liquid protest 25
local state formations 14
location on terrain of governmentality
63–4
logistical power 140–1
Lonmin mine 1–2; *see also* mineworkers,
Marikana
lumpenproletariat 57
Luxemburg, Rosa 142

Malema, Julius 1
Mamdani, Mahmood 13, 55–6, 59–62
Mandela, Nelson 6, 43–4
Marais, Stephen 109
Marikana strike *see* mineworkers,
Marikana
marketization 22; capitalism and 26–7,
32–3; commodification and 27–9;
destruction of nature and 27–8; of
education 23, 28–9; and exclusionary
politics 22–4; waves of 30–1
Marx, Karl 10, 12, 21, 26–7, 33, 57; on
workers' power 138–9
Marxism 12, 137–8; theory of social
movements 38

Mason, Paul 4
massacre, Marikana 1–2, 156, 171, 173
Mathunjwa, Joseph 153
Maxwele, Chumani 183
Mbatha, Siphiwe 154
Mbeki, Thabo 118, 176
McAdam, Doug 154
McCarthy, James 26
McCarthy, John D. 154
McInnes, Patrick 91–2
McKinley, Dale 8, 144
Mdlalose, Bandile 43, 47
mineworkers, Marikana 9–10, 21, 25, 58,
153–4, 165–6; AMCU protected strike,
2014 163–5; Amplat mines strike, 2012
160–2; Commission for Conciliation,
Mediation and Arbitration (CCMA)
160; formation of workers' committee
at Amplats mine 157–60; hegemony,
organic intellectuals, and leadership
among 154–5; Lonmin strike, 2012
1–2; police response to 1–2, 156, 171,
173; setting the context for strikes
among 156–7
Mitchell's Plain *see* Housing Assembly,
Cape Flats
money as fictitious commodity 28
Motsoaledi, South Africa 63, 66
movements beyond movements 9
Munck, Ronaldo 148
municipal workers, Johannesburg 137–8,
147–9; analytical framework of
changing forms of power and 138–41;
contesting the commodification of
public goods 142–4; contesting
the labour regime 141–2; cycles of
contestation and 141–7; mobilising
contract workers, rebuilding union
power 145–7
Murray, Gregor 140

National Democratic Revolution (NDR)
172
National Economic Development and
Labour Council (NEDLAC) 142
National Transport Movement (NTM) 177
National Union of Metalworkers South
Africa (NUMSA) 1, 15, 45, 153
National Union of Mineworkers (NUM) 1,
10, 156–7, 178
nature, destruction of 27–8
neoliberalism 21, 30; defining social
movements in age of 36–8; South

192 *Index*

African social movements in age of 38–49
New Deal 30
Ngubane, China 78
Nhlapo, Stephen 118, 122–4, 127–9
Nilsen, Alf Gunvald 36, 38, 92
Northern Theory 11
Ntuli, Lawrence 137

object of exchange 29
Occupy Movement 3–5, 23, 27, 43, 184; direct democracy and 45–6; invented *versus* invited spaces of 77–8; spinoffs 109–10; Umlazi 73–7, 80–1, 83–5
Operation Khanyisa Movement 44
Opp, Karl-Dieter 37
Oppenheimer, Nicky 172
organic intellectuals 154–5

Parsons, Talcott 33
participatory democracy 24
patronage, political 119–21; shared grievances and competitive networks of 121–4
Pickerill, Jenny 43
Pikitup 145–7, 152n64
Pointer, Rebecca 46
Polanyi, Karl 12–13, 22, 92; on fictitious commodities 26–32, 39; framework of workers' power 138
police repression 1–2, 25, 46–7, 156, 171, 173
political repertoires in social movements 24–5, 42
political society 91
politics: ends of 98–100; exclusionary 22–4; of incorporation 90–2; patronage 119–21; of representation 92–5; strategic 66–7; tenderpreneurship in 131n48; youth 183–5; *see also* Left formations
Politikon 47
"popcorn" protests 41
popular struggles in South Africa 67–9
populism 68
postcolonial politics 55; direct and indirect rule in 59–60; political society and community protests in 63–7; and political society as postcolonial exclusion 61–3; society and urban/rural divide in 56–60; theory of 33, 56–60; underdevelopment and 56; xenophobia and 58
power 138–41; associational 139; institutional 140; logistical 140–1; structural 139; symbolic 140–1

precariat, the 179–80
prefigurative politics 24
protected strike, 2014 AMCU 163–5
protests: as collective claim making 125–7; common demands in 64; as counter hegemonic challenges 73, 83–5; cycles of 37; dual nature of 130n2; first post-apartheid 1–2; liquid 25; police responses to 1–2, 25, 46–7, 156, 171, 173; as political navigation 127–8; political patronage and 119–21; political society and community 63–7; "popcorn" 41; rebellions of the poor 40–2; rise in rate of South African 72, 107–8; service delivery issues 8–9, 63–5, 72, 110–13; strategic politics and 66–7; WSSD march 7–8; in Zandspruit 124–5; *see also* social movements
public goods, commodification of 142–4

Ramatholdi, Ngoako 85
rebellion of the poor 40–2
recommodification of labor 31
representation, politics of 92–5
Rhodes, Cecil John 183
Right 2 Know Campaign 73
Robins, Steven 90–1
Rosenthal, Kelly 72
Rupert, Johann 172

Schneeman, Maureen 118, 121–5, 127
shared grievances and competitive patronage networks 121–4
Sharpeville, South Africa 1
socialism 32
social media 42–3
social movements: assembly points 24–5; common political repertoires in 24–5, 42; defining 36–8; hegemony, organic intellectuals, and leadership 154–5; from marketization to exclusionary politics 22–4; Marxist theory of 38; neoliberalism and South African 36–49; occupying public spaces and police repression 46–7; police repression against 25, 46–7; politics of incorporation and 90–2; of the 1960s 26; sociology as 25, 33–4; sociology for 29–33, 47–8; sociology of 26–9; South Africa at crossroads of 21; *see also* Left formations
Society, Work and Development Institute 34
sociology: as social movement 25, 33–4; for social movements 29–33; of social movements 26–9

Index 193

South Africa: under apartheid 6–7, 43, 59, 171–2; common political repertoires in 42; popular struggles in 67–9; rebellion of the poor 40–2; social movements in neoliberal age 38–49; Truth and Reconciliation Commission 171; xenophobia in 58

South African Commercial, Catering and Allied Workers' Union (SACCAWU) 177

South African Communist Party (SACP) 6, 39

South African Municipal Workers Union (SAMWU) 10, 14, 137–8, 147–9, 177; commodification of public goods and 143–4; mobilising contract workers and rebuilding union power 145–7

South African National Civic Organisation (SANCO) 6

South African resistance: antecedents in global perspective 5–8; contentious democracy and 8–10; fragmented struggles in 4–5; political terrain of 13–15; popular struggles 67–9; protest repertoire 5; rise in 1–2, 72, 107–8; situated in global protests 109–10; *see also* Left formations

South African Students Congress (SASCO) 183

South African Transport and Allied Workers Union (SATAWU) 10, 177

South Durban Community Environmental Alliance (SDCEA) 73, 77

Southern Theory 10–13

Southern Theory 10–11

Soweto, Southj Africa 1, 6, 43–4

Soweto Electricity Crisis Committee (SECC) 72, 91

Stalinism 30

Standing, Guy 5, 21, 27

state-society relation 59–60

strategic politics 66–7

strikes, labor 1–2, 9–10, 25; *see also* mineworkers, Marikana

structural power 139

symbolic power 140–1

Tarrow, Sidney 37

Tatane, Andries 171

tenderpreneurship 131n48

terrains of struggle 13–15

Thembelihle Crisis Committee (TCC) 181–3

Time 2

Touraine, Alain 26, 29

Traveling Theory 11

Treatment Action Campaign 7

Tunisia 3, 23, 109

Twitter 42

Umlazi "Occupy" protest 73–7; challenge to ANC 80–1; as counter hegemonic challenge 83–5; in invented versus invited spaces 77–8

underdevelopment 56

Unemployed Peoples Movement (UPM) 73

United Democratic Front (UDF) 174

United Front (UF) 173, 185–7

urban/rural divide 56–60

Vavi, Zwelinzima 10, 176

Von Holdt, Karl 111, 114, 119, 130n2

Walder, Andrew 55

Ward 68, South Durban, protest 73–4

waves of marketization 30–1

Weber, Max 10, 33

Wentworth Development Forum (WDF) 76–80

Why It's Kicking Off Everywhere 4

Wilkinson, Steven 119, 120

Wood, Lesley J. 47

workplace militancy 9–10

World Bank 7–8, 143

World Conference Against Racism 7

World Social Forum 7

World Summit on Sustainable Development (WSSD) 7–8

World Trade Organization (WTO) 7–8

Wretched of the Earth, The 56

Wright, Erik Olin 139

xenophobia 58

youth politics 183–5

Zald, Mayer 26, 154

Zandspruit informal settlement 118–19, 128–30; political patronage and protest 119–21; protests as political navigation 127–8; protests at collective claim making 125–7; protests in 124–5; shared grievances and competitive patronage networks 121–4

Zuern, Elke 90–1

Zuma, Jacob 118, 124, 164